MINISTRY
of GREED

MINISTRY of GREED

*The Inside Story
of the Televangelists and
Their Holy Wars*

by
LARRY MARTZ
with GINNY CARROLL

A NEWSWEEK BOOK
Weidenfeld & Nicolson
New York

Published by Weidenfeld & Nicolson, New York
A Division of Wheatland Corporation
841 Broadway
New York, New York 10003-4793

Published in Canada by General Publishing Company, Ltd.

Library of Congress Cataloging-in-Publication Data
Martz, Larry.
    Ministry of greed : the inside story of the televangelists and their holy wars / by Larry Martz with Ginny Carroll.—1st ed.
        p.   cm.—(A Newsweek book)
    Includes index.
    ISBN 1-555-84216-X
    1. Bakker, Jim. 2. Bakker, Tammy. 3. Falwell, Jerry.
    4. Television in religion—United States. 5. Evangelists—United States—Biography. I. Carroll, Ginny. II. Title.
    BV3785.B3M27   1988
    269'.2'0922—dc19
    [B]   88-11111
                                                    CIP

Manufactured in the United States of America

Designed by Irving Perkins Associates

First Edition

10 9 8 7 6 5 4 3 2 1

To Anne Martz,
with love and gratitude;
to J.H. Carroll,
father and friend.

Contents

Foreword

It was a story of God, greed, sex, and power, and it played out like a yearlong soap opera in newspaper headlines and TV talk shows. Jim and Tammy Bakker's peccadilloes and the holy wars for control of their PTL empire were far from the most important news story of 1987, but they touched something basic in America. The Bakkers' battle with Jerry Falwell became the stuff of songs, jokes, cartoons, and endless gossip; rival evangelists chose sides and traded denunciations over the air. Jessica Hahn, whose sin with Jim touched off the scandal, metamorphosed from a Long Island "Bible belle" into a *Playboy* playmate. The scandal opened a window on the important but little-known world of televangelism, and the nation was fascinated: One of Ted Koppel's "Nightline" interviews with Jim and Tammy drew the highest ratings in his show's history, and the two *Newsweek* cover stories on the scandal were the magazine's best-selling issues of the year.

Ministry of Greed had its beginnings in *Newsweek*'s week-by-week coverage of the scandal that became known as Gospelgate. As the drama unfolded, *Newsweek*'s reporters across the country uncovered far more information than the magazine could use in its limited space; at the same time, it was increasingly clear that the inside story had still to be pieced together and put into perspective for general readers unfamiliar with born-again believers. In midsummer of 1987, the editors approved a plan to use the magazine's weekly reporting as the basis for a book—not a compendium of

Newsweek's coverage, but a new narrative probing the scandal and what really happened in the struggle for control of the $172 million empire called PTL.

The PTL story was peculiarly suited to newsweekly coverage. Information for each week's piece had to be gathered and integrated from sources all over the country—from Jim and Tammy Bakker's several refuges; from PTL headquarters near Charlotte, North Carolina; from Jessica Hahn on Long Island and her adviser in California; from Jerry Falwell's headquarters in Lynchburg, Virginia, and Jimmy Swaggart's in Baton Rouge, Louisiana; from the Assemblies of God in Springfield, Missouri; and from religious scholars and TV evangelists based around the country. Important facts came from government files and sources in Washington, D.C., and from PTL's faithful donors—a kind of Greek chorus of innocent victims of the scandal —who lived all across the land. At one time or another, all of *Newsweek*'s ten domestic bureaus reported on various segments of the story, and over the months, their files mounted to 450 pages and 175,000 words. As often happens, the writers in New York turned out finished stories perhaps only a tenth as long as the incoming files. The surplus information remained to be developed and used. Even so, a great deal of added reporting was needed to fill in the details and flesh out the human story.

And the news media played major parts in the drama. The *Charlotte Observer* had been digging at the scandal for years, and its knowledge triggered the action. The *Washington Post* and other newspapers broke major angles of the story. *Newsweek* itself also had a role, and the warring evangelists used Ted Koppel, CNN's Larry King, and other television shows as gun platforms to wage their battle. I have tried to give an accurate sense of the role the various media played and to give credit for information developed by others. But this book is a new telling of the story, with a wealth of added details and the perspective of a little time to ponder its meanings.

I was the writer for the project. Among many other subjects, I have written and edited stories on religion for *Newsweek*, including several of the pieces in the continuing PTL scandal. For the book, I coordinated the old and new reporting, participated in some of the interviews, suggested areas to be explored, and finally wrote the finished narrative. But it is a true collaboration. The words and ultimate responsibility are mine; the reporting is from the correspondents; the insights and judgments are largely collective.

Detroit Bureau Chief Ginny Carroll, who had worked extensively on the weekly coverage, was chief reporter for this book. Having grown up in the Carolinas and followed the Bakkers as a reporter for the *News & Observer* in Raleigh before coming to *Newsweek,* she was familiar with the evangelical world and fascinated by the story. She was detached from weekly duty for four months to explore all the facets of the scandal, filling in gaps, developing new facts and insights, and seeking out sources that had been overlooked. Most of the new information in the book came from her painstaking interviews with all the major figures in the story and many others. As with the weekly reporting, however, some of the new questions suggested by her leads were sent to reporters in other bureaus, who contributed short supplementary files.

In addition to Ginny Carroll, the principal reporters were Mariana Gosnell, Michael A. Lerner, John McCormick, Peter McKillop, Mark Miller, Daniel Pedersen, Daniel Shapiro, Vern E. Smith, Rich Thomas, Anne Underwood, Deborah Witherspoon, and Lynda Wright. All did outstanding work. Religion editor Kenneth L. Woodward contributed to the reporting and wrote several of the weekly stories. It was Lynn Povich, *Newsweek*'s senior editor for special projects, who first suggested developing the magazine's coverage into a book. Eileen Clancey assembled the photographs, and Anne Underwood provided extraordinary research and was tireless in tracking down factual mistakes. Any remaining errors, however, are mine. I am grateful to Rollene Saal, *Newsweek*'s literary agent, for getting us together with Weidenfeld & Nicolson, and to William Strachan, whose perceptive editing greatly improved the finished work. Literally dozens of *Newsweek* staffers provided help, patience, and indulgence as we pursued this project; family members and friends lived graciously with our absences and deadlines. *Newsweek*'s editor in chief, Richard M. Smith, and editor Maynard Parker made the book possible, committing themselves along with us to the project. To all, our thanks.

Larry Martz, senior editor
May 15, 1988

MINISTRY
of GREED

Chapter 1

Rich Veins of Sleaze

Was God giving it all back?

Tammy Faye was almost trembling. Edgy, expectant, her face twisting under the makeup, she perched on the sofa. Jim sat bolt upright in the big leather wing chair, his fist drumming up and down, up and down on the chair arm. On the huge TV screen in front of them, their great enemy was resigning, bowing out of the ministry he had stolen from them. "In good conscience," Jerry Falwell was saying, he and his people "cannot sit on a board that could have the slightest potential for the return of Jim Bakker."

Sitting beside her mother, seventeen-year-old Tammy Sue Bakker breathed a soft "Yea." Her brother, Jamie Charles, eleven, was watching from under the coffee table; his shoes stuck out, waggling celebration. On the oversize screen, Falwell was still talking: ". . . probably the greatest scab and cancer on the face of Christianity in two thousand years of church history."

Jim reddened and flared. "I can't believe he said that about me!"

"Unchristian," agreed Tammy Faye, shaking her head sadly.

And then their own images filled the screen, in color-coordinated outfits of bright blue, promising to go back anytime to take care of their baby, the empire they had been forced to give up. It would only be logical to call on them, Jim was telling the camera. "I'd think that if my children had a need, I'd call the mother and father to help with that need."

"Our blues show up real good," said Tammy Faye, and Jim nodded.

A moment later, clumsy editing clipped off one of his on-screen comments in mid-syllable. "See?" he demanded, his mouth twisting. "They cut me off. They always cut me off."

It was a rerun, of course, the fourth or fifth hourly wrap-up on the network news since Falwell's live press conference and Jim and Tammy's quick rejoinder for the cameras. But they watched hungrily over and over, needing to know it had really happened.

It was October 8, 1987, nearly seven months since the Bakkers had turned over the ministry to Falwell. In the glory of the fall color in the Great Smoky Mountains, their hilltop refuge outside Gatlinburg, Tennessee, was beset by reporters. *Newsweek*'s Ginny Carroll had talked herself through the security gate, but a dozen more were prowling outside. In a clutter of movers' boxes and the debris of months of exile, the telephone jangled constantly. Jim and Tammy were scheming a triumphant return to the daily television show, the national audience, and the evangelical theme park called Heritage USA that were their rightful realm. On the screen far into the night, announcers and talk show hosts would ask the question gravely: Will Jim and Tammy come back?

But they weren't coming back. Whether or not Jim knew it in his heart, he was going to be cut off again. The holy war of 1987 was winding down, and nobody was going to win.

Jim and Tammy Bakker burst on the national consciousness only by falling gaudily from grace, stars of the latest in a long line of sex and money scandals in American religion. They seemed at first just funny little people, puppets made for television: he with his outsize boyish features and Howdy Doody grin, she with her baby doll mannerisms, copious tears, and landfill makeup. To people not part of the gospel world, it came as news that Jim and Tammy were giants in the electronic church, builders of an empire that took in $129 million a year and counted its congregation in the millions. Starting as dropouts from a Minneapolis Bible college, they had become powers. They hobnobbed with presidents, lived like high-stepping royalty, commanded devotion and dollars from the faithful, and called down divine wrath on anyone who got in their way.

Their downfall, too, seemed larger than life. The sin charged to Jim wasn't just a fling with a church secretary named Jessica Hahn but bisexual behavior that by some accounts had gone on for years, and they weren't accused merely of dipping into the offering plate but of plundering their ministry of millions of dollars in salaries and bonuses and countless thousands more squandered on high living. When the scandal finally became public, it touched off a public cross fire among rival preachers and a struggle for control of their empire that matched any of the year's takeover battles on Wall Street—or, for that matter, anything seen on television's "Dynasty" or "Dallas." And it was only the beginning of a year of crisis for evangelicals that was to see two other national preachers, Oral Roberts and Jimmy Swaggart, mired in controversy, too.

Jim and Tammy lost their bitter struggle with Jerry Falwell, the good Samaritan who promised to save them from scandal and wound up taking over their empire. Jim's backers and a growing number of Falwell's own allies charged that Falwell, deny it as he would, really meant to steal PTL. But in the end he, too, lost out, leaving the empire floundering in bankruptcy and fighting in vain to survive. It was a story in the rich tradition of American religious scandals, from the fictional lecheries of the Reverend Arthur Dimmesdale and Elmer Gantry to the real-life escapades of Henry Ward Beecher, Aimee Semple McPherson, and Billy James Hargis. But it had no heroes and few grace notes. The kindest thing to be said about most of the preachers is that they deserved each other. The ultimate losers were the people who believed in the Bakkers and sent money to support their works.

The scandal known as Gospelgate also opened a rare window on the world of evangelical Christianity. It is a faith that claims one in three American adults and has power out of proportion to its numbers. Evangelicals helped elect our last two presidents. They influence Congress and the legislatures; they censor textbooks; and they will never give up trying to outlaw abortion, legalize school prayer, and beat back the gay rights movement. The evangelical current in America flows from our oldest history and our current culture; if the scandal hadn't touched some deep part of us, its wealth of sleazy detail would not have been so endlessly fascinating. It would not have inspired the jokes, cartoons, and bumper stickers; it would not have been a staple of newsmagazine covers, TV talk shows, Johnny Carson monologues, and columnists' punditry.

At their best, Jim and Tammy had a childlike quality, an innocence and spontaneity that drew the eye and warmed the heart. They were without irony or self-consciousness. They just loved

Jesus, they said, and they called their empire PTL, an acronym standing interchangeably for Praise the Lord and People That Love. (After the fall, it would become Pay the Lady or Pass the Loot.) For many of the older people who followed their lives on the daily PTL show, they were surrogate children, the lovable stars of a real-life soap opera. There was a vulnerability behind Jim's charm and practiced TV manner; at times he seemed almost camera-shy, nearly at a loss for what to do or say next. But he was the man with the vision, one who could see the future of cable television, the magic of a Christian theme park, and the buying power of a generation of evangelical Christians no longer locked in poverty. "He's the straight man, and I'm kind of his funny little person," said Tammy. That was her pose, the kind of deference to her man that outrages feminists but plays beautifully to the ladies of the Christian right. But behind the giggles, the shopping sprees, and the Kewpie doll makeup, Tammy was the tough, vital spark for the show. Whether she was streaking her mascara with copious tears or laughing uncontrollably at some on-screen disaster, she lived on the edge, with an unpredictable quality that kept people tuned in.

Offscreen, Tammy was warm and likable, a gracious hostess and a generous friend; her impulsiveness had a touching quality. Jim was more guarded, wary. He said he was shy, but the feeling he left with a lot of people was that he wasn't much interested in them. On camera the two of them came into their own: alive with the lights; somehow larger; two halves of a long-practiced telegenic whole. He led the talk, and she supported him. If his phrasing faltered a bit or his thought seemed to wander, she would step in instantly to pick up the patter, amplifying and polishing his idea until he was ready to go on. They were a good team.

The show was the foundation of the empire, the money machine that pulled in ninety-six million dollars from the viewers in 1986 alone. It wasn't just a broadcast religious service, like Jerry Falwell's "Old Time Gospel Hour," or the fire-and-brimstone preaching that Jimmy Swaggart sent over the airwaves. "The Jim and Tammy TV Ministry Hour" began as a talkfest, the kind they had originally created for Pat Robertson and his Christian Broadcasting Network (CBN), but it evolved into a continuing daytime drama, the ongoing story of their lives mixed with segments of gospel music, talk show, and telethon. Beyond the comforts of faith and the reaffirming of

Christian values, Jim and Tammy hooked the viewers with their personal crises.

It was a real-life soap opera. Jim and Tammy "would be down in the dumps one day, very depressed because of some evil things that had happened or because finances were down," said Quentin Schultze, professor of communications at Calvin College in Michigan and a perceptive student of the televangelists. "A week or two later, they would be rejoicing and weeping because they had made it through. But soon another conflict would come." Their children's problems and their marital spats were aired for the cameras. The *Charlotte Observer*, muckraking through PTL's finances, was an agent of Satan out to get them. Even their weight problem became a crisis, and when they shed pounds, they turned out a book about it and sold it to the faithful, along with their autobiographies, endless plaques, gadgets and mementos, and souvenirs including a $675 Tammy Faye doll, lovingly handmade and dressed to kill. As the empire grew, the royal family became a personality cult.

But the physical heart of PTL was the theme park, campground, and corporate campus called Heritage USA, where the faithful could gather to play, worship, and commune. It had already become one of the nation's major tourist attractions, behind only the two Disney parks, drawing more than six million visitors in 1986. In Jim's grand vision, it would also be the future of PTL and his own permanent legacy.

It is a strange, gaudy monument, spread across twenty-three hundred acres of rolling woodland on the border between North and South Carolina. It began as a Christian campground, a modern version of the revival grounds that originated on the American frontier. For most people, the enduring image of such places is a dim, depression-era scene of screenless cabins, naked light bulbs, yellowing mattresses, and rolled flypaper; it is one of the symbols that fix evangelical sects firmly in the lower classes. But Jim understood that his flock had prospered with America. His campground was built for thirty-thousand-dollar Winnebago campers and Airstream trailers, pulled by Buicks and Chryslers with air conditioning and wire wheels.

It may seem odd that there is nothing here that looks like a church. But in a place that lives on television, the studio, a big building fittingly called the Barn, naturally took priority. Only after it had been replaced by a modern broadcasting center did the Barn's primary function become meetings of the Heritage Village Church. Dressed up with a stucco facing, it sits next to the broadcasting center and still looks like a barn.

Nearby, however, is the Upper Room, a facsimile of the building in Jerusalem said to have been the scene of Christ's last supper with his disciples. For the faithful, this is the religious heart of Heritage USA. Several prayer meetings are held each day in the small chamber, where 120 people can sit on backless benches around an altar. To one side is a desk-size chest of clear plastic with a slot in the top. Pads of forms are provided for prayers, and visitors can fill them out and drop them into the hopper. Deciphered through the plastic, the scribbles ask prayers for "More perfect faith," "Resurrect & restore marriage of George and Isobel————," "My sister Bea after 28 weeks of marriage her husband don't [love] her and unfaithful. She is heart broken & a PTL partner & other donations." Believers can also send photos, to be posted on huge stands in the Upper Room. There are thousands: young people and old; babies in respirators; grannies in wheelchairs; twisted and deformed bodies; Nancy Reagan on a billboard; a military jet high in the sky with an arrow pointing to it and the penciled name Rocky.

"If you want to be a fisher of men," Jim Bakker said, "you have to have good bait." Preachers like Jimmy Swaggart might scowl and scorn, but Heritage was also for fun. The idea was that Christian families could come for a vacation, in a Christian atmosphere with decent people—no smoking or drinking. They could pray together, watch the show being taped, see the Passion play in the outdoor amphitheater with its replica of Old Jerusalem, and play together too. Thus Jim created the water park, a thirteen-million-dollar toy on a man-made island in an artificial lake, with a wave machine, rides varying from wild to sedate, and a 163-foot water slide down an artificial mountain of concrete. Heritage USA has swimming pools, a carrousel, a farm and petting zoo, a miniature train chugging around the lake, and a 14-foot-high fiberglass moose at a fork in the road. And there is the shopping mall, a place after Tammy's own heart. It was built alongside the hotel like a brand-new turn-of-the-century Main Street, housed safely indoors under a blue plaster sky with movie projections of clouds drifting across it. Here are the religious books and records, the racks of greeting cards and framed prayers and homiletic plaques: "God Bless Our Happy Home." There are jewelry stores, clothing stores, and restaurants. And there are candy and ice cream shops to cater to the one vice that evangelicals seem to embrace without shame.

The faithful came to Heritage USA from all across the land, in a profusion of accents and license plates, filling acres of parking lots and shaded camping facilities. The unwritten rule was to smile and nod at everyone, to wave at passing cars, to chat easily. The visitors were invariably cheerful, clean, and pleasant, an accurate cross section of the PTL audience. They were older than the American average, more female, more rural, more overweight, more southern and midwestern than the norm. And PTL was more integrated than many TV ministries, with a black membership estimated to be near the U.S. average of 12 percent. But the people who came to Heritage USA, representing all races and ethnic backgrounds, were bound together by faith and a cast of mind. They thought Jim was cute and Tammy was beautiful and Heritage was a wonderful place. It was thrilling to be right there when the show was being taped and awesome to tiptoe through the Upper Room, and the Tammy Faye refrigerator magnets in the gift shop were just darling.

When the scandal broke, the faithful for the most part were hurt but forgiving. Jim and Tammy's followers were not the pursed-lipped, intolerant haters of fundamentalist stereotype. In the first weeks, only a few denounced their pastor for his sin with Jessica Hahn. Most of them told reporters that Jim Bakker was just a man, that God would forgive him and they must, too, that the scandal was a test of their faith, and that they would be stronger for it in the end. The church is the body of Christ, said the Reverend Eugene Stanton, a volunteer counselor at PTL, and "We know the whole body of Christ is being attacked by Satan. The Christian has put on the armor of God, and we stand fast. Hallelujah and praise the Lord!"

It is a slice of America that isn't of much interest to the rich, the media, intellectuals, or manufacturers of anything more upscale than detergents; the demographics of the Bakkers' flock describe the audience that most advertisers would cheerfully lose. But these are sweet people, direct and open in their faith and their eagerness to believe. They defer cheerfully to God and those who speak for him; they are resigned to human frailty, their own and others', and humble before the mysteries of the divine. They try earnestly to live as the Bible directs. Jim and Tammy's followers have strengths that the nation may one day need, as Britain needed Londoners in the blitz. They have endured, and they count.

They are also an increasingly powerful force in America's political and cultural life. "One out of ten homes in America is said to be a trailer, and a lot of folks not too long ago bought light blue leisure suits," said William Martin, a sociologist at Rice University. "I'm not trying to sound like a snob, but we tend to forget that we live in an extremely diverse society." It isn't just a matter of numbers, either, but a reinforcement of classic American values. Evangelicals have traditionally been poor people, but more and more of them are moving up in the world, at least partly because their religion has helped them learn middle-class ways. Creativity counted for less at Heritage than tidiness, obedience, niceness. As one young mother, leaving the taping of the daily show, told her little boy, "You were *very good.* Very *quiet.*"

If evangelicals in the past frowned on worldly pleasures, it was at least partly to make a virtue of necessity; as the old union song sneered, there'll be pie in the sky when you die. It was also comforting to think that the rich who oppressed them weren't going to heaven. But these days, people whose fathers were seasonal coal miners or hardscrabble sharecroppers have become storekeepers, factory foremen, government workers, and white-collar executives; their faith survives, but its austerity chafes. So Jim and Tammy preached prosperity theology, yuppie values for the new middle class. It's okay to want it all and even okay to have most of it, Jim told them. At Heritage USA, the year's big celebration was Christmas, in all its material frenzy. It was the peak season at the shopping mall, and festive displays of more than a million lights started going up by Labor Day. Easter, the central mystery of Christianity with its miracle of resurrection and redemption, was just another holiday. Jim's credo was that God wanted you to prosper, on earth as in heaven: "If you pray for a camper, be sure to tell him what color." And anything you gave God would be returned to you, literally, many times over.

Giving to God, of course, meant giving to PTL, and Jim learned to take advantage of his flock's new prosperity. Evangelists have always had a few wealthy patrons, usually people who made new fortunes in fields like oil or entertainment, but the bulk of the revenues has come from folks who send envelopes every month. Jim was no exception. The backbone of his empire was the mailing list of 507,000 "PTL partners" who were regular correspondents, and about half of them were pledged to make a monthly contribution of $15 or more. Through computerized mailings, the partners could be given the illusion of individual attention, with their names in the body of the letter and even a reference to their latest donations or requests for prayer. They could also be induced to buy endless quantities of religious books, Tammy Faye records, vials of Jordan water, and the like, and they could be nudged into bigger donations and special gifts by telethons for special causes or announcements of financial crisis. The elderly were particularly vulnerable to such appeals. Just before the Bakker scandal, Dorothy Dodd, a social worker in Altoona, Pennsylvania, had to rescue a sixty-seven-year-old widow who couldn't pay her gas bill because she had sent $55 of her $330 monthly Social Security check to Oral Roberts. Roberts had touched off a national fire storm, quickly overtaken by the Bakker scandal, when he announced that if he didn't reach a fundraising goal of $8 million, God was going to "call me home."

Jim's greatest inspiration was a way to bring in the money in larger bundles by creating "lifetime partners." For just a thousand dollars, he promised, a lifetime partner could enjoy a vacation of four days and three nights at the Heritage Grand Hotel or the still-unfinished Heritage Grand Towers, every year for life, with spouse. It was clearly a bargain, and in a little less than three years some 114,000 partners had sent in at least one check for a thousand dollars. Some signed up five or six times, so they could take friends and relatives along, and most of them kept up their regular donations, too. By 1986, more than half of all the money mailed to PTL came for lifetime partnerships. Unfortunately, the state government took the position that Jim was renting hotel rooms and owed the state's hotel occupancy tax on all the revenues he had raised in lifetime partnerships. If the courts uphold that argument, it could open up federal tax liabilities and force PTL to set aside millions in reserves—a blow that could prove fatal. But Jim's insight that the faithful could be tapped in large numbers for a thousand dollars at a crack was revolutionary and would surely be an inspiration to his fellow evangelists when they figured out a safe way to do it.

The beating heart of Heritage USA was the broadcasting studio and the three satellite dishes that beamed the show out to the donors and kept the money coming in. The treasure was the mailing list, housed along with the computers, the mail operation, and the executive offices in a squat pyramidal building called the World Outreach Center on a hill near the hotel. The incoming mail, with its checks and cold cash, was sent to the maximum-security counting room in trays of a thousand envelopes each. On good days after a telethon there might be thirty-five trays, keeping counters at work late into the night until the armored cars came to haul the takings to the bank.

But a vision needs more than money to sustain it. Heritage USA was already a place to live as well as visit; there were six villages of homes and condos, about a thousand residences in all, where the faithful could invest in vacation and retirement homes. Jim was planning more. The five-hundred-room Heritage Grand Towers hotel stood half finished when the scandal halted construction; he had broken ground for a hundred-million-dollar crystal cathedral, modeled on the great Crystal Palace built for the 1851 London world's fair, and he was planning an eighteen-hole golf course with condos along every fairway. There was going to be a monorail, a village called Old Jerusalem, the Heritage School of Evangelism. There would be a Bible theme park with rides to rival Disney World: Noah's Ark; Jonah and the Whale; a trip through heaven and hell to help people keep the faith. And that was just the beginning.

"The guy mesmerizes you," said Doug Oldham, Jim's chief gospel singer and cohost of the show. "You hear all these dreams. Eight years ago there was nothing here but mud and trees. So you get in the car and you ride down the road with him. He says, 'See that ravine back there? You know, at the water park, people love those waves. I've been thinking. If we could build a mountain and put two sets of flaps all around so that we could throw waves out in a circle, then we could build a big hotel there. We could probably have the mountain belch a little smoke and have some fire blow every once in a while. And I think I can put a top on it that will give us year-round water. We'll be able to have the wave flaps year-round.' The guy would be off, running."

Why would anyone want a fake volcano? Perhaps, if you have to ask, you'll never know. But it's a safe bet that the faithful would have loved it.

Jim was also a preacher, with the power of the Holy Spirit. It is a real phenomenon, that moment when a roomful of believers gets the shivery feeling that some larger power is present; it is when unbelievers tend either to become converts or to recoil in a blend of fear and distaste, muttering about mass hysteria. An evangelical preacher like Jim Bakker can help that moment to birth, more often than not, and that is the quality that keeps his followers faithful. Jim and Tammy could transmit at least a mild sensation of the Holy Spirit over the airwaves. When they invited the viewers to give their lives to Christ, the phone bank invariably got busy. But in revival meetings, up in front of the people, Jim could invoke the blessings of the spirit. He could heal the sick and make people speak in tongues.

To nonbelievers, such performances seem like pure fakery. And there is no question that the Gospelgate scandal laid bare rich veins of sleaze, hypocrisy, and cynicism among the preachers. But hypocrisy alone can't explain the preachers caught in sin. Like most people, they live in several roles with several layers of reality, some of them contradictory. Psychologists say most healers, even those who consciously cheat, believe that they can at least sometimes tap a supernatural power. Jim Bakker could joke with his aides about the "Grandma Grunts" gullible enough to send in ten-dollar donations for ten-cent Christmas ornaments, but on some level he believed he was ministering to his flock. The TV preachers generally seem convinced that there is a God and that sin is real. Psychologist Bruce Narramore of the evangelical Biola University in La Mirada, California, said Jimmy Swaggart preached so fiercely about the evils of pornography precisely because he was himself secretly wallowing in it and struggling against his sin. It was Swaggart who led the denunciation of Bakker's philandering, only to be unmasked a year later as a patron of prostitutes himself.

If that seems laughable to most Americans, it is a dead serious drama of sin and repentance to evangelicals—and there are a lot of them. According to Gallup, one of every three adult Americans claims to be born again, an evangelical believer. But to most of the rest of the nation, what the evangelicals believe and why they act as they do remain a mystery; their faith seems as strange as the animism of Zaire. And no part of it is more foreign than Jim Bakker's religion, the Pentecostal branch of evangelical Christianity.

All evangelicals believe in the divinity of Christ and that the Bible is, at least in some sense, true in every word. All of them believe that they attain salvation by being born again in a religious experience and that they must evangelize, proclaiming the good news of resurrection and salvation in word and deed. Fundamentalists like Billy Graham and Jerry Falwell draw the line there. A minority, called charismatic or Pentecostal believers, hold that the Holy Spirit can work directly through them, letting them prophesy or heal the sick. To be saved, a person must not only believe but receive the baptism of the Holy Spirit, a kind of religious ecstasy during which the believer speaks in unearthly tongues, as Christ's disciples were said to have done at the feast of Pentecost. This may include falling to the ground, twitching, and writhing. Often described as "holy rollers," the charismatic Christians have deep doctrinal feuds with their fundamentalist brethren. Nothing in the PTL holy wars astonished knowledgeable observers more than the fact that Falwell, a fundamentalist Baptist, was trying to run a charismatic ministry. In the end, that misfit alone may have doomed the effort.

Like most TV preachers in the charismatic line, Jim Bakker refrained from televising the showier blessings of the spirit. On the cool medium, unbelievers tend to be put off by the sight of people writhing on the floor and babbling. But for the faithful who cared to come to Heritage USA or to attend healing services when Jim preached elsewhere, the full power of his calling was evident. He wasn't usually as gaudy as healers like John Wesley Fletcher, Ernest Angley, or Oral Roberts, stomping and shouting as sufferers swooned under his healing hand. But at least once, he wrote in his autobiography, *Move That Mountain!*, when he stretched out his hand to pray over a woman with cancer, "it appeared a bolt of lightning shot from the tips of my fingers and hit her. Her body was literally picked up and hurled through the air." And her Pap test, which had been positive, showed no illness after that.

By the *Wall Street Journal*'s estimate, one out of every four negative Pap tests in recent years has been a tragic mistake. For the faithful, that isn't the point; true believers don't look to science for proof of miracles. And in the end, it was Jim Bakker's ability to call on such spectacular power that kept at least some of his followers loyal even after the scandal broke. Martha Cravener, a widow and regular PTL contributor from Elizabethtown, Pennsylvania, told a *Newsweek* reporter that she had been upset when she first heard the story about Jim's afternoon with Jessica Hahn. But then she realized that Jim had repented and been forgiven by God. She had seen him preach twice since the sin, she said, and "If he was still sinning, the anointing of God would not have been on him. But the power of God was all over him. I definitely feel he was forgiven."

And Jim and Tammy did some good in the course of doing well. Along with its countinghouse and playgrounds, Heritage USA had Fort Hope, a place where homeless men could straighten themselves out, and Heritage House, a home to offer pregnant girls an alternative to abortion. PTL ran a nationwide prison ministry and claimed to have 679 dropoff points around the country where the needy could go for food and clothing. It also helped other ministries, colleges, charities, and individuals with generous gifts.

Some of these publicized good works, however, were more sham than blessing. In 1986, for instance, Jim had a personable and telegenic guest on the show, Kevin Whittum, the seventeen-year-old victim of a rare bone disease. Impulsively, Jim announced that he would build a home at Heritage USA for Kevin and other handicapped children. In the next few months, more than three million dollars poured in, and a huge blue Victorian house was built. But Kevin's House didn't meet the local fire codes for such residences. Because Jim's cousins, who were to run the place, had legally adopted Kevin, he could legally live there; but this solution had obvious limits, and there were never more than two handicapped children living in Kevin's House.

As the glitz spread, the original Christian vision of Heritage USA blurred and faded. As Jim first sketched it out to his executives, the campground wasn't to be all play for the visitors. The heart of PTL was to be Christian counseling. At every hour of the day, the show was playing on cable TV somewhere, and troubled souls were calling in for help. Every campsite would be fitted with a phone jack, Jim said, and the visitors in their campers and trailers were to take the calls. They would counsel and pray, ease the pain, do some good for hurting people while having their vacation, and go home with a sense of renewed calling. The phone jacks were put in, but their purpose was forgotten; in recent years, nobody has talked to the campers about counseling. It was a symptom of the deeper rot.

In the early days of PTL, old-timers say, Jim and Tammy were warm and open people, generous to their workers and casually friendly to visitors. But a guest on the show in 1976 recalls that Jim was badly shaken by a bomb threat to PTL that day. There had been a rash of crazy calls: A woman claiming to be the mother of Jesus demanded to be on the show; there were threats to kill Jim and Tammy and kidnap Tammy Sue, by then a six-year-old known to all as Susie. "I thought people would love me for this," Jim told his friend plaintively, "but they hate me." Within a few weeks, this visitor says, Jim had beefed up his security force and "started becoming a little Napoleon." Other PTL old-timers say his paranoia was reinforced by his battle with the Federal Communications Commission, which began hearings in 1979 on whether he had mishandled donations. By then he was well along in the subtle process of corruption wrought by money, power, and an abundance of yes-men. To most of the two thousand workers at PTL, Jim and Tammy had become just images on the screen and distant presences, sweeping past with their entourage, bestowing at best empty smiles.

Part of the corruption that afflicted the Bakkers may be built into the evangelical method. It is not a faith that calls for much introspection, and even the best of its practitioners rely on a kind of trickery to win souls for God. More than a century ago the evangelist Charles G. Finney advised his brethren to try "new measures to stir up emotional excitements," and preachers have been trying them ever since. There is outright manipulation, making people feel guilt and shame as a buildup to the altar call: "And that other sin—I don't have to tell you what it is; you feel it in your own heart. . . ." There is also the basic ballyhoo to make everything seem slightly bigger than life, from the blackness of a sinner's guilt to the number of souls being saved. In most congregations, at least half the people responding to the altar call have been there before; they are reaffirming an earlier decision. Even the elder statesman Billy Graham uses shills: The counselors who are to greet his converts and listen to their problems are seated randomly in the audience. After the call, they lead the way to the altar, giving others courage to follow and at least doubling the visible response.

The TV preachers routinely exaggerate the size of their audiences and the amount of their revenues. Many of them use bait-and-switch tactics, raising money for one cause and spending it on another. It is as if such tricks could be winked at in the good cause; in evangelism, the end justifies the means. And if the preachers start their mission sincere and honest, said Russ Reid, a director of the Evangelical Council for Financial Accountability (ECFA), "The crowd seduces them. The sick people feed back to them a message: 'We need you.' The preachers begin to believe it and are seduced by it."

Jim and Tammy may have been more easily seduced than most. There is no question that Jim Bakker's personality subtly encouraged the process; he dreaded confrontation and obviously disliked being contradicted or told bad news. He had always had a tendency to shade facts toward his own wish for the truth, and as time went on, fewer and fewer people would tell him it wasn't so. The result was a wall of insulation built around him by his aides.

"I helped with that," said Don Hardister, the fiercely loyal former undercover cop who headed PTL's security force and spent most of his time close to Bakker. "My job was to keep him in as sterile an environment as I could, and I got pretty good at it. Keep it brief and keep it moving, that kind of thing. I prided myself on breaking any contact that I could. It wasn't something he asked for. But he kind of got used to it, fell into it." Even when Jim sat with the faithful watching the Passion play, Hardister said, two rows of PTL employees surrounded him in the amphitheater, keeping the masses away.

In that kind of atmosphere, Jim and Tammy rapidly came to agree with their courtiers' view of what was due them. Some of the perks came without payment or request, as a matter of course. Hardister's security men were constantly around; it was part of the routine for them to function as servants, too. They stocked the refrigerator, washed the cars, cleaned the swimming pool, carried out the cat litter. Small and large indulgences also became routine. On one road trip, Hardister recalled, he was sent out to buy a hundred dollars worth of cinnamon buns—not because anyone was hungry but because Tammy liked the way they made the hotel room smell. Michael Richardson, another former bodyguard, wrote in his book on life with Jim and Tammy about the time Jim told him to call the state commissioners and have the speed limit lowered to forty-five miles an hour on the road past the main gate, so people would have to slow down and look. When Jim wanted his houseboat moved under a causeway across man-made Lake Wylie, he tried to order the utility company that managed the dam to let out enough water so the boat could float through.

They lived in an increasingly artificial world, with values to match. Tammy had her breasts enlarged and fat sucked from her midriff; Jim had his chin tucked so sharply that his whiskers grew behind his ears, where the face skin had been pulled up. There was no surgical procedure to implant deceit or hypocrisy, but apparently they grew by themselves. There was the day Jim taped a television spot in the California desert, telling movingly how he loved to go into the desert alone to pray and seek guidance, just as Moses and Christ had done. As Frye Gaillard of the *Charlotte Observer* told the story, Jim finished the take; then, without so much as an ironic smile, he gathered up his retinue and his TV crew, climbed into his Rolls, and drove home. Well, Christ and Moses didn't have Jim's responsibilities.

Doug and Laura Lee Oldham were the Best Friends. That is a position recognized in most royal courts and a lot of corporate suites, and it doesn't quite mean what most people mean by the words *best friends* because equality has nothing to do with it. Doug and Laura Lee spent a lot of time with Jim and Tammy, whenever they were wanted. The two couples went places together and laughed a lot, and Doug listened to Jim's grand plans, and Laura Lee went shopping with Tammy; they helped entertain the visiting dignitaries. They had held the post for about a year and a half when the scandal broke out. There had been other Best Friends, of course, a long line; when the Oldhams went to get their perks—the leased car and the PTL-owned house at Tega Cay right next to Jim and Tammy's—one of the businesspeople told them it was known as the house for the rent-a-friends.

But Doug and Laura Lee were good at the job because they genuinely liked Jim and Tammy. "They are great people. Supercreative," said Doug not long after the crash. "Tam is a gem. Jim is a genius. But the price they pay to be that good is terribly high. I love them. Having said that, I have to face myself, and so I could not work for them anymore."

Doug is a tired, aging lion of a man, likable and genial with a shock of white hair and a comfortable paunch; on the show he was a folksy presence and an easy baritone voice, launching into gospel hymns as if they were conversation. He is also a little soft at the core. When his friend was accused of homosexuality, Doug didn't try to find out whether it was true. "I didn't want to hit hard evidence," he said, and he never asked Jim about it either. But he is a shrewd observer with a wry, self-deprecating wit and few illusions. "Jim and Tam were always fighting," he said. "That was our job. Mine was to keep him cool. Laura Lee's was to keep her cool. And the people here said we did a better job than anybody had ever done."

Keeping Jim cool was mainly a matter of listening but occasionally taking a hand in PTL business. Nominally, Doug was president of the recording company, but that didn't mean anything; Jim said there were M.B.A.'s to take care of the business. "I had a lot of power, although there was no power," Doug said. "Because I was with Jim all the time, it appeared I did. In a monarchy, everybody assumes that if you're with the king, you have power." In practice, Doug tried to use his access to tell Jim some of the things others wouldn't. "The people close to him didn't want anybody else to get to him," he said. "It was protecting themselves from what would happen if somebody brought negative information to him. The lower-echelon people never got to see Jim except maybe in the hallway. So I always felt like the little people were a bit abused. There were some people who seemed to take pleasure in making life miserable for people. I'd bring something like that to his attention, and he'd remedy it." There were limits, of course. "I didn't do any more of that than I thought I had to, because I knew I'd run out of grace. There could have been a hundred things a day, and he'd have gotten tired of it."

Looking back on it, Doug said, "I thought we were on a friendship basis. And, probably as close as he comes to friendship, we were." But Jim was a small and essentially inward man who preserved his privacy. In hindsight, what Doug thought was Jim's openness seemed a bit devious. "I realize now that all he told me was what he wanted me to get," Doug said, "and he manipulated my moves by what he fed me." Jim wanted to manipulate Laura Lee, too; toward the end, Doug said, he tried to make her a lackey, sending her on needless errands just to show that he could. Jim didn't much like women, Doug decided. But on the whole, "I'll have to admit

I enjoyed the relationship. To have that genius smile on you makes you a little bit giddy. Everybody's saying, 'Gosh, nobody's ever been that close to him.' And you're wandering around. You say, 'This is fun.' "

Laura Lee's job was harder. She is a motherly, down-home woman, steady of temperament and serene of spirit, and she needed all that to deal with Tammy. "It's a little hard to explain her," Laura Lee said. "I liked her. I liked being with her." Tammy was brilliant, mercurial, restless, and funny, with an almost desperate gaiety. "It was like she had not had the proper nurturing, growing up, and she was bereft in that emotional realm," said Laura Lee. "She wouldn't let you mother her, you couldn't do it overtly, but if you could be a support, in a way she didn't know you were doing it, she relied on it. She rested in it. It was kind of like a little talented bratty sister that you would do anything to try to smooth her way."

Perhaps you had to be there to see the fun in it. In Laura Lee's telling, Tammy's vitality sounded mainly exhausting—and Jim seemed to think so, too. Mostly he kept the business side of PTL to himself; if Tammy found out about something, said Laura Lee, "She'd just chew it. She'd just get ahold of it and shake it like a puppy with a sock until it just drove you nuts. And she'd get an opinion, maybe right, maybe wrong, but she'd bull it through until Jim would throw up his hands and do whatever she wanted. You could see why he tried to keep it away from her." Sometimes, she said, Tammy could be savage. At a booksellers' convention, she tongue-lashed a PTL vice-president because she didn't like the display booth. The man had no choice but to quit on the spot. But Tammy didn't know she had done wrong, Laura Lee said. "It's not hardly Christian, but she does not really see that. I know it's no excuse, but she doesn't see it."

Tammy's strangest trait was a streak of self-destructiveness. The shopping, Laura Lee said, was just barely in control. Tammy spent all her salary on it but never used Jim's money and scrupulously repaid any PTL petty cash she might dip into. Worse, she refused to eat properly, even though she suffered from hypoglycemia, a condition of precariously balanced blood sugar that can lead to emotional storms. To keep from flying off the handle, Tammy should have had carefully balanced meals and well-timed snacks. Instead, she would flush her breakfast down the toilet, then get snappish and shaky; Laura Lee would have to trick her into taking a bite of tuna sandwich to get enough protein into her system to settle her down. And Tammy had the same perverse reaction to doctors' orders the time she had suction lipectomy surgery to remove the fat from her waistline. They told her to be sure to drink lots of fluids, but she simply wouldn't do it. It was scary, Laura Lee said. Tammy "had gone into the fetal position on the bed, like she was withdrawn from life totally. She would not do what she knew she had to do. It was a really strange thing." Laura Lee finally got Tammy to drink—by telling her not to.

The couples split when Jim fell out with Falwell. Doug, who had worked for Falwell before coming to PTL, chose to stay with the show in the new regime, and he and Laura Lee went back to Tega Cay, leaving the Bakkers in their California exile. "I was mad for a while, felt like I had wasted two years of my life," said Laura Lee. "But now that's sort of settled in my mind. I have a great affection for her. I really do. I tried to serve her, and I did it because I liked her."

Just down the road from the Heritage USA gates, Juanita Fitzgerald, who moved here from Ohio to be near Jim and Tammy, sat in her Whole in One doughnut shop a few days after the scandal erupted. "Every time Tammy cried, I cried and grabbed my ol' checkbook," she said. "Millions of people did the same thing. You're so hyped up from the broadcast, when they say 'Give,' you give.

"It's a deception, that whole thing. He was just like a king. He walked around, but he don't speak to the little people. Nothing that happens out there surprises me. The way I look at it, it's just Jim Bakker's kingdom, and I think he's coming back."

Chapter 2

Good News and Clanging Cymbals

"Remember, God loves you," said Jim with his rubbery smile.

"He really, really does," said Tammy, her mascara getting moist again.

That was their daily sign-off on the TV show, and it was the last message the faithful saw as they left Heritage USA. It plumbed the shallows of the Bakkers' beliefs; in eight words, two thousand years of Christian theology had been reduced to a bumper sticker.

The message was also perfectly suited to the medium. Television is notoriously bad at delivering complex ideas and changing people's minds; what it does best is to entertain its audience and reinforce clear, positive values. The TV preachers must convey absolute certainty: If you will believe and love Jesus, you will be happy and go to heaven. That is a ridiculous simplification of Christianity, a faith whose mysteries, ambiguities, and paradoxes have kept theologians arguing for two millennia. But American evangelicals have been whittling away at those complexities for nearly two centuries. By the time Jim and Tammy came along, the faith had been cut down almost to fit the small screen.

Their feel-good theology was one of the most extreme doctrines in the electronic church, a far cry from the righteous moralizing of a Jimmy Swaggart or Billy Graham's stern call to the nation to regain greatness by returning to God's ways. But nearly all the preachers come from a common tradition and share basic beliefs, just as their viewers often watch several preachers with different messages. The evangelical faith has found its home in America; revivalism has both shaped and been shaped by the American experience.

Evangelism is as old as Christianity. The word itself comes from the Greek *euangelion,* "good news," and it was Christ himself who told his disciples, "Go ye into all the world, and preach the Gospel to every creature" (Mark 16:15). Its appeal is summed up in Jessica Hahn's account of her first visit to the revival tent in 1974. As she told *Playboy,* "I thought, this must be what falling in love is like. . . . When you are raised Catholic, it is very quiet, and that is beautiful. They choose to worship that way, and that's nice. But in this church, everything was alive. There were lots and lots of people my age. There were tons and tons of people and activities. And the minute you walked in, they took your hand, told you to just come and be seated. And you felt wanted." The preachers, she said, were *"fierce.* They're real tough in their preaching. And I thought, God, that authority. It was like, *head on."*

It is a style that fits the national stereotypes of warmth, energy, impatience with fine distinctions, even vulgarity, and so it is that the evangelical churches have been thriving and growing in the second half of the twentieth century while the staid old mainline Protestant denominations have been losing worshipers. Ronald H. Nash, a professor of religion and philosophy at Western Kentucky University, estimated in *Evangelicals in America* that the Methodists alone dropped nine hundred thousand members between 1970 and 1977, while the Presbyterians and Episcopalians lost five hundred thousand each. Meanwhile, evangelicals now boast seven thousand colleges and seminaries and six thousand bookstores; they have sent thirty thousand missionaries to foreign countries, eleven times the number of mainline missionaries.

Nobody can agree on how many evangelicals there are in the country. The estimates range from forty million to sixty million. In 1986, a Gallup survey found that 33 percent of the adult civilian population described itself as evangelical; that would be more than fifty-eight million Americans. That includes growing numbers of worshipers in the mainline churches—including four to five million Roman Catholics—who have had born-again experiences and consider themselves evangelical. But not all evangelicals believe the same things or accept one another's beliefs. The forty-three denominations that are members of the National Association of Evangelicals (NAE) managed to agree on a seven-point statement of faith, beginning with the crucial point that the Bible is inspired, infallible, and the only authoritative word of God. But there are other sects that are not members of the NAE and would disagree sharply on finer points of doctrine, most of them involving just how literally which word of God must be taken.

In the beginning, Christianity was a personal faith, passed on from disciple to convert, rich with anecdote and individual meanings. But almost from the start, it was an institution, too, growing layers of ritual and doctrine, and as the centuries passed, it was increasingly defined by the Roman Catholic hierarchy. The stress came to be on the chain of authority, with the church as intermediary between God and worshiper, claiming the power to interpret God's word and relay commands to the sinner. In turn, the faithful were offered the certainty of salvation if only they followed the rules and obeyed the church.

Martin Luther laid the foundations for modern evangelical faith in A.D. 1517, when he challenged that hierarchy. Luther stressed the Bible, not the priest, as the source of authority for believers, and he said no amount of good works would ensure a place among the saints. Only faith in God could bring sinful man to salvation, and it was granted only by the grace of God.

But Luther's theology left the faithful with no solid assurance of salvation, and the search for certainty has preoccupied Protestants ever since. In the seventeenth century, English Puritans began to emphasize the importance of the conversion experience—as they saw it, not a blinding flash but a years-long process of spiritual growth that progressed from indifference to conviction, from terror to reassurance. When they had been through that, the elect could know who they were. And when Puritanism was transplanted to the American colonies, this rebirth became the centerpiece of the faith. Believers in the Congregational Church had to undergo a trial of admission to membership, proving to skeptical older members that they had experienced a true and lasting conversion. It was a serious business, with the applicants detailing their personal journeys and the brethren questioning intently; witnesses offered support or damaging evidence on a candidate's sanctity and moral behavior. Perhaps these trials grew too arduous; in the late seventeenth and early eighteenth centuries, there were periodic crises in American religion as church membership declined. Colonial ministers denounced the impiety and waywardness of their flocks.

Then came the Great Awakening of the 1740s, the first of several such waves of revival in American church history. The English preacher George Whitefield triggered it, in three visits to the colonies. To worshipers who had suffered for years under the nasal dronings of scholarly ministers dissecting fine points of theology, Whitefield was a revelation. He preached in fields and marketplaces as well as churches, and his dramatic oratory, human-interest stories, and well-rehearsed breast-beatings drew hysterical outcries and repentant groans from his listeners. It was a theatrical experience on both sides, under the banner of salvation. Benjamin Franklin wrote a bit acidly that it was extraordinary "how much they admired and respected him, notwithstanding his common abuse of them, by assuring them they were naturally 'half beasts and half devils.' "

Whitefield and his contemporaries did tend to harp on the shortcomings of the faithful. John Calvin had taught that mortal man was naturally sinful; he urged a life of austerity and the shunning of temptation to be worthy of God's grace, and this emphasis on sin was a strong current in American preaching. The best-known sermon of the time was Jonathan Edwards's classic "Sinners in the Hands of an Angry God," which left strong men actually clinging to the pillars of the meetinghouse and crying aloud for mercy from the certainty of damnation. Edwards told them that they were heavy with sin, walking over the pit of hell on a rotten scaffold, kept from falling only by the hand of God. But "The God that holds you over the pit of hell, much as one holds a spider, or some loathsome insect over the fire, abhors you, and is dreadfully provoked . . . you are ten thousand times more abominable in his eyes, than the most hateful venomous serpent is in ours . . . and yet it is nothing but his hand that holds you from falling into the fire every moment."

It was strong stuff. It also built on the complex theology of Luther and Calvin, for Whitefield and his colleagues were not just tub-thumpers but scholars, too. But its effect was to ratify emotion and the conversion experience at the expense of formal doctrine and thus to change the nature of Protestantism in America. In the long run, such traditional churches as the Congregational would lose members to the new Baptists and Methodists.

The trend accelerated in the Second Awakening, beginning in 1790, as revivalism moved west and traded sophistication for a new raw emotional power. Its most memorable event was a huge camp meeting at Cane Ridge, Kentucky, in August 1801; it drew a crowd of at least ten thousand, at a time when the state capital had only two thousand residents, and it was greeted as the "greatest outpouring of the Spirit since the Pentecost." The crowd was made up of frontiersmen, tough, profane, and hard-drinking, with wives described by one scholar as "scarcely demure" and running packs of unruly children. It was an extraordinary scene of tents, wagons, flickering bonfires, strong drink, and stronger emotion; for people living in isolated cabins, the meeting must have been enormously stimulating. Some critics said that the passions roused weren't primarily religious and that "more souls were begot than saved."

But the saving was spectacular. The Spirit moved the converted to frenzies of faith. They barked aloud, twitched uncontrollably, fell to earth, danced solemnly and ecstatically for hours, laughed rapturously or sang with an unearthly resonance. The master of these revels was a Presbyterian minister, Barton Warren Stone, who reverently cataloged in his memoirs the symptoms of salvation. Those who fell, he said, would "generally, with a piercing scream, fall like a log on the floor, earth or mud, and appear as dead." The "jerks" might afflict one part of the body or the whole convert. "When the head alone was affected, it would be jerked backward and forward, or from side to side, so quickly that the features of the face could not be distinguished. When the whole system was affected, I have seen the person stand in one place, and jerk backward and forward in quick succession, their head nearly touching the floor behind and before." But the singing, Stone said, was "more unaccountable than any thing else I ever saw. The subject in a very happy state of mind would sing most melodiously, not from the mouth or nose, but entirely in the breast, the sounds issuing from thence. Such music silenced every thing, and attracted the attention of all. It was most heavenly. None could ever be tired of hearing it."

The elders of Stone's staid church were alarmed and embarrassed by such goings-on. They banned any further camp meetings on Presbyterian ground. But the new sect of Methodists, founded by the English brothers John and Charles Wesley, saw revivals as a great opportunity to win souls. In their book, conversion was only the beginning of salvation. It was John Wesley who developed the concept of the second blessing after conversion, to eradicate "inbred sin." His colleague John Fletcher specified that the second experience should be the baptism in the Holy Spirit—a teaching that led directly to the Pentecostal movement of the twentieth century. For Wesley's followers, "Methodist fits" were a perfectly acceptable way to win souls.

Methodists used camp meetings and circuit-riding preachers to spread the faith and made great inroads on the frontier; by 1844 they were the largest religious denomination in America, with more than a million souls. It was a yeoman church of simple faith and considerable power of preaching, appealing to people impatient with the complex dogma and ecclesiastical formality of the New England Congregationalists and Presbyterians. But the Methodists still insisted on order and authority in churchly affairs, and they began losing to the Baptist Church, an even higher emotional bidder. The Baptists grew nearly as fast as the Methodists had done, not with circuit riders but with farmer-preachers—ordinary men who heard the call to preach and organized their neighbors into congregations, without financial support or theological direction from any central authority.

By the pre-Civil War period, evangelism was almost anything it said it was, and the father of modern revivalism, Charles G. Finney, brought this simple faith to the cities of America. None of the refinements mattered to Finney; he was tormented by the urgent need to save souls from hell by any method that worked, and he called on his brethren to develop "new measures to stir up emotional excitements" in revival meetings. He was the first preacher to popularize the altar call, denouncing sin and then inviting the repentant to come forward and be saved. He would invade a community without invitation, pray for sinners by name, and ask God to inspire his critics with contrition. His protracted meetings met nightly for a week or more, and he would target potential converts by seating them on the "anxious bench," where a sinner would be surrounded by neighbors and relatives, who discussed his faults one by one and prayed over him until he saw the light. By all accounts, that was an experience that few wanted prolonged.

More important, Finney's leveling faith finally made religion democratic. Anyone willing to repent could join the church immediately, and salvation was guaranteed. The Puritan concept of man's total depravity and the Calvinist insistence on original sin were all but dropped. God didn't choose the elect anymore; people could choose to be saved. It was wonderfully fair and open to all. The leveling extended to revival music: no more chanted psalms or complex harmonies, but popular tunes with easily learned words, highly effective in prompting religious feelings. Soon every wandering preacher traveled with a singer to help stir up the crowd, and later in the century the best known of these men, Ira Sankey, compiled a set of gospel hymnals.

There was a clear dash of anti-intellectualism in the movement as a whole. As early as Barton Stone's day, two of his associates wrote that they neither knew nor cared what John Calvin thought, and Charles Finney admitted at his Presbyterian ordination that he hadn't so much as read the denomination's credo, the Westminster Confession of faith. The Methodist circuit rider Peter Cartwright scoffed that an educated preacher was like "a gosling that had got the straddles by wading in the dew." This know-nothing strain persisted, and it helped stamp evangelicalism for decades as a lower-class faith.

In the preaching of Dwight L. Moody after the Civil War, the spiky theology of Luther and Calvin was finally simplified nearly to Jim Bakker's level. A onetime shoe salesman, Moody preached a God of Love who threatened no hellfire or damnation but smiled benevolently on his people. Moody shunned theatrics or dramatic exhortations. His message was simply the "three Rs: Ruin by sin, Redemption by Christ and Regeneration by the Holy Spirit." He told converts to "join some church at once"—which one didn't matter—and he had no concern for the thorny intellectual and social problems of the late nineteenth century, from Darwinism to the Industrial Revolution. All problems, he was sure, could be solved by people getting saved.

It was fitting that Moody was also the first to fashion an evangelical empire. His was a personal ministry, affiliated not with a denomination but with the YMCA, and he founded the Moody Bible Institute and the Mount Hermon School for Boys. "It's not spectacular by modern standards," said George Marsden, a religious historian at Duke University, "but he really built his own denomination. What it amounts to is Dwight L. Moody Enterprises."

But the challenges that Moody chose to ignore wouldn't go away, and the resulting tension split American Protestantism. Urbanization and large-scale Catholic immigration were changing American life. Catholics introduced new customs and values, and with urbanization, the anonymity and temptations of city life were eroding the power of churches that had been able to dominate small towns and farm communities. Both higher education and science were becoming secularized. Most college presidents until then had been clergymen, and scientists had tended to see their purpose as calling attention to the wonders of God's work. Now the natural sciences were on the rise, imposing their own standards and dominating academic thought. Charles Darwin had challenged the Book of Genesis head-on; there was talk of "warfare" between science and religion.

The mainline churches responded with a liberalizing movement. As they came to see the appalling social conditions and new needs created by the Industrial Revolution, the liberals started giving priority to a "social gospel" that threatened to become more important than evangelism itself. At the same time, the intellectual roots of the faith were losing strength. The Old Testament was no longer universally read as the literal word of God, but more as a religious history of the Jews; Jesus was coming to be seen more as a moral teacher than as the actual son of God whose death mysteriously redeemed human sin and promised individual salvation. By the early twentieth century, liberal thought had taken over most of the Protestant seminaries and ruled the mainline denominations. Even the evangelical churches were losing their fire; impelled to respectability, the Baptists and Methodists were drifting into the mainstream.

The inevitable backlash to the liberal movement became known as fundamentalism. It was a militantly evangelical and antimodern movement, and it took as its guiding principle the doctrine of biblical inerrancy. Until the 1880s, the literal truth of the Bible had been not so much proclaimed as assumed; as sociologist James Davison Hunter of the University of Virginia pointed out, it didn't occur to anyone to defend the credo until it was under attack. But within a few years, conservative theologians had worked out the lines of defense.

Inerrancy came to mean that the statements and teachings of the

Bible are inspired by God and are completely without error. The new natural science had established the primacy of facts, and now the fundamentalists saw the Bible as a book of facts. All its historic and scientific statements are true and accurate, they declared; any statement of history or science that contradicts the Bible must be untrue. As it has evolved over the years, inerrancy leaves room for poetry and metaphor. When the psalmist wrote, "Lift up your heads, O ye gates" (Psalms 24:7), he did not mean that gates had grown heads. There is also room for scholarship to correct bad translations and even, in some cases at least, to explain inconsistencies by recognizing that ancient writers used hyperbole and set little store by precision of language.

Fundamentalism had been gaining force for twenty years before it got its name. Between 1910 and 1915, a set of twelve paperback books defending conservative doctrines were published. They were financed by two wealthy laymen in Los Angeles and collectively called *The Fundamentals.* Each volume set out basic arguments for conservative doctrine and went on to defend them against the liberal heresies. More than three million copies of the books were distributed, and in 1920 the preacher Curtis Lee Laws extended the name to the whole conservative movement, calling it fundamentalism.

Meanwhile, the movement was gaining momentum and political force, particularly in the battle to defend Prohibition and ban the teaching of evolutionary theory.

Fundamentalists could claim only part of the credit for the passage in 1919 of the Eighteenth Amendment, which banned commerce in alcoholic beverages. The temperance movement was a broad coalition that had been growing for a century, and by the time the amendment was ratified, thirty-three states already had their own prohibition statutes. But it soon became evident that the contempt for law spawned by Prohibition was corrupting the nation, and support for it dwindled through the 1920s. The fundamentalists, however, kept the faith. By the time Prohibition was repealed in 1933, they were practically alone in defending it—a stance that heightened their image as cranky zealots.

It was the war on Darwinism, however, that brought the movement its worst defeat. This, too, began with a series of victories. Fundamentalists had introduced bills in twenty states to ban the teaching of evolution in public schools and won passage in nine states. The American Civil Liberties Union was looking for a test case to try to overturn these laws and found it when John Scopes, a young teacher, agreed to defy the ban in Tennessee. William Jennings Bryan, the widely admired populist orator, prosecuted Scopes in the sensational "monkey trial" in Dayton, Tennessee, in 1925. Bryan won the jury's verdict, but Clarence Darrow for the defense made Bryan—and, by extension, fundamentalism—look ridiculous.

A climax in the trial came when Darrow put Bryan on the witness stand and quizzed him about the faith. It soon became plain that Bryan didn't know much about it, or many other things either; he said he had never wondered about any other religions and didn't believe any civilization on earth could predate Noah's flood, which he said had happened in 2348 B.C. Nor did he expect to learn anything new. "I have all the information I want to live by and to die by," he declared. He believed that snakes crawl on their bellies as God's punishment for tempting Eve. But when Darrow asked how snakes had traveled before that, Bryan couldn't say. After that, the pack of northern journalists headed by H. L. Mencken gave fundamentalism a permanent brand as backward, bigoted, and ignorant— a creed for the "booboisie."

That image was reinforced by the prominent evangelists of the day. Billy Sunday was a farm boy and professional baseball player for the Chicago White Stockings before he was converted and took to the revival tent, where he and his chorister, Homer A. Rodeheaver, combined elements of music hall and low theater to electrify the faithful. By 1904, he was successful enough to be able to demand that expense money be raised in advance of his crusades. In 1917, his peak year, 1.4 million people came to hear him preach in New York, and he won 98,264 converts. It was an age in love with statistics, and Billy liked to boast that his system had cut the cost of making converts to two dollars per soul.

Billy called himself "a rube of the rubes," and he behaved accordingly. He would shout, rant, smash furniture, hurl himself across the stage, and rip off his shirt to dramatize his torrents of words. What the church needed, he preached, were fighting men of God, not "hog-jowled, weasel-eyed, sponge-columned, mushy-fisted, jelly-spined, pussy-footing, four-flushing, Charlotte-russe Christians." More delicate souls might urge Christians to hate the sin but love the sinner. Not Billy. Any man who wasn't a teetotaler was a "dirty, low-down, whiskey-soaked, beer-guzzling, bull-necked, foul-mouthed hypocrite."

Aimee Semple McPherson was almost as dramatic. One of the first evangelists to see the possibilities of radio, she was the first woman to preach on the airwaves and the first preacher to build a radio station owned by her church. She used it to build support for her Angelus Temple in Los Angeles, then the largest church in America, seating fifty-three hundred believers. A flamboyant, attractive woman in flowing robes, she personally conducted twenty-one weekly services, many of them with theatrical flourishes to drive home what she called the Foursquare Gospel. Sister Aimee's idea of a socko opening for a sermon was to drive into the church dressed as a policeman, blow a whistle, and shout, "Stop! You are going to hell!"

Sister Aimee's ministry suffered a major setback in 1926, when she disappeared for a month. She turned up in a Mexican border town, saying she had been kidnapped but had escaped and walked to safety across the desert. It was noticed, however, that her shoes were unscuffed by the ordeal, and she was accused of spending the month sinning in Carmel with a married man. It was a national sensation. She was charged with conspiracy to impair public morals; but the key witness changed her story, and the case was dropped. If Sister Aimee's national image was a bit tarnished after that, her own faithful seemed largely unflustered by the escapade. She established her own denomination, the International Church of the Four-square Gospel, the next year, and it went on to flourish under the ministry of her son, Rolf McPherson.

That was far from the first sex scandal in the American clergy. The most notorious case involved Henry Ward Beecher, a popular minister in Brooklyn and the brother of Harriet Beecher Stowe, author of *Uncle Tom's Cabin*. Beecher was called the "greatest preacher since St. Paul," and he earned forty thousand dollars a year from his sermons and writing, a vast sum in those post-Civil War days. In 1874 his friend and protégé Theodore Tilton accused Beecher of having an affair with Tilton's wife, Elizabeth, and sued him for alienation of affections. The six-month trial was a sensation but ended in a hung jury. Beecher, only slightly tainted, stayed in his pulpit. He was very much a mainstream minister, but like some of the modern televangelists, he preached a message revolving around God's love. Some historians think he rationalized his behavior with his theology. "Even if he didn't commit adultery, he stepped beyond acceptable behavior," said Mark Noll, professor of religious history at Wheaton College in Illinois.

Still earlier, there was the case of Ephraim K. Avery, a Methodist revivalist who was accused of murdering a pregnant mill girl in Bristol, Rhode Island, in 1832. He was acquitted, but the people ran him out of town. Some years later another Methodist, John Newland Maffitt, was disgraced in Washington when he was accused of persuading a friend to seduce Maffitt's wife to provide him with grounds for a divorce. And in this century, Aimee Semple McPherson was only one of the preachers who preceded Jim Bakker and Jimmy Swaggart as figures of notoriety. They all helped bolster the stereotype of evangelistic cynicism, hypocrisy, lechery, and greed that had been promoted by H. L. Mencken and driven home by Sinclair Lewis in his 1927 novel *Elmer Gantry.*

In spite of this unlovely image, evangelical faith never really lost ground, particularly in the Bible Belt of the rural South and Midwest and its outposts in Texas, Oklahoma, and California. The fundamentalists grimly kept the faith and won enough converts to keep their churches growing. But the old-time religion was effectively ignored in the mainstream for two decades, until Billy Graham's dramatic emergence in the early 1950s began the era of televangelism.

Long before television, the evangelical movement had split and diversified in matters of doctrine. Beginning in the 1920s, fundamentalists became increasingly isolated from the conservative Protestant mainstream; then fundamentalism itself split into warring camps. Meanwhile, the Pentecostal branch of the faith sprang up in the first decade of the century and grew with considerable vigor. By 1987, the umbrella of evangelicalism covered at least three main rival groups, with countless offshoots.

The central faith remained simple: The Bible was the word of God, and what it said was infallibly true. Christ was divine, born of a virgin, the incarnation of God. His death would atone for the sins of all believers; he rose from the dead and will return to earth in the flesh at the end of the present age. But no matter how hard the preachers tried to take the Bible literally, differing interpretations kept cropping up, and these gave rise to doctrinal disputes—not over major theological problems like free will or the nature of the Trinity, but over points of emphasis and details of prophecy.

And there was a deeper problem: Conservative fundamentalists were retreating from the world into their own hard shell. An evangelical Anglican historian, James Packer, described the process:

> Partly in self-defense, the movement developed a pronounced anti-intellectual bias; it grew distrustful of scholarship, skeptical as to the value of reasoning in matters of religion and truculent in its attitude towards the arguments of its opponents. Something less than intellectual integrity appeared in its readiness to support a good cause with a bad argument. . . . Its adventures in the field of the natural sciences, especially with reference to evolution, were most unfortunate. Here, where the fundamentalists' confidence was greatest, their competence was least, and their performance brought ridicule and discredit on themselves. Generally, fundamentalism lacked theological energy and concern for Christian learning. It grew intellectually barren. Culture became suspect . . . [and] fundamentalism turned in upon itself.

One symptom of this syndrome was the doctrine of separatism, requiring fundamentalists to keep their distance from unbelievers. It was ordered in 2 Corinthians 6:17: "Wherefore come out from among them, and be ye separate, saith the Lord, and touch not the unclean thing; and I will receive you." As applied in practice over the past fifty years, this has meant shunning not only godless and immoral people but Catholics, Jews, liberal Protestants, and even fellow conservatives whose orthodoxy wasn't fierce enough. Terry Muck, executive editor of the magazine *Christianity Today*, says that in practice, the hard-shell fundamentalists gave up on "a hopelessly sinful world" and could only denounce it. In response, the more moderate conservative Protestants regrouped under the nineteenth-century name of evangelicals. They agreed that the world was sinful but hoped it could be at least partly redeemed.

By the 1970s, the fundamentalists had taken separatism so far that they classified three kinds of believers: those who separate themselves from the ungodly; those who refuse to associate with believers who have unbelieving friends; and the truly righteous who fear contamination twice removed, shunning even people whose friends have friends who don't believe. These third-order separatists were the clenched fist of the religious right, and their fortress mentality made their less self-righteous brethren increasingly uncomfortable. That led to a second schism, with Jerry Falwell leading a movement of neofundamentalists back toward the evangelical position. The moderates kept their various labels, but the doctrinal lines between evangelicals and fundamentalists grew blurry.

Meanwhile, Pentecostal or charismatic worship had emerged as a separate branch of conservative Protestantism. Starting in 1901, an itinerant minister, Charles Fox Parham, preached that the gifts of the Holy Spirit (*charisma* is Greek for "favor" or "gift") can still give ordinary Christians the ability to prophesy, have revelations, and heal the sick by faith. Moreover, he said, the baptism of the Holy Spirit is always proved by speaking in tongues, as Christ's disciples are said to have done at the feast of Pentecost. There is some disagreement about what this means, but most Pentecostals say speaking in tongues, or glossolalia, is the God-given ability to pray or speak in a nonearthly or heavenly language. Phoneticians who have studied the subject note skeptically that charismatic worshipers always use the phonemes of their mother tongue in their heavenly language, and hard-line fundamentalists say flatly that glossolalia any time after the first century A.D. is the work of the devil. What matters is love, they say; as St. Paul put it (1 Corinthians 13:1), "If I speak in the tongues of men and of angels, but have not love, I am a noisy gong or a clanging cymbal."

Nonetheless, Parham's message quickly spread to Texas and California, to Chicago and New York. Pentecostalism was color-blind almost from the start; William Seymour, a black evangelist, learned it from Parham and led a tumultuous revival in the black ghetto of Los Angeles in 1906, beginning with a handful of worshipers in a small house and ending several days later in an abandoned warehouse on Azusa Street. Then, in 1914, several thousand midwestern believers joined to form the Assemblies of God, a loose confederation of Pentecostal churches. The Assemblies in turn gave birth to several other schismatic denominations, but even so it has become one of the fastest-growing churches in America.

The original Pentecostals tended to come from the lower social orders, and the faith was regarded condescendingly at best. A reporter at the Azusa Street revival wrote that "night is made hideous . . . by the howlings of the worshipers. The devotees of the weird doctrine practice the most fanatical rites, preach the wildest theories and work themselves into a state of mad excitement." But that stigma has faded with the rising tide of prosperity. In addition, the charismatic faith has spread since 1960 to many middle- and upper-class mainline churches, starting with an Episcopal minister, Dennis Bennett, in Van Nuys, California.

While fundamentalists cling to the Calvinist belief in austerity, hard work, atonement for sin, and abhorrence of worldly pleasures, charismatics tend to put their stress on God's love. It is an old dichotomy in the Protestant faith. As far back as the Puritan movement of sixteenth-century Britain, the pious have been arguing that the Lord loves his people and will not neglect his elect in this life. Indeed, no matter what Calvin said, some prosperous burghers maintained complacently that rich meant right; they were manifestly enjoying God's grace, and the poor were just as obviously destined for hell.

But one wing of the Pentecostal movement has found in this notion the key to millions of Christian hearts. In the late 1930s, in a sermon called "Acres of Diamonds," the preacher Russell Conwell told his flock: "I say you ought to get rich and it is your duty to get rich . . . because to make money honestly is to preach the Gospel. The men who get rich may be the most honest men you find in the community." In recent years, the doctrine has been developed into all-out prosperity theology: God will make you rich, Jim Bakker and his colleagues promised, if you give him your money first as a token of faith.

In Tulsa, Oklahoma, Oral Roberts developed the doctrine of Seed Faith. Giving is just like agriculture, he discovered; the farmer plants a tiny handful of seed and reaps a great harvest. So Roberts sent his contributors Seed Faith booklets, with monthly coupons to clip and mail in to request prayers and note the amount donated. God wants you to succeed, Pat Robertson told his flock; there is an earthly store of abundance waiting for you. It's all there in Luke 6:38: "Give that it may be given unto you." Dozens of other verses reinforced the message, and the preachers told endless stories of pious folk parting with their last dollars in a good cause, only to receive several times as much from a surprise benefactor.

To preachers with a sterner view of God and reality, prosperity theology was outright heresy, a perversion of the faith that turned Calvinism upside down. As Jerry Falwell was to say upon taking over PTL, the Bakkers' message made God into a slot machine and insulted the faith of every poor person whose belief was not rewarded with riches. And it was far from universally tolerated even among charismatics. Jimmy Swaggart, who condemned Bakker and his operation for years, was a fellow minister in the Assemblies of God—until he resigned in his own fall from grace.

For the preachers who held it, however, prosperity theology had an interesting side effect. If they were seen to be rich, it was no disgrace but a proof that their message was true. "Oral recognized what the popes knew long ago," said Roberts's disillusioned old friend Jenkin Lloyd Jones, editor of the *Tulsa Tribune.* "Little people are impressed by wealth. That's why the silver is on display at the Vatican."

And when they come under fire, preachers like Jim Bakker have kept their flocks loyal by explaining their troubles as the work of the devil. In 1978, reformers, including Billy Graham, organized the Evangelical Council for Financial Accountability to enforce rules on the brethren. But in the year of the Bakker scandal, none of the nationally famous television preachers felt constrained to be members. "The preacher lives like a king, but nobody cares," said ECFA board member Russ Reid. "You can't bring them under control because the people who give them their money don't think they need to be brought under control."

Pentecostals are still a minority in the evangelical movement, and hard-line fundamentalists form another minority on the opposite wing. Ronald Nash has pictured the movement as three overlapping circles, with the evangelical mainstream in the center. For practical purposes, most evangelicals pay at least lip service to each other's beliefs and acknowledge each other as Christians, members of the "body of Christ" that is the church. But fundamentalists still shun charismatics; Jerry Falwell, for instance, is widely quoted as having said that speakers in tongues "ate too much pizza last night." And at the extremes, neither hard-line fundamentalists nor Pentecostals fit comfortably in the mainline creed. Some Pentecostals are outright unitarians who deny the Trinity.

For the most part, however, the great disputes that keep the religious right in turmoil involve not major issues of theology but fine points of interpretation and prophecy. All fundamentalists believe that Christ will actually return to earth; many think the End Time is near. But there are deep divisions over the precise scenario of the return.

Most fundamentalists believe Christ will come back and rule a kingdom on earth for a thousand years. This position is called premillennialism, meaning that the Second Coming will occur before the thousand-year reign, or millennium, predicted in Revelation 20:1–10. Some premillennialists are also pretribulationists, who believe that seven years before the Second Coming, the miracle of the Rapture will happen. Christ will return, not in person but in clouds of glory, to take all the saved to heaven. Dead believers from all ages will be restored to life and caught up, and so will the living Christians, all in an instant. Believers sometimes worry about the practical results: surgeons whisked away in the midst of operations; flight crews taken from jetliner cockpits in midair. There are said to be bumper stickers: WARNING: IN CASE OF THE RAPTURE, DRIVER WILL DISAPPEAR.

But the Rapture will usher in the Great Tribulation, seven terrible years in which an evil leader, the Antichrist, will gain control of the world. There will be massacres, and people who become believers during this period will be persecuted mercilessly. Famines, pestilences, and earthquakes will plague the earth. Finally, the armies of the world will converge at a place called Armageddon; then Christ, with the armies of heaven, will return in the true Second Coming to destroy the wicked and set up the millennial kingdom. The writer Hal Lindsey has popularized these predictions in several books, one of which, *The Late Great Planet Earth*, has sold at least twelve million copies.

Among the televangelists, Jerry Falwell, James Robison, Jimmy Swaggart, and Jim Bakker all preach some form of millennialism. But there are other readings of the prophecy. Postmillennialists think there will be no Rapture and no Second Coming until after the thousand-year period in which the kingdom of God will be established on earth. The doctrine called amillennialism holds that the whole passage in the Book of Revelation should be read symbolically: At the end of the present era, there will be only the Second Coming and the Last Judgment. Disputes among the rival factions can be fierce. When Jerry Falwell was called the "most dangerous man in America," Ronald Nash noted, the accusation came not from a liberal Democrat but from a fellow fundamentalist Baptist, the head of Bob Jones University.

Whatever the differences in detail, any such intricate script is ripe with certainty. It has a powerful appeal for people who don't want to wrestle with the implications of free will or the ambiguity of "Lord, I believe: help thou mine unbelief."

Perhaps the same need for certainty leads evangelicals to identify with conservative positions in political and social issues. They generally believe that right and wrong in temporal affairs are defined by the Bible, that there is no legitimate room for compromise on such issues, and that the nation is in moral decline and must turn back to God, old-fashioned morality, and family values. Doctrine even dictates stands on international affairs. Many evangelicals identify the Antichrist with communism and take it as given that he plans to attack Israel. Thus a good Christian has no choice but to fight communism and all its works and support Israel unconditionally. And while the record doesn't warrant alarm over evangelical intolerance and fanaticism, that stereotype, as James Davison Hunter conceded, is not just a caricature. In fact, he said, it "is accurate in many ways."

To most evangelicals, abortion is simply murder; it can't be tolerated. Women are not equal to men; they are simultaneously superior creatures and subservient to men, and they have no interest in giving up their separate status. As Jerry Falwell said once, "God made men to take care of women, to protect them, to help them with their jackets and make sure nobody else messes with them." And as Jeffrey Hadden and Charles E. Swann noted in their 1981 book *Prime Time Preachers*, the hottest issue of all may be homosexual rights. When James Robison attacked homosexuality as "despicable" and "perversion of the highest order," a Dallas TV station had to grant equal time to a gay rights group, and it canceled Robison's program until he promised to abide by the fairness doctrine. He was bewildered. "I did not attack an individual or any group," he protested, "but rather a life-style condemned by the Bible."

In recent years, evangelicals have even tried to invent a devil's religion labeled "secular humanism," derived from the nontheistic, rationalist philosophy known as humanism. There is no such faith or any proof of its existence; there are no secular humanist churches, ministers, doctrines, or congregations. But evangelicals have tried to persuade courts to recognize secular humanism as a full-fledged religion, subject to the same rules that bind other faiths in public debate. This could mean that evangelicals could demand equal time in schools or other public forums to rebut practically any liberal concept, from evolutionary theory to cultural relativism, that doesn't acknowledge the supreme authority of the Bible.

When evangelicals join in political movements like Moral Majority, they are advocating policies driven by biblical prophecy. These commitments may not always be clear. For the purposes of his presidential campaign, Pat Robertson played down some of his earlier statements, including the dictum that only Christians and Jews are qualified to hold public office. And according to Jeffrey Hadden, Robertson once identified the European Common Market as the ten-nation confederacy mentioned in a prophecy of Daniel. Robertson warned that when Greece joined as the tenth member, it set the stage for the rise of the Antichrist, the Rapture, and the Tribulation. Robertson has also said that the Soviet Union will attack Israel and that the Bible "specifically, clearly, unequivocally" foretells that God will destroy Russia in a series of natural calamities. It has never been clear how such a view of events would shape Robertson's foreign policy if he were president, but unbelievers tend to find it a little spooky.

Still, the notion of a monolithic Christian right in American politics is also mythical. Doctrine aside, evangelicals in America are a diverse social and economic lot, running a gamut from Appalachian coal miners to university presidents. On most issues, they vote not for religious reasons but from a blend of social, political, and economic interests. Even on the litmus issues, they are not wholly predictable: The Evangelical Women's Caucus adopted a gay rights resolution in 1986, and evangelicals in Utah oppose prayer in school because Mormons run the schools.

Evangelicals probably made a crucial difference in the narrow victory of the born-again Jimmy Carter over Gerald Ford, but when they deserted Carter for Ronald Reagan four years later, they were part of a national tide. Jerry Falwell was quick to claim that the Moral Majority had created that landslide, but the truth was considerably more complicated. What it showed was that Reagan knew how to include evangelicals as part of his broader majority. Pat Robertson's campaign in 1987 and 1988 proved again that evangelicals can turn out thousands of highly motivated troops to ring doorbells, take over party machinery, and dominate straw polls and caucuses. But to win national elections, a candidate can't count on unified support from the faithful and in any case has to put together a broader coalition.

But if the religious right is still a long way from running the country, its television preachers have built an industry on the millions of faithful—ever hopeful, ever yearning for more perfect faith, ever willing to send money.

Gail Jauregui was born again at the age of seventeen. "I was desperate," she recalled. "I was on drugs, alcohol. My life was terrible! Then it happened. I got on my knees, and I didn't know who I was praying to. But I knew there was somebody up there listening. Since then, my life has just changed totally.

"It's a good life. When I didn't have God, I didn't have anything. With God, I have everything. I have faith to move a mountain. I have joy; I have peace. If I need something, there's somebody there that's going to help me, guide me, direct me. He's my provider; he's my peace. He's everything to me. I wake up, and there he is. I go to sleep, and there he is. Without him, there's no telling where I'd be. He's everything to me. That's my life. God's my life."

Now she was twenty-eight, a laundry worker in Tulsa, Oklahoma. "People shouldn't stop giving," she said. "The devil tries to get you not to give. When a scandal happens, people should be giving more. Because you're not giving to a man, you're giving to God."

Chapter 3
Gospel Economics

To most Americans, the electronic church is a channel to be flipped past or perhaps to be stared at for a minute or two, while a preacher raves about sin and salvation or somebody tells a treacly tale of buying God's favors. Prosperity theology offers a daily catalog of bathos, but the classic moment may have come on Pat Robertson's "700 Club" as far back as 1979. As Dick Dabney wrote it in *Harper's,* Pat's black cohost, Ben Kinchlow, brought the good news from the telephone bank, where volunteers were taking calls from the viewers.

"We have a report just in from Charlottesville, Va.," Ben said. "A lady with an ingrown toenail sent in $100 along with her Seven Lifetime Prayer Requests. Within a week—get this—*three* of those *lifetime* prayer requests have been answered!"

"Praise *God*!" said Pat.

"And that's not all," said Ben. "The toenail was miraculously healed *the very next day*!"

"Praise God," said Pat again. "You know, you can't outgive God."

Televangelism is big business. Across America in 1987, there were 221 television and 1,370 radio stations broadcasting mostly religious programming. Seven cable TV networks did the same, and preachers bought time on hundreds of commercial stations. Hardly a home in America can't be reached by the electronic church, and the ratings services maintain that in four out of ten homes, somebody tunes in to a televangelist at least once a month.

Billy Graham started the boom in televangelism, and he remains its elder statesman. But it is both ironic and fitting that he has no regular TV program, appearing only on special programs or when he is leading a crusade somewhere. A conservative Baptist and a rectitudinous man, Graham has been accused of snuggling up too eagerly to presidents but never of the sleazier excesses associated with televangelism. Perhaps he was wise enough to see that the new medium for reaching the unsaved would become a Frankenstein's monster—technically, financially, and ethically.

The technical development was swift. In the 1950s, Graham used the camera only to record his traditional revival meetings, as a sort of journalistic adjunct. It was Oral Roberts who brought TV into the tent and played to the camera, letting the audience participate in the meeting. If people in their living rooms would place their hands on the TV set, Roberts promised, they could be healed by faith at long distance. And it was Rex Humbard, then an obscure preacher in Akron, Ohio, who saw the full entertainment potential of the new medium. He organized his service as a TV production and built his Cathedral of Tomorrow as a TV studio. Modeled on variety shows of the 1960s, the meeting featured Humbard and his entire pastel-clad family standing on a huge revolving stage, singing "God Is Love" for an applauding studio audience. Robertson's "700 Club" pioneered the talk show format, and he went on to start the first religious network. With each step in the process, of course, the TV format became more important, and the message was correspondingly reduced.

In the process, the preachers turned television into a giant collection plate. Evangelists have always been good fund-raisers; Benjamin Franklin made the point in describing his reaction to one of George Whitefield's appeals. First he resolved not to give anything; as Whitefield waxed eloquent, Franklin thought he might part with his copper and then, grudgingly, the silver, "and he finished so admirably that I emptied my pocket wholly into the collector's dish, gold and all." As Aimee Semple McPherson discovered, radio broadened the audience and the fund-raising possibilities. But the power of television opened a whole new horizon.

In television's early days, stations thought of religious broadcasting mainly as a way to discharge their obligation to the Federal Communications Commission (FCC) to provide "public-service"

programming. The major networks formed religious advisory com-
mittees to give away time for spreading the word, and mainline
denominations got most of it. But with the exception of a few
pioneers like Bishop Fulton J. Sheen, they used it tentatively and
ineffectively. The smaller sects, frozen out, chose to buy time and
pay for it by making direct—and increasingly lucrative—appeals to
the viewers for funds. But then the FCC relaxed its rules, deciding
in 1960 that paid religious programming would count as public-
service time. Suddenly the mainline churches found themselves out
of the action while the televangelists were buying the desirable time
and paying for it with their enormous donations. Estimates of the
total funds given to TV preachers are gauzy, if only because of the
number of local shows and the total absence of reporting requirements, but reasonable estimates run as high as a billion dollars a
year.

There is a catch: Television is expensive. Production costs are
high, and time on commercial stations is costly. Half an hour on
Sunday morning in one of the top five urban markets can cost as
much as ten thousand dollars, and the TV preachers must constantly adjust their schedules to reach the markets that provide the
most donations, thus maximizing their returns. Even so, the cost of
programming and airtime soaks up huge percentages of the money
that comes in.

Only estimates are possible on how much of the revenue goes to
keep the process running. The ministries are sparing with figures,
and those they do report may confuse more than enlighten; the
preachers are sensitive about their fund-raising costs and try to
disguise many of them as ministerial expenses. The cost of broadcasting in Africa, for instance, may be listed as missionary work even
though it produces donations. The cost of a gospel album sent as a
premium for a donation may be counted as ministering. Analyzing
Jerry Falwell's operations, Frances FitzGerald calculated in 1981
that he spent five of every seven dollars he raised just to keep his
show going, and Jimmy Swaggart is said to spend as much as 80
percent of his total income on TV. Most knowledgeable observers
agree that those figures are in the ballpark.

Conservative columnist Cal Thomas, who was once an executive
with Falwell's organization, says the result of the cost squeeze is "a
certain Wall Street mentality. Bigger is better." The preachers must

not only stay on the air but compete for prime time in the most lucrative markets. Thus they find themselves spending more money to buy more TV time to send out more appeals for more money to buy more time. At the extreme, as in the PTL case, the race turns into a classic Ponzi scheme, with the latest donations being used to pay off the angriest creditors. Broadcasting sources say most of the ministers habitually run behind in paying for airtime.

Revenues depend heavily on the size of the audience. And whatever the doctrinal differences of the evangelists, they pale in comparison with the debate over how many people watch their shows. The preachers evangelize their figures along with the rest of their message. Jerry Falwell maintained regularly in 1980 that 25 million people watched his "Old Time Gospel Hour" every week, and Jeffrey Hadden has said one of Falwell's associates once doubled that claim to 50 million. A Gallup poll in 1981 found that 32 percent of a national sampling said they had watched religious programming in the past week. On the basis of that figure, the broadcasters said confidently that they had a total of 71 million weekly viewers—a third of the nation then.

But people don't always do what they say they do. To refine the numbers, Gallup and the Annenberg School of Communications at the University of Pennsylvania teamed up for an analysis in 1984. By studying months of diaries kept by viewers for the Arbitron audience ratings, the Annenberg researchers found 24.7 million weekly viewers of religious programs. This was a duplicated audience, meaning that some viewers watched several shows each week. Correcting for the duplication and making an offsetting estimate of underreporting, the study concluded that only 13.3 million people were watching at least fifteen minutes of televangelism each week. The audience is even smaller if the number of viewers per set is cut to reflect the time of day such programming appears. William F. Fore, television expert for the National Council of Churches, wrote in his book *Television and Religion* that the true audience by that reckoning would be only 7.2 million. And if the audience were limited to those watching an hour or more a week, Fore said, the number would be just 3.8 million.

But that figure is only part of the total audience, since it counts only the viewers of stations in the twelve channels of very high frequency (VHF). There are many more in the ultrahigh frequency

(UHF) band, and many of them are linked in the four principal religious cable networks. Pat Robertson's CBN, the first such network, hired the A. C. Nielsen Company in 1985 to measure the electronic church, including cable, and announced that the study found a monthly audience of 40 percent of all American households, or 61 million homes. On further analysis, however, that number also shrank dramatically. One of the Annenberg researchers concluded that the total unduplicated audience for televangelism, including cable, is probably no larger than the 13.3 million weekly viewers found in the original study.

That is a far cry from Falwell's claim of 25 million viewers for the "Old Time Gospel Hour" alone. But it is hardly an insignificant audience. In perspective, 13.3 million is 5.4 percent of the total population, only one-eighth the number of people who watched the top-rated weekly Bill Cosby show in the 1986 season. But it is two-thirds the number of weekly readers that *Time* and *Newsweek* each claim. And it is nearly eight times the number of votes by which Jimmy Carter beat Gerald Ford.

The audience is generally downscale. The Annenberg study confirmed the picture of the electronic congregation as older, poorer, less educated, and more conservative than the general population, and as concentrated in the South and Midwest. "There is considerable evidence that many of them tend to be somewhat alienated from mainline America," said Fore. "They feel they are on the short end of things, that they haven't gotten what others have." But contrary to the image so earnestly promoted by the TV preachers themselves, their viewers are not sinners waiting to be saved; they are overwhelmingly believers. True to its nature, TV preaches to the converted. Seventy-seven percent of the viewers are church members, and nearly all attend church regularly.

The size of each preacher's audience triggers another debate, and Falwell is not the only one who makes exaggerated claims. "They are as evangelistic in their accounting as they are in their preaching, which means they add about forty-five percent onto any number they put out," said Steve Haner, a former Virginia journalist who studies the televangelists. But there are objective measurements. By the Arbitron ratings of February 1987, Jimmy Swaggart had the largest audience just before the PTL scandal hit, with more than 2 million households tuned to his weekly show (not counting cable viewers). California's Robert Schuller, an heir to Norman Vincent Peale's positive-thinking credo, came in second. Oral Roberts, once the undisputed leader, had seen his audience fall more than 50 percent, to just over 1.1 million households. Falwell had 616,000; Robertson's "700 Club" and the PTL show fell below that. And some preachers who are household words in evangelical homes are total unknowns to the nongospel audience. "The World Tomorrow," for instance, whose cohosts are David Hulme, David Alpert, and Richard Ames, was the fourth-ranked religious show in the ratings with just over 1 million households. That put it ahead of Falwell, "the 700 Club," and PTL.

But the audience for the preachers has stopped growing. Although it rose rapidly by any count in the early 1970s, the total peaked around 1977 and has stayed flat or drifted down ever since. Meanwhile, the number of televangelists continues to grow. There are hundreds of preachers with national, regional, and local shows; more than ninety of them broadcast over five or more stations. The proliferation has turned what was already hot competition into a mad scramble. "Some one of them is now soaking almost everyone out there who wants to be soaked," said Nelson Keener, a former Falwell executive who now works for the reformed Watergate figure Charles Colson in his Prison Fellowship.

It was to ease the TV cost squeeze that Pat Robertson, Paul Crouch, and Jim Bakker created their cable networks. At the time, in the early 1970s, new cable systems were being created all over the country, and their operators were hungry for programming. The preachers could buy time cheaply or even get it free, guaranteeing to fill a channel with round-the-clock wholesomeness that would count toward a system's public-service obligation. They could also get a cheap lease for a transponder on a communications satellite to feed their programs to the cable systems. They could even turn a profit on the operation by selling time on their channels to other preachers or by broadcasting reruns of commercial TV shows and selling advertising around them.

More than any other asset, it was PTL's Inspirational Network that made Jim Bakker's empire a prize to fight over. Bakker had negotiated long-term contracts with more than 1,200 cable systems reaching into 13 million households. PTL was an all-religious network, without commercial reruns. By *Newsweek*'s informed estimate, other preachers paid a total of about $6.5 million for the time Bakker sold them in 1986, at rates of $2,600 for a prime-time hour or $15,000 for a special on Saturday night. Costs of cable system contracts and the satellite lease came to about $5.5 million, leaving $1 million in profit. But Bakker was also getting free airtime on PTL worth $6.5 million, allowing him to use his budget of $15 million to broadcast his show on more than 170 commercial TV stations. Falwell was paying more than $14 million a year for airtime, some of it on PTL, but since his own Liberty Broadcasting Network (LBN) was insignificant, he reached far fewer viewers for the money.

Some minor-league TV preachers have actually given up the struggle to stay on the air. In Delaware, Ohio, Leroy Jenkins had built his Sunday morning show to thirty-four stations, but it was costing $1.5 million a year. "A few months ago, the Spirit spoke to me and said to go off TV and into radio," he reported early in 1987. His revenues plummeted. But with costs down to $200,000, he said, the net takings actually increased.

The preachers who stay on TV have no choice but to be very good at it. They are practiced showmen—Jerry Falwell is said to have asked one talk show host whether he preferred answers in thirty-second, sixty-second, or ninety-second bites—and they use the most sophisticated marketing techniques known to Madison Avenue. Computer data banks are used to tabulate the ratios of donations to expenses in various markets, and surveys of viewer preferences turn up subjects for new shows or specials. Pat Robertson's CBN once asked its viewers what ten questions they would most like to ask God and built a show around the winner: Why is there suffering? Before it was telecast, the show was viewed by focus groups, then taken back to the studio for a quick retuning.

Given the static market, the TV preachers have just two real alternatives: They must try to pry more money from their current givers or steal followers from their rivals. "This is hamburger wars, Wendy's fighting McDonald's," said Richard Gaylord Briley, a religious fund-raiser who has worked for several celebrity preachers. "They are trying to maintain income and market shares in a declining market." And under this pressure, some of the tactics they use are anything but godly.

Later, Oral Roberts complained that he had been woefully misinterpreted. When God said he would call Oral home if the eight million dollars didn't come in, that wasn't a *threat.* "Being called home is what it's all about," he said. "Heaven is my home. I expect to meet the Lord." Still, it seemed clear enough that when he first reported God's ultimatum, Oral wasn't hoping that his flock would hold back their dollars to hasten his time of bliss. And that was just one in a series of increasingly outrageous statements, all forced by his monumental spending and dwindling revenues.

Born dirt poor and part Cherokee near Ada, Oklahoma, Roberts discovered that God had blessed his hand with healing powers. Starting in a tent, he became one of the first TV preachers and, in the mid-seventies, by far the biggest; at one point, his audience was conservatively estimated at more than two million households. With the proceeds, he built the $150 million Oral Roberts University and a two-hundred-foot space needle Prayer Tower on the prairie near Tulsa.

The complex was already Oklahoma's biggest tourist attraction when God told Oral to create the City of Faith, a hospital, clinic, and medical research center. Oral said God appeared to him in a vision, nine hundred feet high, commanding that the hospital be equally tall and have precisely 777 beds. That touched off a national hoot of derision (a popular poster showed a road sign: DANGER: 900-FOOT JESUS CROSSING), and the local authorities, arguing that the hospital was unneeded in any case, never authorized the full complement of beds. Still, the money came in.

The hospital ate up the building fund and more, but failed to draw patients. In practice, the staff has had trouble keeping more than 100 of the 294 beds in use. Oral's TV ratings were dwindling, and donations were down from eighty-eight million dollars in 1980 to fifty-eight million dollars in 1986. Roberts had to close his dental school, hand over his law school to Pat Robertson, and slow construction of a new religious center for lack of funds. It was in rising desperation that he made his announcement in January 1987 that God would end his days on earth if he failed to reach his eight-million-dollar goal by the end of March.

The target was reached, thanks largely to a crotchety Florida dog track owner who came up with a check for $1.3 million and advised Oral to see a psychiatrist. But Roberts kept feeling the pressure to make ever more dramatic announcements. Within months, he had disclosed that the devil had tried to strangle him in his bedroom but Evelyn, his wife, had rescued him. Then he said he had raised several people from the dead and that he expected to return with Christ for the millennium and rule again over the Oral Roberts empire. "People always say, 'What next?' " said Oral's biographer, David E. Harrell, Jr., a historian at the University of Alabama at Birmingham. "I mean, how do you top a nine-hundred-foot Jesus? Well, he did. I would never bet against Oral Roberts or Richard Nixon."

A showy public crisis is a TV preacher's most reliable fund-raising tactic. "It is the first rule of the game," says columnist Cal Thomas. "You can't raise money on positives. Unfortunately, only scare scenarios and negative appeals bring in the bucks." Falwell himself once said in a speech, "A man from whom I took great inspiration used to say, 'Fellows, if you're going to be successful, keep a fight going all the time.' " The enemy is always Satan, who is a real and tangible force in the evangelical worldview, though the devil can take any number of guises. He might be the *Charlotte Observer* hounding Jim Bakker, or he might be prompting the misgivings a donor feels when Oral Roberts asks for the rent money.

There is a cynicism in all this that the more thoughtful evangelicals deplore. Shortly before the PTL scandal broke, theologian Carl F. H. Henry assailed the "end justifies the means" rationalization that as long as the cause is just, "whatever turns a quick dollar" is okay. Robert Schuller, whose operation draws fewer complaints than most, was caught in what amounted to a technical deception in one of his letters to the faithful in 1981: "I am writing to you today from Peking, China. *The impossibility thinkers were wrong. I am here!* I cannot give you any details of my conversations with the leading Chinese personalities. I must honor their privacy." What Schuller neglected to say was that he had written the letter before leaving on his trip and sent along a faked photo of himself at the Great Wall.

When the truth about the letter was finally told in the glare of the PTL scandal, Schuller's people danced around it. The letter had to be written in advance, a spokesman explained, to allow time for handling. "Obviously," he said, "there was never any intent to deceive or engage in any dishonesty." Well, a white lie. But people expect more from a preacher. And in a field where bigger is seen to be better and evangelistic "stretching" is no sin, a serious lie can begin as a small deception. "I've heard many sermons about the danger of beginning to tell little white lies," Cal Thomas told ABC's Ted Koppel in a "Nightline" discussion of the PTL story. "We've seen that in government, with Watergate . . . we see it on Wall Street . . . and now we're seeing it in religion. I think there's a kind of moral receivership here."

Well short of outright cheating, the TV preachers commonly play by very loose rules. While few of them operate on anything like Jim Bakker's scale of ethical conduct, hardly any (with the possible exception of Billy Graham) can claim to be without sin in raising and handling money. Among the routine practices:

Distorting financial facts. Thanks to their tax exemption, the ministries have hardly any reporting requirements. While many promise audited financial statements, few actually provide them. Conceding that he hadn't put out a statement in two years, Falwell joked in 1987: "I just got ornery." But between statements, Falwell said publicly that his annual revenues in 1985 came to $100 million. As it turned out, the total that year was $73.5 million. Similarly, CBN gave estimates of its total income for fiscal 1985 as high as $233 million. The true figure was $159.2 million.

When statements are issued, they are often unrevealing. The preachers' salaries usually seem modest. Before he resigned from CBN, for instance, Pat Robertson said he got a salary of $60,000 (CBN's report to the IRS for fiscal 1985 listed his total compensation as $78,367) and said he returned it all as a donation. But he gets an undisclosed amount in royalties on books, some of which have sold as many as half a million copies. Huge bonuses may be hidden, as in the PTL case. The preachers may receive gifts from wealthy followers ranging from mink coats to complete homes. They are free to give jobs to their families; Robert Schuller has eight relatives on his payroll, and Jimmy Swaggart's wife, his son, and his son's wife all sit on his board of directors.

The preacher's finances are often tangled up with his ministry's. Falwell, for instance, got a salary of $100,000 in 1987. But he gets as much as $5,000 a speech and speaks a dozen or more times a year, often flying to the date in the ministry's private jet—taking care of ministry business en route, of course. He got a $1 million advance for his autobiography in 1986; he said that after paying his taxes, his agent, and his ghostwriter, he donated the rest to his church. But like Robertson and others, he has accepted royalties on previous books. Some of those books have been bought in large numbers by his ministry, to be sold to the faithful or used as premiums for donations. Thus the ministry indirectly subsidizes Falwell's royalties. All told, a spokesman said, Falwell's income about doubles his published salary. (A few weeks after that estimate, however, Falwell himself doubled it again. He said his 1986 income was $435,000, and he would do a little better in 1987.)

The Internal Revenue Service has a rule that compensation for the preachers and their families must be "reasonable." But that is a standard open to much debate; as Jim Bakker argues, who's to say that a man capable of raising $96 million in donations isn't worth $2 million a year? The IRS has challenged PTL's tax exemption largely on this basis, but the case is a long way from proved.

Spending figures for the ministries are especially murky. To enhance their image, they try to minimize fund-raising costs and allocate as much spending as possible to actual good works at home and abroad. But in any strict accounting, a good deal of this money would be listed as a cost of fund-raising. Premiums given in return for donations, for instance, may be books or other gifts with religious meaning—anything from lapel pins to framed prayers. The cost of the gifts, and often the postage to send them, is usually listed under "ministries," not "fund-raising." In Falwell's 1985 statement —one of the few detailed enough for this kind of scrutiny—"mission work" was listed as $3 million. But journalist Steve Haner said most of that was spent for overseas airtime and for scholarships for foreign students and the children of overseas missionaries at Falwell's Liberty University. Actual mission work, Haner said, came to $328,116.

Working the computer. Given a mailing list of hundreds of thousands of people who have sent money for the cause, the TV preachers have a money machine for producing more. "The transaction only begins on television," said religious fund-raiser Richard Gaylord Briley. "The rest of the business is by mail." The first aim is to get more frequent and larger donations, and the ministries go about that with the businesslike calculation of the folks at American Express cheering on their cardholders to raise the monthly bill. Roger Flessing, a former top television executive at PTL, ran a study of its donor base in 1982 and found that it was a rotating group: The average donor gave to five other ministries and contributed to PTL four to five times a year. An increase of just one gift a year per donor, he realized, could raise the total by 20 percent.

To achieve that, computerized mailings can be sent with individually tailored messages. The name of the recipient appears several times in the body of the letter, perhaps with a reference to the previous gift or a reassurance that the preacher is praying for an errant son. A giver who hasn't contributed for a while can be gently chided, then warned that he or she is in danger of being cut off. In what Jeffrey Hadden called the "whammy letter," Rex Humbard (who has since partially retired) used to write that he yearned to pray for his old friend, but the name was no longer on the list. There was no outright threat that being taken off the list was tantamount to damnation, but it clearly wasn't going to help.

Most of the preachers try to package their appeal in what Rosser Reeves, the father of the hard sell in advertising, used to call a "unique selling proposition." Givers can be Partners of PTL, or Faith Partners of Oral Roberts, or believers in Pat Robertson's Kingdom Principles. For varying amounts of money, donors can have their names inscribed on Roberts's Prayer Tower, on individual chairs in Schuller's Crystal Cathedral, on "Living Memorial" bricks in Falwell's Liberty Mountain prayer chapel. Or they can sign up for special "clubs," an escalating aristocracy depending on how much they promise: $1,000 a year, $2,500 a year, even $5,000 a year to be a member of CBN's Founders' Club. At that level, of course, a donor can expect personal attention from the preacher—perhaps even a dinner.

That can lead to another kind of request. Perhaps the ultimate in fund-raising is the search for wealthy followers who will leave money to the ministry in their wills. Nearly all the preachers comb their lists for such potential benefactors and find them surprisingly often. The preachers may also collide with bereaved and angry relatives when the bequest comes due. In 1981, Jimmy Swaggart was left about twelve million dollars by a wealthy California widow, Zoe Vance. Her relatives sued, and the case was eventually settled out of court. Swaggart reportedly kept about 70 percent of the money, and the relatives are still bitter. "She was ill with cancer and blind in one eye," said a source close to the case. "She was too ill and weak, and they talked her into it. I think they're a bunch of con men." Similarly, Jerry Falwell was sued by the relatives of Johnnie Eureka Jackson, a victim of Alzheimer's disease, after she had left him her life savings of seventy-nine thousand dollars. Asked for comment, Falwell said he didn't recall the case. It was settled out of court.

As the fund-raising escalates, the preaching inevitably dwindles. There's no overall estimate on how much airtime is given to the endless begging, but it is considerable. According to the *Freedom Writer* newsletter, Falwell spent twenty-six minutes of every "Old Time Gospel Hour" in 1987 pleading for money. There are also out-and-out telethons and pleas for special causes with telegenic beneficiaries, such as Vietnamese refugees or Kevin Whittum.

The relics trade. In addition to offering books and gifts as premiums for donations, items can be sold outright at something like their retail value, with the ministry taking the retailer's markup. Carol Flake, author of *Redemptorama: Culture, Politics, and the New Evangelicalism,* calls this "hawking holy molies." The goods can range from twigs from the Holy Land or "pocket prayer coins" to a special edition of the Bible. Oral Roberts once sold small pieces of cloth bearing the imprint of his healing hand; another time he offered a plastic bag full of holy water, advising the viewers to anoint their wallets with it for a quick return on their investment. Nearly all the ministries sell travel packages. Swaggart once offered a trip to the Holy Land or to Hawaii, "depending on the season."

Shaking the death rattle. Oral Roberts made it personal, but at one time or another, most of the preachers have told their followers that the ministry itself would have to shrink or go out of business if the current drive didn't go over the top. On the dubious theory that the TV shows are converting hundreds of sinners daily, this is presented as a triumph for the devil and a devastating defeat for the cause of Christ. "I'm going to be as frank and honest with you as I know how to be," Swaggart wrote to his flock in 1987. "If I have to cancel just one station because I don't get your support, then people will die and go to hell by the thousands."

The Bakkers probably held the record for going-out-of-business fund drives, and the chaotic state of their finances made them more or less believable. But at least one of their frequent guests, a now disillusioned preacher turned circus ringmaster named Austin Miles, said he lost faith in the operation after one such telethon.

Tammy had wept copiously, telling the viewers, "If we don't have a million by Thursday, they're going to pull the plug on the satellite. I don't know how we're going to make it." Over lunch, Miles said, he asked Bakker's brother Norman whether PTL would survive, and Norm told him not to worry, the money was already in the bank. Jim liked to hold up payments as long as possible, Norm said, and the ultimatum on the satellite provided a handy excuse to raise money.

Bait-and-switch fund-raising. It's illegal tactics in business, but many of the televangelists manage to raise money for one cause and spend it on another. What makes this legitimate for the preachers is what Calvin College's Quentin Schultze called the "weasel clause": The preacher announces a fund drive for, say, two hundred thousand dollars to get food to starving Ethiopians. Film clips of the pathetic victims are taken and can be shown for weeks. The appeal may raise millions, but the ministry is committed to send only two hundred thousand dollars to the cause. Falwell, who has been criticized for such practices, defends them as not only legal but ethical. His former aide Nelson Keener is more dubious. "I wouldn't say fraudulent because the money is always applied to the general evangelical mission," he said, "but it's just terribly manipulative."

Even this permissive standard was too strict for Jim Bakker. What got him in trouble with the FCC was his raising of funds for TV ministries abroad, including one in South Korea. Bakker had suggested this venture impulsively on his show one morning. He raised funds specifically for the project, sending donors at the $100 level a plastic-encased replica of the Korean crown jewels. He told repeated lies about the project on the air: PTL had been given an $800,000 building in South Korea; the studios were being built; and "We are getting ready to ship the cameras." In South Korea, the Reverend Cho Yonggi was upset. He complained that visitors from the States kept asking to see his studios, and where was the money, please? In the end, he never got any of it, but several weeks after the FCC investigation began, Bakker gave $350,000 to the Assemblies of God to be used for TV ministries in Asia.

Bakker at least halfway apologized, telling the FCC, "In those days my faith was a little bit reckless. I believed God would do anything. We now have budget controls." But as he told it in his autobiography, reckless was an understatement. At one point in the early days of PTL, he wrote, God ordered him to send a creditor a check for twenty thousand dollars that wasn't in the bank, guaranteeing that the money would turn up in the mail on Monday morning. "Just send him the check," God said, "and I'll do the miracle for you." Jim took that as a trial of faith. He didn't quite kite the check himself; he ordered one of his aides to do it. Sure enough, in rolled the money to cover it.

Creeping corruption. For the most part, the lapses of televangelism come from cutting corners. It is a matter of money coming first, ahead of everything else, sometimes at the price of simple decency. When Oral Roberts's eldest son, Ronnie, committed suicide after a drug problem, Oral grieved publicly for him—and Ronnie's brother, Richard, sent a letter to the flock: "This would be a wonderful time to show how much you love my daddy." Mailing out his Seed Faith booklets with their monthly donation forms, Oral advised his flock to keep the book with the monthly bills, and on "the first of each month put God's work first in your life." Jerry Falwell, among others, doesn't hesitate to suggest that borrowing money to send him wouldn't be amiss, what with the importance of the cause. In a letter asking for a four-hundred-dollar check to fight abortion by becoming a "Save-a-Baby Godparent," Falwell added a postscript: "Several concerned persons have actually borrowed $400 in order to become a Godparent. Some have taken $400 out of their savings. Please do what you can."

Isn't this going too far? Dinesh D'Souza, a Heritage Foundation conservative who generally approves of the televangelists, concedes that there is a "morally problematic image" in the thought of an elderly woman endorsing her Social Security check over to a televangelist. "But on the other hand," he said, "if you are old and a believer and you don't have much of interest and excitement except your religion—well, it's hard to condemn voluntary giving." Somewhere, however, a line has to be drawn; Pat Robertson and Ben Kinchlow were well past it the day they rejoiced over a California woman who decided to send them the money she had budgeted for her cancer medicine.

In part, these dubious practices reflect the fact that the preacher is pretty remote from the flock. His pretense is that each letter is read and prayed over, each donation personally welcomed. But there aren't enough hours in the day for a TV minister to pay that kind of attention, even if he wanted to. In practice, he sees the faithful not as a congregation but as a golden cornucopia, made up of computerized bits and bytes.

In part, too, the rot traces to the preachers' own lack of broad education and experience. "I don't think the ministers set out to deceive people. They aren't bad," said Rice University sociologist William Martin. "But they become seduced by their celebrity and power, and they fall into a trap. They work under the foolish premise that 'God will protect us' or 'no one will find us out.' "

The premise is not all that foolish. The chances are excellent that no matter what a minister does, he will get away with no worse than a slap on the wrist. The constitutional mandate to separate church from state has been interpreted for years largely as a ban on government interference in religious affairs. Although officials can legitimately prosecute criminal acts by ministers or regulate churches in their purely commercial activity, the political power of organized religion has made sure that regulation is usually applied with a light hand. In addition, the Reagan administration's ties to the religious right may have made the regulators even more hesitant than usual to crack down on TV ministers.

Thus, when Jim Bakker came under fire in 1979 from the *Charlotte Observer* for his diversion of the South Korean funds and a similar case in Brazil, the FCC began an investigation. After three years of probing and thousands of pages of testimony, there was massive evidence that money had been diverted. Also, in eleven days of testimony under oath, Bakker himself was contradicted at least twenty-seven times by other witnesses, eighteen times by written evidence, and thirty-six times by his own testimony. He could have been prosecuted for fraud or perjury. But the FCC, in a bitterly disputed four-to-three vote, decided in 1982 to settle the case by letting PTL sell its only television station, which removed it from FCC jurisdiction. The Justice Department declined to pursue the criminal charges. The Internal Revenue Service began investigating in 1983 whether PTL's tax exemption should be lifted, but by the time the scandal erupted, IRS agents hadn't yet reached a decision on the years 1981–1983 and were just beginning to look at later years.

Was this deliberate foot-dragging? In early 1988, the public broadcasting program "Frontline" strongly suggested that the Reagan administration was trying to protect a preacher who had both personal and political ties to the White House. An FCC staff investigator told "Frontline" he had been told to water down his report on PTL, deleting 134 factual passages and softening some of his conclusions. But there were denials all around of any kind of pressure from the top. And without proof, in view of the long record of governmental reluctance to hound churches, the denials were plausible enough.

The PTL scandal did give new life to a self-policing movement within the National Religious Broadcasters, which formally adopted new rules for its 1,350 members at its 1988 meeting. Under the new code, major ministries would have to disclose a good deal more financial data and make annual reports available to the public. Family-dominated boards of directors were banned. But there was still no requirement to disclose ministerial salaries and bonuses, and there weren't many teeth in the penalties. The NRB said it would deny its seal of compliance to a ministry that didn't follow the rules, but it had no plans to point fingers by saying publicly which ministries weren't complying. It remained to be proved whether the donors would notice that the seal wasn't there or, if they did, whether they would care enough to stop sending money.

Since the scandal, "I'm probably a little more cautious about where we put our finances," said Bonnie Kohlen, forty, a homemaker and hospital volunteer in Yorba Linda, California. "But I still feel that if I felt led to contribute money somewhere and they used it wrong, then they have to answer for that.

"I think our focus should be on God and not on people anyway. 'Let him among you who is without sin cast the first stone.'"

Chapter 4

Going First Class, with God

It was no secret that the Bakkers were living high off the hog. There wasn't even much effort to hide it; as Jim himself often said, "God doesn't want his people to go second class." But the full scale of the excess didn't come out until after Jim and Tammy were disgraced and the Falwell people got a look at the books. They were dumbfounded. Jerry Nims, the new PTL chief executive, told reporters that it was flat-out "fiscal sin." It wasn't a matter of edging over the line, he said. "There was absolutely no line. For these folks, there were no rules."

There were, however, cars: an ever-changing fleet of Cadillacs and Mercedeses and a vintage Rolls-Royce. There were also houses. The one at Tega Cay on Lake Wylie, just fifteen minutes' drive from Heritage USA, was valued in 1985 at $1.3 million. It had three kitchens, a fish-shaped swimming pool, a two-level, carpeted, air-conditioned tree house for Jamie Charles, and an air-conditioned doghouse for the family pets, and PTL was deeding it over to the Bakkers a little at a time. That would make up for the vacation condo on Florida's gold coast—bought and decorated for them by the ministry in 1982 for a total of $593,000—that had to be sold when the *Charlotte Observer* went on a crusade about it. Jim and Tammy owned three more condos on the Heritage grounds, occupied by various relatives on the payroll, and they had the use of the Presidential Suite at the Heritage Grand Hotel, a four-bedroom apartment with gold-plated swan faucets and a fifty-foot walk-in closet with its own chandeliers. That layout was supposed to cost visitors $2,000 a night when Jim and Tammy weren't in residence, but there's no record of anybody renting it; it was mainly used to put up visiting dignitaries. The house in Gatlinburg, with its spectacular mountain views, had cost them only $148,500, but they were adding $90,000 in renovations, including a two-foot-thick spike-topped stone security fence that became known as the Great Wall of Gatlinburg. The house in Palm Desert, California, had cost them $449,000; they put it up for sale while Tammy was being treated at the Betty Ford Clinic and bought another in Palm Springs for $600,000. It was hard to keep track of the real estate. By one count, they lived in seven houses in one six-year stretch.

The Bakkers saw nothing to apologize for; it was all part of Jim's prosperity theology. "Why should God have junk?" he demanded. "Why should I apologize because God throws in crystal chandeliers, mahogany floors, and the best construction in the world?" But God didn't stop there. There were permanent wardrobes for Jim and Tammy in most of their homes, and more clothes in the dressing rooms at the PTL studio, which also had an eleven-thousand-dollar Jacuzzi and a workout room. There were Tammy's legendary shopping sprees for fur coats and jewels; there were dresses in those closets with the price tags still dangling from them and toys in Jamie Charles's rooms that had never been taken out of their boxes. There were parties for PTL executives. One festive occasion called for nine thousand dollars' worth of truffles imported from Brussels. There was the forty-three-foot houseboat. And there was the entourage, the cronies and bodyguards and high PTL officials who swept grandly before and behind the royal couple, flying along on their trips, competing for favor and learning to anticipate every wish before it had to be spoken.

All that was plain to be seen for anyone who wanted to look. But the faithful, the people who were spending their lives working for PTL and the others who sent in the money, preferred not to see, or perhaps preferred to look selectively. Ellen Baker was one of the workers. At the time of the scandal she described herself delicately as a large woman in spite of having lost thirty pounds, but she still carried a wallet photo of the slim young girl who had come to PTL in 1973, when it was just Channel 36 in Charlotte. That was a year before Jim Bakker drove up in his white Cadillac to host a telethon and stayed to found the empire. After the fall, Ellen was one of just four people from the 1975 organization chart who were still with PTL, and she was its institutional memory, running the archives of television tapes. She devised the filing system that could locate any given segment from fifteen years of programs in a matter of minutes. She could have done even better, she told a visitor, if she had good fast tape-editing machines, not this old junk; she'd kept arguing for proper equipment and explaining how it would pay for itself, but there was never enough money. Now she knew why. What hurt, she said, was not so much the sex stuff as the betrayal of faith. "There are people here," she said, "getting only eleven thousand dollars a year, people with holes in their shoes working because they believe in it, and then those two were taking all that money."

After it all came out, some of the bitter people at PTL said Jim and Tammy had been corrupt from the start. But as Ellen Baker saw it in the early years, they were sincere and loving Christians with a great vision. They never got really close to the people who worked for them; but they could be kind and considerate, and what they wanted was for the glory of God. Sometime around 1978 or 1979, she said, the rot began to set in. That was after the evangelist John Wesley Fletcher had become a regular guest on the show. He was a secret drinker who sometimes had to be routed out of bed and cleaned up for the cameras, but Jim Bakker wouldn't hear of having him fired. Fletcher, a burly man with a black mane of blow-dried hair and dead, expressionless eyes, showed up in 1976. He performed miracles of faith healing. "You, sir, yes, come here. . . . I never saw you before, right? Never laid eyes on you. . . . I feel you have something in your belly. . . . You have a *cancer* in your belly. . . . Heal! HEAL! . . . That cancer is dead." Ellen Baker heard later he had sent agents around the campground to find out who was suffering from what and how desperate they might be. Fletcher dropped out of the picture after he was defrocked as a drunk by the Assemblies of God, but he had already done enough damage: He was the one who brought Jessica Hahn from Long Island for the afternoon with Jim in Florida.

Fletcher was only one of the people who truckled to the Bakkers, surrounding them and insulating them from bad news, doing anything necessary to share the growing pot of money and power. Gary Smith, PTL's chief operating officer in 1979 and 1980, told reporters after the blowup that he was fired because he tried to curb the extravagances and mismanagement that were rife even then.

Richard Dortch took over as Jim Bakker's top aide in 1983, supposedly to tighten procedures; he was a polished, executive churchman who at one time was said to be in the running for the top job at the Assemblies of God national headquarters. Dortch soon told staffers that his first priority was to help Jim Bakker. That grated on David Taggart, the smart, stylish Detroiter who had used his position as Bakker's executive assistant to become the de facto number two at PTL. Bakker's former bodyguard Mike Richardson wrote that when Dortch started installing his own people, Taggart complained furiously about the "age of the Dortchites" at PTL.

Taggart and Dortch soon learned to get along. Taggart's brother James, an interior decorator, was paid a $120,000 annual retainer to work on the hotel and various Bakker homes. In turn, Dortch's son, Rich, became PTL's finance director, and his daughter, Deanna Dortch Collins, rose to be a producer on the show. Nepotism was in the PTL tradition: Bakker had put his brother Norm on the payroll as a greeter in the theme park, and his sister, Donna Puckett, was a finance officer. Even Jim's parents, Raleigh and Furnia Bakker, were wandering around the grounds, hailed by affectionate visitors as Mom and Dad. And Dortch and Taggart cemented their standing with the boss by getting all the money Jim wanted from the board of directors.

PTL's directors had never been particularly feisty, but now their subjugation was complete. "I used to joke about it," said Roger Flessing, who served two hitches with Bakker in ten years and later became a TV consultant for Billy Graham. "Bakker only called a board meeting when he needed money. And every bonus was set up by Dortch, or Dortch took credit for it. So, are you going to fire this guy who's getting you all this money? No way." After the crash, board members were to say that they seldom questioned what Jim Bakker told them and didn't know what had been spent. "We directed very little," said one of them, Texas evangelist J. Don George, "but we approved a considerable amount." Taggart didn't even give them copies of the minutes that they routinely accepted without a reading.

And the money flowed. According to the Falwell aides trying later to piece records together, the directors sometimes approved blank bonuses for top executives, with amounts to be filled in by Taggart and Dortch. They each drew more than $600,000 in salary and bonus in the final fifteen months of the great boondoggle. But as courtiers they knew what was due to royalty, and it was the Bakkers who profited most from this cozy arrangement. As the IRS finally totted it up, the top officials of PTL had been paid $14.9 million more than their services were worth in the years 1981–1987. Of that, Jim and Tammy had taken $9.36 million.

When the figures finally began coming out, Jim and Tammy protested that they were wrong, fantasies created to blacken their names. And it seemed likely that the IRS figures were the equivalent of a bargaining position, to be whittled down in negotiations as the Bakkers proved which expenditures were legitimate. But if only half the charges were true, the excesses would still be awesome.

Jim and Tammy had always tried to maintain a delicate distinction: While God wanted them to live well, they weren't getting rich. Jim liked to say that their combined salary in 1979 was $72,800, and as recently as 1986 he said the couple's savings had sometimes dropped to $500. In 1984, pleading for contributions on a PTL broadcast, Tammy told the viewers it was up to them to pay the bills, because "Jim and I can't. We've given everything we have, and literally we have given everything. I have offered to sell everything I have, because things don't really mean that much when it comes to getting the Gospel of Jesus Christ out. But if I sold every single thing I own, Jim, it would probably keep us on the air one more day."

"Oh, no, it wouldn't be that long," he told her.

In truth, they might have been a bit tapped out at the time. They had only recently made a $149,000 down payment on the Palm Desert house and paid $100,000 for a Mercedes and a Rolls. But if there was any pinch, it was brief. In 1984, 1985, and 1986, Falwell's people were to learn, the Bakkers received salaries and bonuses totaling $4 million, with another $792,000 in the first three months of 1987.

Even that wasn't enough. Falwell's men found that a special executive account had been set up, under David Taggart's control and administered directly by PTL's auditors, to handle $620,000 in cash advances on the PTL credit cards. Among other things, Taggart reportedly used $45,000 to pay for a European vacation. But most of the money was unaccounted for, part of a total of $1.3 million that the Internal Revenue Service said might have been used for personal expenses by the Bakkers and their friends in the years 1981–1983.

Tammy always pictured herself as the family's champion shopper, and she was no slouch. After taping a show she would announce, "My shoppin' demons are hoppin'," and she would drive off with a friend for a session at the nearby malls. Her CB moniker was the Bargainhunter, and her usual taste ran to inexpensive clothes from the bargain outlets, though she spread herself a bit on costly leather outfits and fancy jewels when she went to the big city. She was generous with gifts and flat-out mawkish when it came to her pets. The air-conditioned doghouse actually came about because Tammy woke up one winter night, worrying that the dogs might be cold. Jim got Don Hardister out of bed, and he rigged an emergency heater in the doghouse. But Tammy wanted permanent central heating. Hardister's solution was the old air conditioner, which could be set to heat as well. It didn't do much good, though; the dogs hated it and wouldn't sleep there.

Tammy's terminal whimsy may have been the wedding she staged in 1986 for her Yorkshire terrier Corky. When Corky took up with Peaches, a neighbor's poodle bitch, Tammy dressed them in tuxedo and bridal gown, had them exchange *arfs* and gold-plated collars, and videotaped the ceremony for posterity. But her sentimentality about animals didn't run deep. She wrote casually about having sold or given away pets at least twice when moving the family, and according to Falwell's people, two of the five dogs left behind at Tega Cay wound up in the pound when Tammy neglected to send for them. What she really liked was make-believe animals, and she had hundreds of them, covering every available surface in all the houses, the hotel rooms, even the corporate offices. They ranged from cuddly toys to sculptures. The Gatlinburg house had a lifelike German shepherd, taxidermically preserved and stuffed. The Falwell people found a seven-foot bronze giraffe along with the teddy bears, oversize pandas, and floppy puppies in the corporate suite.

Jim liked to shop, too, and David Taggart is said to have been his guide and fashion mentor, buying dozens of shirts at a time and paying as much as $4,000 in one day for suits. Taggart himself was something of a mystery, a secretive man who disliked appearing on

TV and let it be known that his father was an auto dealer; in truth, the elder Taggart was said to have managed an auto body shop. Wherever he got his money, Taggart was a notable clotheshorse, with an extensive wardrobe and jewelry. He told friends at PTL that his watch had cost $20,000. He was close to his brother, with whom he shared an apartment, and the two of them bought a condo for $640,000 in 1986 in New York's Trump Tower. In all, the IRS said, he managed to take $2.26 million in unreasonable compensation from PTL.

When Jim decided one day in Palm Desert to go shopping for another Rolls, Taggart chartered a Learjet for the trip to Concannon's Horseless Carriages in Santa Ana, at a cost reported to be $3,000. They wound up buying two cars that day. One was a vintage Rolls that cost $35,000, plus $27,438 in renovations; Jim thought it would look nice in a Plexiglas box on top of the Heritage Grand Hotel.

Road trips were a real bonanza for the retinue. Jim and Tammy never traveled alone, and seldom without half a dozen friends, relatives, aides, and bodyguards, all on the PTL tab. There was a flight to Europe on the Concorde, with seats at more than $2,000 apiece. On a trip to Hawaii, the Bakkers occupied the $350-a-night Presidential Suite at the Ilachi Hotel, while the courtiers stayed in rooms priced up to $200. They made copious use of room service, and the credit cards tracked their purchases across the land: an $800 briefcase; a $70 address book; a $74 toilet kit from Gucci; a $120 pen. They spent $4,015 one day at a crystal boutique in Laguna Beach, California, and $2,833 five days later at Louis Vuitton in Beverly Hills. The loot became a nuisance of sorts. A former executive who often traveled with Jim and Tammy recalled that on one trip to Bermuda, "We left Charlotte with eight people and fifteen bags. We came back with eight people and twenty-seven bags."

Other possessions came through more devious routes. According to the *Washington Post*, Jim, Tammy, and Dortch each got a Mercedes-Benz 500 SEL for Christmas in 1986. The cars were sold to an Alabama businessman, Charles Woodall, and then leased by his company to PTL. Mark Burgund, PTL financial director in the Falwell regime, told the newspaper that Woodall then billed PTL for $150,000 in consulting fees, an amount reached by totaling the price tags of the cars.

If Jerry Nims saw all that as fiscal sin, Jim Bakker saw it as a blessing: "The Lord has us on a roller-coaster ride, and we're holding on for dear life." The two back-road revivalists from North Central Bible College had wealth, power, and adulation; they had prayed with Jimmy Carter aboard Air Force One, attended Ronald Reagan's inaugural as honored guests, and heard Reagan tell the NRB convention, "The PTL TV network is carrying out a master plan for people that love." Jim and Tammy were two little people "on a roll," said Jeffrey Hadden, the University of Virginia sociologist and a longtime student of the televangelists. "Suddenly there was no wish that could not be fulfilled." They had come a long, long way.

By his own story, Jim Bakker was raised in poverty, bitterly conscious of his stunted size and his frayed blue baseball jacket. "It seemed like anything I had was inferior to what other kids had," he wrote in his autobiography, *Move That Mountain!* The truth was both better and a bit worse than that: He was not Huck Finn but Clyde Griffiths in Theodore Dreiser's *An American Tragedy.* Jim's father, Raleigh, was a well-paid machinist in a piston ring plant in Muskegon, Michigan, and one of Jim's boyhood friends recalled after the scandal that the family house was in a mainly middle-class neighborhood of teachers, small storekeepers, and the like. Chafing near the bottom of that bourgeois mixture, Jim would feel none of the easy community of the small-town poor in those early postwar days. His was the desperate shame of the striver whose parents didn't measure up. He owned the standard red coaster wagon of a midwestern boyhood and used it to earn movie money by selling flowers and melons door to door. His father even had a home movie camera, no small thing in those days, and the neighborhood kids gathered for shows in the Bakker basement. But the house was cement block, covered in what Raleigh Bakker thought would be buff-colored paint. The color turned out to be orange, and it embarrassed Jim so much that he would ask to be dropped off blocks from home so his tonier friends wouldn't see it.

Jim was born small and grew slowly, and Raleigh and Furnia Bakker feared for a while that their fourth child was going to be a midget. He was afraid of nearly everything, from the first day of school to the huge eye that he took to be God's, painted on the Sunday school classroom wall. He was also a slow learner, barely passing from grade to grade. He pictured himself as a shy and friendless boy, but his playmates remembered him as ingratiating and sentimental. When his dog Prince died, young Jim bought a marker in a cut-rate tombstone yard, dragged it home in the red wagon, and conducted an ecumenical funeral service. Later, finding a stray puppy, he not only advertised the dog in the local paper but found a home for it and visited it regularly.

In his autobiography, Jim confessed to cutting classes and experimenting with smoking in an effort to win popularity through vice. But he recorded no worse sins, and an early turning point in his life came when a teacher in junior high school offered to teach him photography if he would clean up the darkroom. That led to work for the school newspaper, where Jim eventually became an editor. He stood out in speech classes and stumbled into a vocation when he first tried being disc jockey at a school dance. He was still a shy boy with deep-seated feelings of inferiority, but with a microphone between him and the world, he discovered a talent for warm, easy patter.

By then the family had moved to a decayed old mansion built by a lumber baron a century before, and Raleigh Bakker was driving a five-year-old Cadillac; Jim the striver was on his way. He emceed one dance after another and directed the annual variety shows, and at one gorgeous peak of social success, he threw an afterparty in the old mansion that drew four hundred students, the reigning Miss Michigan, and a live band. He was in the limelight, and glowing.

Religion was a fixture of the Bakkers' life, and the family church was the Pentecostal Assembly of God. It is a powerful faith, short on theological subtleties and heavy with certainty, and it has never had much appeal for the upper crust. On the social scale of western Michigan, such "holy roller" churches, with their God-touched twitching and speaking in tongues, ranked far below the staid dullness of Episcopalians, Presbyterians, Methodists, and even Baptists and Catholics. If that added to Jim's social discomfort, he did not confess it, but he wrote with a touch of envy that his oldest brother, Bob, "had long since escaped" the routine of churchgoing. For Jim, Norman, and Donna, attendance was mandatory, not only at Sunday sermons but at prayer meetings, revivals, and frequent special services.

And the message followed him like the eye of God. Once, at the height of his popularity, he heard a voice cutting through the dance music he was playing: "Jim, what are you doing here? You don't belong here." He tried to smother the voice in furious activity, he wrote later, but finally he got the unmistakable sign that drove him to his true calling. On a snowy night in 1958, when he had ducked out of church to cruise around with his girlfriend in his father's car, Jim Bakker, then eighteen, ran over little Jimmy Summerfield.

The story became a staple of his ministry, and it lost nothing in the telling: how Fats Domino was singing "Blueberry Hill" on the car radio as Jim drove back to church to meet his parents; how he ignored the small bump he felt turning into the parking lot; how somebody yelled and Jim looked back to see a man picking up a small body. "The child's legs hung down," Jim wrote in *Move That Mountain!* "His tiny arms were limp. Both wheels of the heavy Cadillac had completely run over his body, crushing his lungs immediately." In truth, the injuries weren't life-threatening: a broken collarbone, several cracked ribs, and a punctured lung. Witnesses said it wasn't Jim's fault, that the boy had slipped down a snowbank and under the wheels. But Jim agonized all night, until word came that Jimmy would recover. It was a miracle, he decided, and "at that moment Jesus became the only thing in my life."

He tried hard to be a Christian, hazarding his newfound popularity by refusing any more disc jockey jobs. He studied the Bible and tried to ignore the way it kept falling open to Acts 10:42, "And he commanded us to preach. . . ." He finally yielded, deciding to go to North Central Bible College in Minneapolis to learn to be a minister. There, one night after months of trying, he managed to open his heart and receive the baptism of the Holy Spirit. "I began speaking in a language I hadn't learned," he wrote. "For what seemed like hours I was lost with God. When I drifted back to earth, the room was practically empty of people and I was singing. . . ."

That first year at college, he turned his back on nearly everything but God. He fasted often, led prayers and Bible readings in the school basement, and became known as a "Holy Joe." But the next year he met a freshman named Tammy Faye LaValley.

She was tiny and vivid, a spark of a girl, four feet eleven inches high, and shining. The church of her youth was bleaker and more repressive than Jim's, and her life was a lot harder. Tammy remembered her father only as an angry voice in the night, abandoning his family; she was brought up by a loving stepfather as part of a mixed brood of eight in a hardscrabble house in International Falls, Minnesota.

Tammy recalled the outdoor privy and the tin-tub baths without shame or rancor, as a simple fact of childhood, but she kept an abiding resentment at the way her divorced mother was treated as a fallen woman by the local Assembly of God. The family attended faithfully, Tammy wrote in her autobiography, *I Gotta Be Me*, and her mother was the kind who would give her last thirty dollars in the offering. But the other women were jealous of her musical talents, Tammy said, and "the church would do without a pianist before they let my mother play. . . . I don't know why she stuck it out. I would have quit and told them all to just play their game."

Somehow her faith survived, along with her spirit. "I knew I had a Jesus who was able to cover all of this," she wrote. She discovered on the school playground the power God could wield through her own small frame: "Can you imagine 100 kids following me in a big, long line and all singing 'Jesus Loves Me'? I have been singing for Jesus ever since."

And whenever Tammy felt a conflict with her religion, she managed to reconcile it—mostly in her own favor. When she was fifteen and collided with her "can't-do" church over its ban on cosmetics, the church simply had to be mistaken. Tammy had already bought her first bra, for twenty cents at a garage sale, and her mother had explained that she couldn't get pregnant just from kissing a boy, so she wasn't lacking in sophistication. But when she first put eye makeup on her lashes, she became terrified that it was the devil's work and wiped it off. Then she reconsidered: "Why can't I do this? If it makes me look prettier, why can't I do this?"

People talked about her, but she didn't care. "I was very close to the Lord. . . . I didn't feel condemned. Way down deep in my heart I felt many of the people at our church had been old fuddy-duddies on such things and that there was a place of liberation with the Lord." It was pure Tammy Faye, and sure enough, the Lord did love her. When the time came to welcome Jesus into her heart, he walked right in. First she felt like the tallest person in the world; then: "For hours I lay on the floor and spoke in an unknown language. I wasn't aware of anyone else. I was walking with Jesus."

Tammy said later that she never felt pretty enough, thin enough, or talented enough, and her feelings of inadequacy bothered her for years; it wasn't until she had a teenage daughter of her own that an IQ test finally persuaded her she wasn't stupid. But she clearly caught the eye. She was elected queen of her summer Bible camp two years in a row, and she had already been through two boyfriends by the time she met Jim. The first one was a problem. Ron was nice enough, and he didn't smoke or drink, but he was a nonbeliever who actually went to the movies, and this conflict was too much. So when Ken, the preacher's son, fell in love with her, she handed Ron his walking papers, and he stood all night on her lawn, yelling, "Tammy! Tammy!"

Ken was a believer. But he was a bit of a flirt even after they got engaged, and domineering, too; even though she felt a true vocation to the ministry and her aunt Gin was ready to pay the tuition, he didn't want her to come to Bible college with him. She went anyway, prodded by God. "Hey, girl, this is it," God told her. "You've got to make up your mind." Ken was miffed when she showed up, and the relationship was strained after that. She decided in the end that he had wanted her to stay home so that he could look over the field—and make sure she couldn't.

After she gave Ken his ring back, Jim Bakker asked her out. It took a while and a couple of misunderstandings before they connected; but they went to church on their first date, and on the way home he commanded her to kiss him. She did. The next night they decided to go steady; the night after that they were engaged. Nobody was in favor of that. The school had a rule against students marrying, and Jim's parents got upset. Tammy borrowed his sister Donna's wedding gown, but Raleigh Bakker took it back. In spite of them all, Jim went ahead. With sixty dollars borrowed from Tammy, he made the down payment on a wedding ring. They found a small apartment, left school, and got married, on April Fools' Day 1961, in the same prayer room where Jim had received the Holy Spirit.

The storybook beginning led to a long, hard road. There was no honeymoon. Jim kept his job as a busboy at Rothchild's Restaurant, and Tammy was clerking at the Three Sisters Clothing Store. But then she got a kidney infection; she couldn't work and couldn't help wetting the bed every night. After that she got homesick, and they went to visit her parents, a scene Jim found straight out of "The Beverly Hillbillies." Perhaps worst of all, he seemed to be losing his vocation; he just wanted to stay home and play house. Sister Fern had to call from church, warning him that Tammy was going to be the minister in the family if he didn't look sharp, before Jim started showing up again.

When a preacher turned up from the Amazon at a local revival, the Bakkers heard God calling again and committed themselves to be missionaries. They gave away their belongings and set out to raise support, heading first for a revival in North Carolina. But that was a disaster. After Tammy sang and Jim preached, nothing happened. The Holy Spirit never drew near, and nobody answered the altar call to give their lives to Christ. Jim lay on the carpet and sobbed. He gave up his ministry for the first time that night.

They struggled on. After three barren nights that first revival caught fire. The missionary from the Amazon turned out to be a phony and a thief, but they decided that was a blessing in disguise; God really wanted them on the revival circuit, so they bought a much used white Valiant and drove it from one meeting to the next. They stayed in guest rooms and attics with pastors or parishioners, yearning for privacy and accepting whatever money the Lord sent.

They swallowed a good deal of humble pie and often not much else. Years later, Jim remembered "love offerings" of rusty canned goods without labels, mystery meals that were supposed to be received with gratitude, and his resentment festered. Tammy's most vivid memory was of a scrawny live chicken; unable to slaughter and pluck it, she fed it crumbs and left it behind for less tender sensibilities. They somehow saved enough to buy a trailer, so that at least they could have their own thin roof over their heads. The first day on the road its defective hitch broke; they watched, helpless and horrified, as the trailer cruised past them and demolished itself on a telephone pole. But that disaster, too, turned out to be a blessing. The weeping over their sad story turned the next revival meeting into a bonanza, and three weeks later the trailer company gave them a new and better model to atone for the bad weld.

The story of the trailer was just one more lesson in what became prosperity theology. The crystallizing message for both of them came during a church service, when Jim felt the Lord telling him to put their last twenty-five dollars in the collection plate. That was the grocery money. But they both somehow felt it was the right thing to do, and sure enough, God rewarded them many times over. On the way out of church, a wealthy parishioner asked them out to a restaurant. After dinner he gave them twenty dollars, and before the day was out, two more benefactors had matched the gift. It was a revelation for both of them, and they were to preach it for years and write about it in both their autobiographies. They found dozens of biblical texts to bolster the bargain: Luke 6:38, "Give, and it shall be given unto you"; Proverbs 11:24, "It is possible to give away and become richer"; 2 Corinthians 9:6, ". . . he which soweth bountifully shall reap also bountifully."

As Jerry Falwell was to say, the theology was worse than dubious, and the life it led them to was thoroughly corrupt. For Jim and Tammy, however, the doctrine came straight from heaven, to be proved again and again in the rich drama of their own lives.

That drama took a turn for the better in the spring of 1965, when Jim and Tammy came to the attention of Pat Robertson. The son of a U.S. senator and scion of an old Virginia family, Robertson had heard God's call after a mildly riotous young manhood and already owned one of the first Christian television stations, in Portsmouth, Virginia. What the Bakkers brought to the enterprise was a children's show: They had created a cast of puppets, built around the central characters of Susie Moppet and Allie Alligator, and used them to tell parables of the Christian life. But Jim already had a larger vision. "God meant me to be on television," he would say. "I was made for TV." He joined Robertson's struggling station on condition that Pat would let him do a show modeled on Johnny Carson's late-night talkfest. That idea became "The 700 Club," the centerpiece of what was to be cable television's first religious chain, Robertson's Christian Broadcasting Network.

The Bakkers stayed with CBN for seven years, learning the tricks of television and building their shows as the network grew. Almost by chance, Jim discovered a knack for fund-raising. It happened in an early financial crisis at CBN; a telethon was producing nothing, and Jim finally pleaded with the audience, openly weeping: If people wouldn't open their hearts and their purses, CBN would be dead. The camera "focused on Jim's face as the tears rolled down and spattered on the concrete floor," Robertson wrote in his autobiography, *Shout It from the Housetops.* "Immediately the phones in the studio started ringing. . . . People called in weeping . . . [and] by 2:30 A.M. we had raised $105,000." In the years to come, Jeffrey Hadden observed dryly, tears would be Jim's greatest asset, whether they could be said to flow at God's orders or not. "Some of Bakker's financial scrapes are enough to make any man cry," wrote Hadden, "but when he does it on camera, it's like money in the bank."

The CBN years also produced several of the periodic storms in the Bakker marriage. First Jim had a nervous breakdown, a monthlong crisis of faith and identity that held him immobile and brooding. He took to his bed, as he often did later in lesser troubles, while Tammy, frightened by the illness and feuding bitterly with rival CBN staffers, struggled through the shows alone.

When Jim recovered, Tammy prevailed on him to have a baby, but then it was her turn for trouble. Susie's birth was followed by a depression so deep that Tammy lost touch with God and Jim, too. On the brink of separation after a year of misery, she was actually dialing a psychologist for help when God finally spoke to her again: "Tammy, let me be your psychologist." She burst into tears of grateful relief. A few weeks later, she wrote, while she was singing at a revival, the Holy Spirit set her free in such a coruscation of power that "scores of people came to the altar and found Jesus as their Saviour that night." But she wasn't really free. That depression marked the beginning of a pill habit that nearly killed her seventeen years later.

When it came, the parting with Robertson was strained; both sides seemed to feel badly used. They patched it up later, dealing gently with each other in print, until the PTL scandal broke out. After that, Tammy said bitterly, Robertson "never mentioned our name again. It was like Jim had died almost." By then Robertson was running for president, and he issued a new authorized biography. This one recalled the Bakkers as high-living prima donnas who were charging CBN thousands of dollars for personal expenses, including Tammy's clothes and hairdos.

The Bakkers next joined forces with two California evangelists, Paul and Jan Crouch, a Jim-and-Tammy look-alike team that was starting another TV venture, the Trinity Broadcasting Network. At first the two couples were inseparable, but only two years later the Bakkers stormed out in an angry dispute over the network's independence. Two dozen staffers left with them, and when Jim and Tammy's triumphant telethon in Charlotte resulted in an invitation to stay on at Channel 36, many of those tested troops followed them eastward. They were to be the nucleus of PTL.

The name, too, was imported from California. "The PTL Club" was what they called their show there, a kind of code that Christians could recognize as "Praise the Lord" while dial-flipping unbelievers straying into the show would not be put off. Jim and Tammy had been sending tapes of the show to the Charlotte station; after the telethon, they transferred the whole operation there. It was the show, not the station, that grew into the PTL empire. First Jim built a new studio, in a onetime furniture showroom in a downscale neighborhood of stores, warehouses, and light industry on East Independence Boulevard. He raised funds and recruited volunteer carpenters over the air. Then he set out to build a network modeled on CBN and Trinity, leasing time from stations around the Southeast to carry the PTL show. By the end of 1975 the network had gone national, with 46 stations; eventually it was to transmit by satellite to more than 170 TV stations and an additional cable TV network with thirteen million subscribers. The furniture showroom was left behind when Jim built Heritage Village, a colonial-style complex of studios and offices in a classier part of town. But the paint was hardly dry there when Jim had his grand vision of Heritage USA.

There were frictions on the way to the top. For all his vision, Jim was never much of a business manager; he went through periodic financial crises, hiring and firing executives in the process. At one point he shrugged off a thirteen-million-dollar discrepancy by saying, "The devil got into the computer." PTL's bills were often overdue, and some former executives say that was Jim's conscious strategy. A station wasn't likely to cancel your show, he explained, as long as you owed it money. Station owners have called that a common practice among televangelists. Jim was also an impulsive man at both spending and giving; in the heat of the show, the Lord would prompt him to announce that PTL would give money for a guest's favorite cause, and sometimes it was money that PTL didn't have. That was what got him into trouble in 1977, with his promise to support Christian broadcasting as a missionary effort in Brazil and South Korea. When the *Charlotte Observer* touched off the FCC investigation in 1979, Bakker denounced the inquiry as a satanic plot, and the newspaper was deluged with angry letters from PTL viewers all over the country. The crisis passed when the FCC dropped the case.

Just about then, Jim and Tammy's imperial tendencies came to full flower, and their lives hit the gaudiest pitch of soap opera.

The trouble in the marriage came to a head in 1980. The Bakkers had been through rough patches before. In 1977 Tammy spent several weeks in Hawaii on a trial separation before God told her to go home. That crisis had kept the viewers in suspense for weeks, and it brought some good: PTL established a singles' ministry and marriage seminars to help others in trouble. But now Jim and Tammy were drifting apart again. The FCC case was consuming Jim, and he was spending the rest of his time supervising construction at Heritage USA. He built like a man possessed, pouring millions in donations from the faithful into his vision, tramping through the dust and mud of the construction sites, sketching new wonders for the architects to refine. He would stay on the site long into the night.

Tammy was restless and bored and maybe confused about herself. She complained that PTL had become like a mistress to Jim, and she only wished it were another woman, so she would know what to do about it. It was about this time that her makeup got so heavy, and more than one PTL staffer observed that it was as if she were wearing a mask. It was funny, Ellen Baker recalled, but the dressers at the show who saw Tammy without makeup said she looked younger that way. Tammy started spending more and more time with their new friend Gary Paxton, the heavily bearded country singer who had made his biggest hit with a novelty number called "Alley Oop." Tammy and Gary's wife, Karen, were shopping chums and clowned around a lot, once posing for a photo dressed as dance hall girls. But it was Gary who was giving Tammy singing lessons in Nashville.

Both of them insisted afterward that it was just a flirtation. But the singing lessons and recording sessions sometimes went on all night. Tongues were wagging, and Linda Wilson, who was then Tammy's secretary, said later that she warned Tammy not to get too close to Gary. Jim Bakker reacted at first by sending roses, one a day, to Tammy in Nashville. But then he called Gary, accusing him of having an affair with her; there were bitter words on both sides, and Gary called Jim a "short son of a bitch."

Jim banned Gary from the show. Later, while Jim was in Hawaii,

Tammy asked Gary to appear again, and when Jim returned, he confronted the staff. Red-faced with fury, he demanded to know who had booked Paxton. Reluctantly, the staff told him the truth. He was convinced Tammy and Gary were sleeping together. For Christmas that year, he had his wedding ring melted down to a brooch and gave it to Tammy as a sardonic twenty-year service pin.

Parting with the Paxtons was stormy. Gary Smith, PTL's chief operating officer at the time, tells a melodramatic story of sending two people to intercept Tammy at a shopping center and prevent her from running away with Paxton; by his account, they actually dragged her into a car and hauled her back to Heritage USA, where Smith put her under guard. Whatever she had with Paxton cooled down after that, but the problems were still there. By some accounts, Tammy had more than a flirtation with a second man from the show, music director Thurlow Spurr, before she actually left Jim for a month or so in California. Again God told her to go back. This time the Bakkers talked with Vi Azvedo, the head of PTL's counseling service, and the marriage was patched up again. Vi stayed close at hand for years.

The marriage after that was pretty much as the Oldhams found it: Jim and Tammy clearly had their ups and downs, but they had reached an accommodation. For Tammy, the shopping was some kind of emotional surrogate. Billy Robinson, the court-appointed examiner in PTL's eventual bankruptcy, told of wandering into her closet with its price-tagged dresses and feeling a sudden, deep sorrow for her. "It's like she had a hole in her life," Robinson said, "and she was trying to fill it with all this conspicuous consumption. And no matter how much she spent, she could never fill the void." But there was something else in her life, and it was to catch up with her just before the scandal finally erupted.

In mid-January 1987, the family was spending a long weekend at the Gatlinburg house, the vacation hideout on the Tennessee side of the Great Smoky Mountains. Tammy hadn't been feeling well; on the three-hour drive from the Tega Cay house, near PTL headquarters at Heritage, even a stop for fried chicken at the Po' Folks in Hendersonville hadn't helped her hacking cough. Shortly after midnight on Friday, Don Hardister made a run to the shopping center for aspirin, nose spray, and a vaporizer. Tammy used them and felt better, but the truth was she was coming down with viral pneumonia. On Saturday afternoon Jim got cabin fever and went shopping with Vi Azvedo. Dee Oldham, Doug and Laura Lee's daughter, took Susie and her brother, Jamie Charles, to an amusement park for the afternoon. Hardister was left with Tammy, and she was acting strange.

"My head's just roaring. It's just roaring," she complained. She was chewing Aspergum for a sore throat and couldn't remember how many aspirin she had taken; she had probably had too many, he figured, and he told her to stop. A few minutes later she started giggling uncontrollably at a television program, and he started worrying. Then she wanted to open the sliding doors, in the middle of winter. In itself, that wasn't unusual. Jim and Tammy liked to build a roaring fire in the fireplace and open the doors. But this time she told Hardister, "I'm just burning up. I've gotta take my clothes off and go outside and stand. It's the only way I can cool down." She was quite matter-of-fact, not suggestive at all; Tammy was always very careful that way, Hardister said, "So, I knew that this lady's nuts." He locked her in the house and stood in the driveway for two hours, waiting for Jim and Vi to come home. He was careful, too.

In the next two days, Tammy got sicker. At one point she thought Susie was a baby again and tried to tell Jim how to fix her formula. When the family doctor was flown in from California, he found her so sick he was worried about brain damage. But he also found twenty-seven different nonprescription drugs she had been taking, some of them by the handful. It turned out that she had been popping pills of all kinds ever since the depression she had after Susie was born. So Tammy was flown to Eisenhower Medical Center near Palm Springs, California. That was near another of their vacation places, but it was also the location of the Betty Ford Center for alcohol and drug rehabilitation. The flight out in a chartered jet was not pleasant. Tammy saw demons, bugs crawling on the floor, and a cat and a marching band outside on the wing. Once, she put on her coat and tried to walk out the door.

Jim left the show to join her in California, and they were treated as a family. Rumors began spreading about Tammy, so in March they appeared together in a taped bit on the show and explained her illness, one more crisis in the long drama. But there were rumors about Jim, too: That he was drinking, having affairs, visiting prostitutes, even that he was too fond of some of his male aides. And at least one of the rumors was true. Back in 1980, it had been John Wesley Fletcher's idea that Jim should make Tammy jealous by having a fling with a Long Island secretary just before a telethon in Clearwater Beach, Florida. There, in room 538 of the Sheraton Sand Key Resort, Jim Bakker set the time bomb that destroyed him seven years later.

"It's a good thing God's merciful, or he would have zapped them dead long ago," said Paul Clem, thirty-four, an electrical contractor from Olathe, Kansas. "It was so blatantly mercenary. I realize they're human beings, and they falter; but I believe Christ was not the center of their ministry. Jim and Tammy were the center.

"So many unsuspecting people were victimized by the Bakkers. These were people who really wanted someone they could adulate, a king, a queen. Many of them were probably blue-collar, working-class, and the opulence was something they could never attain. But they thought, since it was religious, it was okay.

"I've been around a lot of people who kid about it. Everyone yuks it up when it comes to Jim and Tammy. The whole thing has been a joke. I think that says the church has taken a real black eye about this."

Chapter 5
Jessica

In the end, people will believe what they want about Jessica Hahn. Perhaps she was just as she pictured herself: The virginal victim, a devout and lonely girl who lived for her church and was betrayed over and over by men she longed to trust. Or maybe she was the whore of West Babylon, Long Island, the gold-digging Bible Belle of the tabloids who dressed like a tart, had a series of cheap affairs, took advantage of Jim Bakker's weakness, and finally cashed in on her notoriety for a cool million dollars.

Most people would come down on the cynical side, and the weight of the evidence seems to be with them. Nobody disputed that Jessica Hahn had carnal relations with Jim Bakker that December afternoon in 1980; or that she negotiated a $265,000 settlement to keep quiet about it; or that after the scandal finally erupted, she peddled her story to *Playboy* magazine for a sum widely reported as $1 million, posed topless for photos with the story, and moved into the Playboy mansion as one of Hugh Hefner's entourage. Her own mother said she was behaving like a bimbo. *Penthouse* found an ex-madam who said Jessica had worked as a hooker; *Penthouse* even found a neighbor youth who said she had seduced him when he was fourteen years old. And when Jessica protested over and over, in interviews and talk shows and the pages of *Playboy*, "I am not a bimbo," it had precisely the perverse effect of Richard Nixon's "I am not a crook."

In fact, Jessica led the calendar in what became the Year of the

Bimbo. First her story started the PTL scandal; then a Washington secretary named Fawn Hall smuggled Iran-contra secrets in her underwear for her boss, Oliver North; and finally Gary Hart was knocked out as front runner in the presidential sweepstakes by his escapades with a party girl, Donna Rice. All three women, with varying credibility, argued that they were guilty of nothing worse than being good-looking females trapped in publicity storms. What that got them was scorn, or at best knowing winks. "Go for it, baby," a phone-in radio caller told Jessica; why not have it all, celebrity, money, and sympathy, too?

The first reporter to track her down was a woman from *New York Newsday,* who found Jessica's small apartment in the top half of an old house covered in mustard-colored asbestos shingles. The reporter said Jim Bakker had resigned from his TV ministry, saying he had been "wickedly manipulated" into a sexual encounter with Jessica Hahn; what did she have to say about that? She wasn't going to talk about it, she replied. But she did talk about herself: her quiet childhood in Massapequa; how she found God; her life as a secretary in the Full Gospel Tabernacle. The interview was low-key, and she posed for the camera in what she was wearing around the house, jeans and boots and a gold chain. That was fairly standard dress for Babylon, a gritty blue-collar bastion in the suburbs of New York. But Jessica was a pretty woman, slim but full-busted, with a cloud of dark hair and sensuous lips; the tight jeans, in combination with the sunglasses she often wore to mask her close-set eyes, looked sexy on the tabloid page. The image went all too well with the story.

With that, the media rush was on. Jessica's unlisted number seemed to be no secret, and her phone rang constantly. After a few calls, she switched on the answering machine and climbed onto her exercise bike. Then, through the taped rock music in her headset, she heard a rumble outside. The heralds of celebrity had arrived, dozens of them: cars and vans; mobile TV crews with mikes on booms; photographers and reporters with blankets and lawn chairs for the stakeout. At first, she tried to hide. Then she pleaded with them to go away. "I don't want to hurt anybody," she told them. "I don't want to say anything about anybody." But they were a clamorous lot, ringing her bell, pushing notes under her door, cajoling her little black dog, Missy, and harassing the neighbors. They trampled the lawn, littered the place with their coffee cartons and pizza boxes, threw pebbles at her windows to get her to appear for the zoom lenses. It is a standard comic scene right out of *The Front Page,* but an ugly one, too. And when Jessica, not knowing what else to do, finally walked out to face the cameras, her appearance set off a scrimmage that actually knocked her down.

That first press conference was strained and not very informative. No, Jessica couldn't talk about what had happened between her and Bakker. "I could say a lot; I could say many things." But her adviser, a California businessman named Paul Roper, had told her not to. She was worried, she said, about the effect of the scandal on her family and on the church. "I feel deeply concerned about the people who attend all these churches. I hope they see this will pass and that this is no reflection, obviously, on the Lord. . . . My greatest concern is that people are under the impression that this goes on everywhere. It does not go on everywhere." That sounded just a touch smarmy, and the reporters decided that Jessica seemed to be basking a bit in the attention. She wandered around the yard, politely declining interviews but plainly flirting with the cameras; from time to time she dropped an offhand word or slipped off her sunglasses with a shy smile.

It made for some vivid film clips on the evening news, and she repeated the performance often in the days to come. Her adviser, Roper, a self-elected scourge of evangelical hypocrisy and the head of an organization he called Operation Anti-Christ, told reporters in California he wished Jessica would stop "walking around in skin-tight jeans in her backyard, making cute little throwaway remarks to the press." But she didn't know what else to do, she protested later; her clothes were simply what she wore—"I try to keep myself nice"—and she was alone with the insatiable media machine. Whatever messages Roper was sending through the press, she said, he wasn't answering his phone.

It continued like that, on and off, for months. In early June, again under siege after a spate of speculative headlines linking her name with another scandal, she brooded to a *Newsweek* reporter that the whole thing was crazy, out of hand. "At the rate they're going I wouldn't be surprised if they link me to Iran. It's scary." She was trying to protect her family from the worst of it, but sometimes she felt so alone that she called a shock radio show because its dirty-mouthed host, Howard Stern, seemed to want to know how she actually felt.

She seemed permanently cast as a victim, even of those who said they wanted to help. She had just called a new lawyer, she said, but he wouldn't even come to her apartment or help her through the press gauntlet. In fact, he put her on notice to make it snappy. She was to come to his office after lunch, but before his three o'clock appointment, and since it was Friday, he was counting on a long lunch. Jessica had confided in many reporters; she had gotten to like and trust a few of them, but even some of those had turned on her. One woman had given her a warning, a word of friendly caution that Jessica took as a threat: "Whatever you do now is never off the record. We will use whatever we have; we will almost create it." She had become notorious, and it was as if the truth about her didn't matter.

What got her first was the music. There was a big yellow and white tent, with a searchlight sweeping the sky, and the joyous hymn "Let's Just Praise the Lord" was filling the summer evening. It was June 1974. Jessica, chubby and shy a month away from her fifteenth birthday, walked into the tent. It wasn't anything like the remote, dark place of her Catholic worship; it was alive, filled with music and young people. Someone took her hand, welcomed her, led her to a seat. The preacher was dark and intense, fierce in his power and authority. He summoned the Holy Spirit, and something happened; the tent filled with an awesome presence. The preacher gave the altar call: "Come up if you want to know Jesus. Come up!" And then he called out directly to her, to Jessica Hahn: "Young lady, you are very alone." It was as if he could see into her soul. God had a special plan for her, he said; he took her by the shoulders, there in front of the congregation, and put his hand on her head. She was overwhelmed by the Spirit. She experienced God.

The preacher was John Wesley Fletcher, and six years later he was to have his own special plan for Jessica Hahn. But now she had entered a new world, one that changed her life completely.

Jessica didn't remember her real father; all she knew of him was that he had treated the family badly and that when she was born, he had refused to hold her. Her stepfather, Ed Moylan, was a New York cop, and he was a strong and loving father to Jessica and her older brother and sister. Her mother, Jessica, was loving, too, a woman who cared about making a home; there were candles on her dining table. But Jessica yearned for the warmth and closeness of TV

families like the Waltons and the Bradys. Until that night in the
tent, the best thing that had happened to her was the birth of her
little brother, Danny, when she was twelve. "I practically raised
him," she said. "When I got off the school bus, Mother would take
my books and I would take Danny." She dressed him, fed him,
helped him learn to walk and speak, and that filled her life.

When the scandal broke, reporters scoured Long Island to find
people who could tell them about Jessica. But "it was almost impossible for them to find somebody who would know me," she said. "I
never got involved with people my age. I didn't go to parties. I
socialize occasionally, have coffee with somebody. But I go to the
movies alone, I go to stores alone. I have always been that way."

For a while, Jessica did have a girlfriend, Carol. But Carol died
suddenly, of a stroke or brain hemorrhage, the year she was fourteen. Jessica's mother told her about it, holding her in her arms.
"Just like I am holding you, God is holding her," she said.

John Wesley Fletcher was a traveling evangelist. He took his tent
from one small Pentecostal church to the next, staying for a month
or so to preach revival of the faith and swell the congregation. The
local minister who actually ran Jessica's church was Gene Profeta,
a powerful preacher and flamboyant man whose taste ran to big cars,
a private plane, and a mink coat, given to him by a member of his
congregation. The tabloids were to learn he had taken out licenses
for two guns, so in their pages he became the pistol-packing
preacher, and in the year of the scandal, Profeta came under scrutiny
by a grand jury in Albany for possible tax fraud. Profeta had founded
the Full Gospel Tabernacle four years before Jessica joined it, with
only forty worshipers. It was still small and struggling when she
found a second home there.

"I started out doing little things," she said. "I cleaned the church;
I started by cleaning the toilet bowls." Often she simply hung
around, visiting with Profeta's wife, Glenda, and she baby-sat with
Profeta's children and with Fletcher's when he was visiting. "They
took me under their wing," she said. "It was an amazing relationship. The church was beautiful; the pastor and his family were like
a second family to me." As she learned more about her new faith,
she began counseling and praying over the phone with troubled
people who called the church for help.

Jessica's parents were a little disturbed by her consuming new interest but became reconciled, she said, as they saw her growing with it. She was still going to Massapequa High School, where classmates were to recall her as pretty but uninteresting; she was graduated as an honor student, but then her immersion in the church became total. She signed on as one of Profeta's secretaries, starting at eighty dollars a week, and the church was her entire life. "I'd often work to midnight," she said. "I loved it. I joined the choir. If I wasn't working, I was in church for every one of the six [weekly] services. There was a Friday service and a Saturday night choir rehearsal. Work and church, and the rest of the time services. To me that was the best time of my life."

What did she find there? Jessica's religious conviction seemed genuine enough; throughout her public statements in the months of stress there ran a consistent thread of faith and concern for her fellow believers. "I know God has a reason for everything," she told *Newsweek* in a long, rambling interview at the depth of her depression in June. "Maybe he will use this in a positive way. I know he will." She is an intelligent woman whose native wit shows clearly through a limited education, and she was smart enough to recognize that faith wasn't her only motivation. In her *Playboy* interview, Jessica said it was "obvious now" that she had been looking for "somebody in authority to kind of lead me around. . . . I mean, I had a sign on my back reading GIVE ME SOME DIRECTION." She was also to recall another facet of her obsession with the church: "I always wanted to be special. I always wanted to be in on something. I hated being on the outside looking in; I still do."

According to some of her fellow workers at the church, that drive for inside knowledge and power soon got out of hand. Jessica did indeed have a special relationship with the Profetas, said Norma Ferretti, another of the preacher's former secretaries, and she wasn't shy about using it. "She was the queen of the tabernacle," said Ferretti. "She really pushed her weight around." At first little more than a receptionist who had to be taught to type and answer letters, Jessica grew autocratic and increasingly jealous as her influence with Profeta increased. As Ferretti told it, if the preacher asked one of the other women to do something Jessica couldn't do, "She would get tingly and moody . . . [and] when you encounter this girl's wrath, you know you are in trouble." She could be sweet and gentle with an elderly parishioner or fly into a rage over a fancied slight. In fact,

Ferretti said, Jessica threatened to get her fired in a spat over a phone call, and six weeks later Ferretti was out of a job.

Norma Ferretti clearly harbored a grudge, but three other former workers at the church agreed with her on another point: When it came to men, Jessica was very like a bimbo. As Jessica pictured herself, she was a shy church mouse who had to learn about sex by reading books and was too reticent to date; when boys would ask her out, she would agree because she didn't know how to say no and then ask her mother to tell the swains she was sick. But her former friends said Jessica was an experienced woman who flirted provocatively, manipulated men at the church, boasted of her sexual exploits, and was no virgin when she went to meet Bakker in Florida. Rocco Riccobono, an electrician and former church handyman, said he and Jessica made love twice in 1978, two years before the Bakker incident, and Joanne Posner, another of Profeta's secretaries, said she had inadvertently witnessed one of these episodes, which happened at her house. Even before that, said Riccobono's former wife, Evelyn, Jessica had told her of spending a weekend at a New York hotel at the age of seventeen with John Wesley Fletcher himself. And when Jessica returned from her 1980 visit to Florida, her former friends said, she wasn't acting like the victim of a near rape; she seemed "very happy, very up."

Jessica's tale of outraged virtue was further undermined when the *New York Post* ran a story about two more men—a black guitarist and a Vietnamese refugee—who claimed to have been her lovers in post-Bakker years. One of them said she had told him Bakker had not been her first man, and both of them said Preacher Profeta had behaved toward Jessica with something like possessive jealousy, ordering them out of her life. That made her image increasingly brazen, especially after the *Playboy* photos appeared.

Jessica was by then a convert to the Playboy philosophy, arguing that the photos had nothing to do with lust or her own state of grace. They were a token of her feminist rebirth, she said, and showed that her body was soft and beautiful, not something to be abused. For that, she was booed and heckled on a publicity tour to hype the magazine. But she furiously denied the stories of her depravity and denounced her onetime friends as a bunch of nobodies. "People are going to be coming out of the woodwork wanting to get their names in the paper," she said; there would probably be fifteen thousand men claiming to have slept with her. In the end, the figure seemed almost that high. According to *Penthouse*'s ex-madam and clients of hers who reportedly supported parts of her story, Jessica did indeed know all the tricks of the trade. She was a seasoned hooker by the time she was seventeen, the ex-madam said, and sometimes serviced forty men at a single party. Jessica's lawyer threatened to sue.

It was true that a lot of people had an interest in discrediting Jessica and her story. Suspicion that they might be trying just that was bolstered by the fact that the names and phone numbers of the turncoat friends were being supplied to New York reporters by a woman who identified herself as a supporter of Jim Bakker's and a property owner at Heritage USA. But Jessica's critics denied any conspiracy. They said they were speaking out only because, as Riccobono put it, "Jessica is detrimental to Christianity."

It was not clear how Christianity, or that part of it represented by the Full Gospel Tabernacle, felt about Jessica. For her part, Jessica at first had nothing but good to say of Profeta, portraying him as a caring man who tried hard to help her. When she first told him what Bakker and Fletcher had done to her, she said, he cried; he wanted to kill both of them. But that story was hard to square with Profeta's public stance. In his first sermon after the story got out, he asked the congregation to pray for an erring brother and sister, adding, "I know Jim Bakker is still a hero." He kept his silence after that, putting his new stone church off limits to reporters and telling his followers, numbering two thousand by then, not to discuss Jessica. He refused any interviews about her, saying only that he knew her as a nice girl and a "homebody."

As she told it, Profeta's nonsupport was her own doing. She had told him not to become part of the scandal; she knew she couldn't go through life depending on him. But he had taken her at her word, and more. She no longer felt welcome at his church. Later, she reportedly testified about him to the grand jury in Albany, and after that any pretense of the old closeness was gone; she would hint that it was Profeta who had encouraged his flock to tell nasty tales about her. But by then she had found her new life in the Playboy mansion.

So Jessica's story of sin with Jim Bakker may be viewed through either of two lenses: the clear outrage of her own tale of betrayal and violation, or the peephole view of a sly assignation set up with a willing woman by two corrupt preachers. The curious thing is how well the two coincide. The facts fit neatly into either interpretation.

Nobody denies that Fletcher, meeting Jessica again when he visited Massapequa early in 1980, remarked admiringly on how she had grown up or that he called sometime later to invite her to a telethon he and Bakker were to do in Florida. She told the story in the taped affidavit that Roper used to win her settlement from PTL and again in *Playboy*: how she flew to Tampa; how Fletcher met her there and told her about Jim and Tammy's marital problems; how he took her to a hotel, had her walk behind him as they passed the front desk, and took her upstairs to a room. There he gave her a glass of wine, and Jim Bakker walked in, wearing only a white terry-cloth swimsuit, still sandy from the beach. But agreement stops there.

Jessica told it starkly, in near-pornographic detail. First Fletcher left them alone together, suggesting that she give Jim a back rub with some Vaseline Intensive Care lotion—"I kept that little yellow bottle all these years"—but she felt ill and dizzy from the wine. In fact, she said, she was so sick that she was unable to resist as Jim undressed her, saying he needed someone, that he had been going through hell. She protested that she was a virgin; she asked why he didn't just hire somebody. But then, she said, she felt it was useless to protest. He forced her to have oral sex, then full intercourse. "He had to keep finding new things to do." When she kept protesting, he kept repeating two of the scene's most callously memorable lines: "You'll appreciate this later. . . . When you help the shepherd, you're helping the sheep." She tried to push him off, but he wouldn't stop. "He just did everything he could do to a woman." Finally, reduced to impotence, he said he wanted to see her again. "I have jets. I can make any kind of arrangements." Then he brushed his hair with her hairbrush,* put on the bathing suit, and left, saying, "Look, I'll see ya."

Jessica said she staggered into the shower, threw up, brushed her teeth; she was still feeling sick when Fletcher returned. He told her how happy she had made Jim, how she had saved PTL that day. She told him she was sick, but he refused to leave and started talking like a character in a cheap porn novel: "You're not going to just give it to Jim, you're going to give it to me, too. . . . You're not going to forget this. . . . You won't remember Jim, you'll remember me." He was brutal and acrobatic, taking her on the floor, scraping her back until it bled, seeming to need pain for his own pleasure. She was

* He should've spanked her bottom with it!

screaming, she said, but nobody seemed to hear. When he finally got up to go, he told her all she needed was something to eat. Then he tuned the TV so that she could watch the telethon and went to serve God.

Jessica was having chills and fever. She fell into a light doze in spite of her pain, she said. Then she turned on the television, partly to make sure the two preachers were still busy and couldn't persecute her anymore. She said they were sniggering to each other, right in front of the altar: "Jim, we really had a good rest today." "Yeah, I need more rest like that." "The Lord really ministered to us today." They were making fun of her, she thought. She called room service and ordered a cheeseburger. The man who brought it asked if she wanted a doctor, but she said no; she was scared and dazed. After one bite she had to cover the cheeseburger; she couldn't stand even the smell. Finally Fletcher came back, bringing a television producer with him. Fletcher hinted that she should entertain the third man, too. Bitterly she refused, and demanded to be sent home. At last he booked her return flight to New York, gave her the precise fare—$129—and left. She dozed through the night and flew home next day, her world shattered. She told nobody what had happened. She was just twenty-one.

In the cynical view of the episode, the facts stay the same, but whether or not Jessica knew the purpose of the trip in advance, she was a willing and practiced victim. After all, if Fletcher had wanted to curry favor with Bakker and perhaps get a blackmailer's edge on him by providing a woman, it would not make much sense to bring him an innocent girl who might resist or even cry rape. She went to the room without complaint, sneaking past the front desk; she serviced first Bakker and then Fletcher. Nobody heard any protest. She lay in bed, watching the show on television, and ordered a cheeseburger. When it came, she passed up a chance to complain of her treatment or get medical help. She went home and didn't tell her story. In fact, according to Evelyn Riccobono, she told her co-workers that she had had a great time in Florida. And she continued to wear the plum-colored wraparound dress that Bakker had supposedly stripped from her.

When the story finally came out seven years later, Fletcher first tried to shrug off his role in the affair with a sarcastic wisecrack: Yes, he had introduced Jessica to Jim, but "Nowhere in the Bible is it written, 'Thou shalt not introduce one another.' " Then, in an interview with the *Charlotte Observer,* he conceded that he had summoned Jessica because Jim, near suicidal over his troubles, needed an understanding woman and wanted to make Tammy jealous. But Fletcher insisted, however implausibly, that he hadn't known sex was going to be involved and didn't know what happened after he left them together. The next day, however, he told a congregation in upstate New York that he was overwhelmed with guilt; eyes filled with tears, he asked forgiveness. Nearly everyone in the congregation of five hundred stood and applauded. But he never made it clear what he was guilty of, and in the next few months, Fletcher stopped talking about it. He was back on the revival circuit. The only thing he would say was that Jessica wasn't telling the truth; he had not had relations with her.

Bakker's story, when he finally told it to Jerry Falwell on resigning his ministry, was more straightforward—up to a point. Yes, it had happened. But it was no more than a fifteen-minute episode. Jessica had very nearly raped *him*, aggressively undressing him and taking the lead; he was so scared and confused that he was impotent, and the next thing he knew he was in his own shower, crying, "Oh, God, I've been with a whore." Jamie Buckingham, a friend of Bakker's and a columnist for the religious magazine *Charisma & Christian Life,* told the press that Jim had been victimized by a hussy who, though only twenty-one, "knew all the tricks of the trade. . . . She just got hold of a Pentecostal preacher who didn't know how to handle it and it just devastated him. He felt terrible guilt." If so, the shame didn't show in the telethon. But that was also somehow irrelevant to the Jessica question. It seemed curiously old-fashioned in the feminist age, but the issue in most people's minds was whether she was pure, and Jim's guilt or contrition had nothing to do with that. Whatever he had done, most people were ready to convict her as everything Buckingham said she was.

But there was another problem with the cynical view of Jessica: As a gold digger—at least in this case—she was a flop. For years, she got nothing for her supposed whoredom. She left Florida without so much as taxi fare for her trouble, and despite Bakker's talk of jets and future assignations, she didn't date either preacher again. Back home, if Jessica was indeed queen of the Full Gospel Tabernacle, it was an unrewarding reign. Her salary had inched up to something like ten thousand dollars a year; she was still working till midnight at the church. She moved from her parents' home to a tiny apartment, but her social life was dreary at best. The idea of blackmail could surely have occurred to her. By her own account, Bakker himself had told her she was picked because she could be trusted, because "you're not someone who is going to try and hurt me like the others." But for more than three years Jessica asked for nothing. Why did she wait so long?

Bakker called Jessica within a few days after her return to Massapequa. His story of the call laid stress on his apology for what had happened and his insistence that he could never see her again. He even advised her to repent and said he would pray for her. Her version emphasized his urging her to keep quiet about it. "I would be accountable to God if I caused trouble," she said bitterly. Later, Fletcher called with the same message, adding what sounded like a warning, that it might cause trouble for her family if she talked. And from time to time after that, she got calls from David Taggart and then Richard Dortch; when she was to return a call like that, a secretary would give her a phony name to use—Jennifer Lee or Elizabeth Anderson. Sometimes, she said, they threatened her. Fletcher once warned her there would be trouble, and Dortch said Fletcher was merciless.

That time, the two men were aiming more at each other than at Jessica. In 1981, Fletcher had been summoned to the Assemblies of God, which had ordained both him and Bakker, to answer for a series of sins. Dortch, who was then a district superintendent for the denomination and also a board member at PTL, was in charge of Fletcher's case, and Fletcher told the *Charlotte Observer* that he had told Dortch then about the Jessica Hahn episode. It was widely rumored in the Assemblies that Fletcher had made a kind of plea bargain with Dortch: To head off a major scandal, Fletcher would be defrocked only for alcoholism, and Dortch would try to get him reinstated after two years. When Dortch either couldn't or wouldn't deliver on his part of the bargain, the story went, Fletcher began spreading Jessica's name around to show what damage he could do. Late in 1983, he called a reporter at the *Observer* and told him to remember the name Jessica Hahn in connection with Jim Bakker.

Jessica said she heard part of that scenario from Dortch, who became PTL's chief operating officer in 1983. Someone had called PTL with the Hahn story, he told her, and it had to be either Jessica or Fletcher. He explained that Fletcher was making trouble because Dortch wouldn't let him back into the Assemblies. Jessica replied that she hadn't been making any calls. That was when Dortch first suggested that she sign some papers, for her own sake, so that PTL could guarantee her protection and even a job for her if she would protect PTL.

Jessica wasn't interested in that bargain or much of anything else. Her life had become a nightmare, she said. She was trying to sort out what had happened to her and not having much success; for years, she said, she kept thinking that these men could do no wrong, and therefore, somehow, she must have been guilty. Her church laid considerable stress on a scriptural verse, "Touch not mine anointed" (1 Chronicles 16:22). That was also a warning Bakker liked to quote on the infrequent occasions when someone ventured to criticize him. What it meant to Jessica was that if she were to accuse a man of God, even if the charge was just, God would curse her.

She felt punished already; she couldn't worship or really listen to sermons anymore. Whenever she wasn't working, she would go home and lie in bed, not sleeping, just brooding. She would throw away the trays of food her mother fixed for her. Her weight dropped from 145 pounds to 112, and her parents began worrying about anorexia. She knew she needed help, and at one point, she told *Playboy*, she tried seeing a Christian psychiatrist. But when she brought up Jim Bakker's name, he said, "Yeah, I've been on his TV show." She felt surrounded.

The telephone talks with PTL continued. As Bakker's people told it, it was Jessica who kept calling them, a seemingly obsessed woman whose crazy story was only gradually taken seriously. But in her version, the approach was always theirs, and the message was always the same: Don't talk; don't hurt the ministry; don't damage the kingdom of God. Both sides agree, however, that it wasn't until March 1984, more than three years after the encounter in room 538, that PTL heard any concrete demands. Then Taggart got an unsigned letter, purportedly from "a Christian lady" who was a friend of Jessica's, describing her long torment and the permanent scars it had left. Jessica's work was suffering, the letter said; she couldn't expect marriage and a happy future; her life was in ruins. The letter asked for a hundred thousand dollars in reparations and commented: "That amount would not seem excessive to you if it had been your daughter or my daughter who had been violated."

Dortch set up a meeting with Jessica on March 31, in room 616 of the Holiday Inn at New York's La Guardia Airport. To quiet any troubling echoes from another hotel room, a woman would also be there: Aimee Cortese, pastor of a church in the Bronx and another member of the PTL board. Dortch was a smooth and persuasive man, silver of hair and tongue; long after he had left the PTL scene, other players in the drama marveled at the things he had made them believe. Cortese was short, powerfully built, and gruff, and Jessica said she looked like a prison warden waiting to meet her.

They wanted her to sign a statement that her whole story had never happened, and their tactics were the classic Mutt-and-Jeff alternation of police interrogations, switching from intimidation to protestations of love for her. But she held them off, and Dortch fell back to let the idea sink in. He called her again in October, saying it was time to sign and be done with it. When he reminded her that she didn't want her parents and her beloved brother Danny to know what had happened, she agreed to sign.

Even so, Jessica said, she dug in her heels when she went to Cortese's Crossroads Tabernacle on November 1 and saw the document. "It's all lies," she protested. She would be admitting to defamation and extortion, and she would have to stipulate that Bakker had never so much as touched her. Sign, Cortese said, or you will never have any peace. Cortese said that there was no time to argue, that she had to go to a meeting; then she wept, saying she loved Jessica like a daughter and would deny the truth of the papers if need be. They had to be signed, she said, but they would never leave New York. In the end, Jessica signed. There had been no bargaining, but afterward Cortese tossed her an envelope and a curt word of advice: "Get some counseling." When Jessica got to her car, she said, she found ten thousand dollars in the envelope.

The source of that money became a matter of intense speculation. When word of the payment first got out, Cortese's brother, Bronx Congressman Robert Garcia, was a target of investigation in the unfolding Wedtech scandal, an intricate scam built around preferential contracts for minority contractors. Ultimately, Wedtech en-

meshed dozens of officials and reached high into the Reagan administration. Federal investigators said eighty thousand dollars in
Wedtech money had been channeled through Cortese's church, and
they could trace only twenty thousand of that. There was no reason
on the surface why the two scandals should be more than coincidentally linked, but the coincidence was conspicuous. And though PTL
gave Cortese's church a gift of fifty thousand dollars, ostensibly for
church renovations, that payment wasn't made until four months
after the payoff to Jessica. Had Jessica's money come from Wedtech?
If so, why?

Cortese refused to discuss either scandal; her lawyer said that
whatever she did in Jessica's case, she was merely following instructions and didn't know what the whole affair was about. And months
later, it turned out that Jessica's ten thousand dollars, and another
two thousand that Cortese had given her several weeks earlier, had
been lent to PTL by Sam Johnson, who was later to be pastor of the
Heritage Village Church. Johnson may or may not have known how
it was to be used. But Jessica was mystified when she saw the *Daily
News* headline linking her name to Wedtech. "I don't even know
what Wedtech is," she protested the next day. "I have seen it on
the news and just turned the channel. It didn't hold my interest."

After she had signed the papers, however, she started thinking
seriously about pressing a case against Bakker and PTL. What she
wanted, she insisted later, was not money but the return of that
statement; she wanted acknowledgment that she had been hurt. But
she needed a legal lever, and now she finally told Profeta what had
happened to her that day in 1980. He flew into a rage, she said. But
he also told her about Paul Roper and his Operation Anti-Christ.

Roper was an odd choice for a champion. He was an enigmatic
Orange County businessman, with real estate and banking interests,
who was also studying law at the age of forty. Jessica said she
thought for years that he really was a lawyer and learned otherwise
only from the press. While he was managing a debt-ridden fundamentalist church, Melodyland Christian Center, in Anaheim in
1980, Roper had a long dispute with the church over what he said
was the minister's personal use of church funds. Later he announced
he was forming Operation Anti-Christ, with a staff of twelve and five
hundred thousand dollars in funding, to expose televangelists who
fleeced their followers. The whole crusade seemed to die quietly

soon after its publicized birth, and Roper himself became one of twenty-two defendants in a 1985 civil case charging fraud in the sale of a savings and loan association in Seattle. His portion of that suit was ultimately settled for $10 million.

Roper was to make a good many statements about Jessica's case, including the vivid remark that Bakker had made her feel "like a piece of hamburger somebody threw out in the street." But he wouldn't discuss his own affairs, and Jessica's feelings about him were to vary considerably as the facts came out. When she told him her story, however, she knew only that he was a man interested in exposing cases like hers. In January 1985 he flew to New York and taped what became a twenty-three-page question-and-answer deposition.

Roper tried to call Bakker to discuss the accusation, he said; when that failed, he got a friend, a lawyer and Christian radio personality named John Stewart, to draw up a suit based on the deposition, demanding $12.3 million in reparations for Jessica. Then he sent it to PTL with the suggestion that a committee of prominent pastors investigate the whole mess.

By this time, Dortch said much later, Profeta had called him, threatening that "when he got finished with Jim Bakker and me, we would never be able to do anything else with a woman for the rest of our lives. . . . I felt a gun was at my head, an extortion was in operation." Profeta denied that story. In any case, Dortch flew to California, hired his own lawyer, and promptly drew up a settlement.

Maybe Jessica was born to lose. The headlines would say the settlement was $265,000 in hush money, and so in a way it was, with $115,000 paid up front and $150,000 to be put in trust for her at the Bank of Los Angeles. But of the $115,000 initial payment, she got only about $20,000, while Roper and Stewart took $95,000. Roper told *Playboy* that the fee was $2,500 a year for the twenty-year trust, plus expenses; Jessica said she didn't know what was usual and simply agreed to the sums. Jessica would get the interest from the trust in monthly checks, and if she kept the secret for twenty years, the whole $150,000 would be hers.

Jessica was going to be set for life, Roper told her, and he would be her trustee. But the trust was never legally established. Roper did have occasional correspondence with Scott Furstman, a lawyer for

PTL, over the details of the agreement. Roper explained later that Furstman never sent him the final draft to be signed, but he refused to discuss how hard he had pressed for it. Jessica got her monthly checks, amounting to $10,045 in 1985 and presumably a similar amount in 1986. But after the story broke, PTL simply announced that it was stopping the interest payments. Jessica never publicly totaled what she got from PTL, but including Cortese's envelope, it was probably about $50,000—slightly more than half the sum her benefactors took.

Spread over a little more than two years and added to her secretary's paycheck, the PTL money couldn't have funded much riotous living for Jessica. As she told it, she paid some bills and bought a few things for her apartment. The one conspicuous sign of better times in her life was a sleek black 1985 Olds Toronado in her driveway. There were some curious discordances that never were explained: stories of her traveling in limousines with bodyguards for her meetings with Cortese; hints that she might have received other payments; traces of a life totally out of keeping with her style in West Babylon. The *Daily News* quoted her boasting of a friendship with the entertainer Liberace; the story said that she had spent several evenings with him in New York and California and that she took (and passed) a test for AIDS after he died of the disease, since she had sometimes eaten from his plate. But if she did get a taste of it, the high life was fleeting. The public scandal found her in West Babylon, still alone.

Even after the story came out, she spent months brooding in her apartment and turning down offers to capitalize on her notoriety. In her eyes, the settlement she had taken wasn't hush money; it was the kind of damages she might have been awarded if she had been hit by a car. "If I were that kind of woman, I would be posing for *Penthouse*," she protested three months after the press siege began. *Penthouse* had actually offered her $350,000, she said, and other bids, involving books, films, and a modeling career, were stacking up in her answering machine.

But then, just a month later, she took a trip to Hollywood to check out all the possibilities. "I would consider anything if the price was right and it helped my life in a positive way," she said. And whatever she had been or done, that was the right decision. For the purposes of the PTL drama, Jessica's virtue had become a secondary issue, to be invoked or besmirched as the players saw fit; in the public eye, like it or not, she *was* "that kind of woman." The realistic choice that faced her was posed best by Steven M. L. Aronson, author of a study of celebrities titled *Hype:* "Do you want to be poor, honest and forgotten, or rich, sleazy and famous?" She had waited so long because that's how long it took to figure it out.

"I've been disgusted by it all, but there is a small thread of pity running through that," said Paul Clem's wife, Susan, a homemaker raising two children in Olathe, Kansas. "At first I thought she was a victim. But if she was, she's not behaving in a very credible way. I don't have a lot of the sympathy for her that I once had. It's hard to believe that Jessica is living out God's will for her by being in the Playboy mansion."

Chapter 6

The Cuckoo's Chick

Even before Jessica Hahn signed her agreement with Richard Dortch, the scandal was spreading. Once the deal was made, the number of people who knew the secret grew almost daily.

The *Charlotte Observer* had most of the story. Fletcher himself had called the *Observer* at least once, and the paper apparently had additional sources. In December 1984, Jessica said later, she heard that a reporter named Charlie Shepard had her name; she called him to find out what he knew. He told her he had heard Jim Bakker was having a torrid affair with her, and she set him right, but without saying anything about Fletcher or the money Aimee Cortese had given her. The newspaper said later that Jessica's story didn't quite track with the deposition that turned up later; among other discrepancies, she said she had been given water, not wine, in the hotel room. The paper continued to dig at the story, as it had been chasing tips about PTL for a decade. But the *Observer*'s pursuit was both cautious and determinedly unsensational. Although its knowledge played a major part in forcing the final disclosure of the scandal and the *Observer* was ahead on many key details as it unfolded, the newspaper didn't get to break the story it had been nursing so long.

Some cynics thought this caution reflected the bruising the *Observer* had taken from readers and advertisers when Bakker singled it out for retaliation, as he had done most recently in the spring of 1986. Several thousand letters flooded in, and editor Richard A. Oppel said they were negative by eight to one. "We were told that

we were anti-Christian, that we were satanic, that we were evil,"
Oppel said. But that wasn't why the *Observer* held the story. Oppel,
a conservative old pro, explained to his readers later that the sexual
peccadilloes of celebrities aren't necessarily news and that he certainly wasn't about to print them without ironclad confirmation.
The editors had known about Tammy's alleged affair with Gary
Paxton, Oppel said, and about a local prostitute's story that Jim
Bakker had visited her. But even if all that was true, so what? The
newspaper wasn't interested unless it looked as if church money
might have been involved. "The story of PTL and the Bakkers is a
story of misuse of money and abuse of trust," he said. His peers
applauded: The National Press Foundation was to name Oppel Editor of the Year for his paper's coverage of the scandal. The *Observer*
also won the Pulitzer Prize for national reporting, and editorial
cartoonist Doug Marlette won his own Pulitzer for his sardonic
comments on the unfolding story.

If the *Observer* wasn't being aggressive about the sex story, there
was plenty of interest in the evangelical community. In part, this
reflected the normal human trait of prurient curiosity. But the
preachers also felt a sense of vulnerability; as Jerry Falwell candidly
put it, he had known for a long time that a major scandal in any of
the top TV ministries "could do great, great damage to the credibility of every media minister." So it was a matter of self-protection to
know what was going on and even to take a hand in events when
necessary. Getting involved was also a Christian duty. In a way that
seems foreign to those outside the community, evangelicals are
supposed to be their brothers' keepers.

From the outside, the PTL holy wars looked like a farrago of
unctuousness and hypocrisy, with very little Christian charity in
the mix. Rival preachers used headlines and TV talk shows to air
each other's dirty linen, seemingly without a care for their rivals'
personal welfare or the harm they might be doing the church at
large. And all the while, they called each other "dear brother" and
sweetly insisted that they were speaking only out of love.

To evangelicals, however, the preachers were acting on a basic
tenet of their faith: the commandment to bear witness. A person is
asked not merely to believe but to spread the faith, and that means
not only telling others the "good news" of Christianity but living
a life that shows Christianity in action. Everyone will fail and fall

into sin from time to time. But the sin will be forgiven, if it is sincerely repented. Thus, as evangelicals see it, it would hardly be Christian for a man to find his brother in sin and let him go to hell for lack of someone to point out his error. And if repentance is not forthcoming, the charges should be taken to the elders of the church for judgment and punishment. In the PTL holy wars, hardly any of the players had totally pure motives in following this credo; but it provided a rationale for what they did, and their actions don't make sense unless their code is taken into account.

The mechanism for confrontation and repentance began cranking up with the first important leak of the Jessica Hahn story, to Jimmy Swaggart. Swaggart had replaced Oral Roberts as the nation's leading televangelist, with an audience measured by Arbitron in 1986 at more than two million households and revenues totaling $142 million. Like Bakker and Fletcher, Swaggart was affiliated with the Pentecostal Assemblies of God. He was also one of its main sources of income, contributing $12 million a year or more to the national denomination from his headquarters in Baton Rouge, Louisiana. But he was in the conservative wing of the order, a thunder-and-brimstone preacher, contemptuously opposed to Bakker's prosperity theology and withering in his denunciation of such fripperies as water slides for a Christian campground.

Swaggart took a personal interest in preacherly peccadilloes, especially in his own denomination. In the summer of 1986, when the rumors about Bakker's misbehavior started heating up, Swaggart was helping force the resignation of a New Orleans televangelist, Marvin Gorman. Gorman had admitted one episode of adultery, but Swaggart insisted there had been more. Gorman stepped down but later filed a defamation suit against Swaggart for ninety million dollars. (And it was Gorman who later came up with the evidence in Swaggart's own disgrace.)

Now Swaggart was on Jim Bakker's case. In July, at a meeting with elders of the Assemblies of God at their national headquarters in Springfield, Missouri, Swaggart warned them that he was hearing rumors about Bakker. As he recalled it later, he said: "Some of them I know are true; others I cannot substantiate. There's an awful lot of smoke and bound to be some fire." But it wasn't until September, Swaggart said, that Fletcher called him and told him specifically about Jessica Hahn. Swaggart called PTL, asking for a meeting with

Bakker to confront him with the story. Instead, Dortch flew to meet him and denied it. Swaggart said he let the matter drop, preferring Dortch's word to Fletcher's. At about the same time, Dortch was fending off a similar question from one of his own board members, J. Don George. George said Dortch told him that a woman had made some hysterical accusations about Bakker but had withdrawn them.

The next significant leak reportedly came from Walter Martin, a California evangelist who knew Roper and Stewart. Martin told the story to John Ankerberg, a wispy-looking but tenacious preacher with a relatively small TV ministry based in Chattanooga, Tennessee, and Ankerberg became the catalyst for the next round of the action.

Ankerberg said his only interest was in helping an errant brother. Others in the drama, however, pointed out that Bakker had recently dropped Ankerberg's show from the PTL network. Ankerberg could also have hoped that his image would be enhanced if he got involved in a sensational case with the top men in the field. In any event, Ankerberg mentioned the story to Swaggart at the annual convention of the National Religious Broadcasters in February 1987 at the Washington Hilton Hotel. Swaggart, miffed at the thought that Dortch might have lied to him, told Ankerberg to look for evidence, and Ankerberg soon got a copy of Jessica Hahn's complaint.

That was enough to convince Swaggart, who had been saying privately for some time that PTL was "a cesspool of sin and filth." He and Ankerberg began warning ministers who were to attend a major conference at Heritage USA that they might prefer to be elsewhere because a major scandal was about to break. But Swaggart did not want to take any open role in lancing the boil. His show, too, had been removed from the PTL network because of a "scheduling problem," and he didn't want to seem to be out for petty revenge. Ankerberg, however, saw a way to pursue Bakker according to the rules of Matthew 18:15–20. In those verses Christ ordered that a brother in sin first should be confronted alone, but if he will not listen, "then take with thee one or two more, that in the mouth of two or three witnesses every word may be established." Ankerberg proposed writing Bakker a letter detailing the evidence, to be signed by himself and Swaggart and any other prominent evangelists they could enlist.

In California, Jim and Tammy had settled in for a long stay at the

Betty Ford Clinic. Tammy first signed in as a patient, Laura Lee Oldham said, but "she can't stand to feel like she's trapped. If she can't get out, she's wild." After just one tempestuous night, the clinic agreed to outpatient status. Jim and Tammy bought another house in Palm Springs, a Spanish-style mansion with a walled compound that covers a quarter of a city block, and put the Palm Desert house up for sale.

They were surprisingly serious about the drug treatment, Don Hardister said. Tammy attended meetings of Alcoholics Anonymous, confessing her drug addiction and telling her story. Jim had no real drug problem, Hardister said, and only occasionally drank a little wine, but he had a psychological dependency: He would break a tiny Valium tablet into four pieces and take one piece per day. The effect must have been negligible, Hardister said, but "Jim thought he was wired." So he was going through the program to help him understand the problem and help Tammy recover. What impressed Hardister most was that Jim and Tammy got so close to their fellow patients. Each of them had a list of seven people to stay in touch with. "Each day you called somebody and asked, 'How are you?'" Don said. "And every day you got a call from somebody with the same thing, 'How are you?' I'd say, 'It's Mark from the program,' and Jim would take the call. He would come to the phone. It was awesome. Those people, their life was depending on getting each other through this program." The Bakkers were finally graduated, in a moving ceremony that stressed again how all the patients depended on each other.

At the *Observer,* meanwhile, at least one of Rich Oppel's conditions for running the Jessica Hahn story had been met: Shepard had evidence that PTL money had been used to pay her off. On February 23 the newspaper got that word to Dortch, who agreed to an interview the next day. But then he insisted on knowing the questions in advance. When they were delivered, PTL spokesman Neil Eskelin called the paper and asked, "I assume you have an affidavit . . . is that correct? We're not on a fishing expedition, are we?" Later he called off the interview. Instead, Dortch sent a vague, wordy statement neither confirming nor denying the charges but saying, "We are prepared to face our accusers before the church, which is what the Bible tells us to do." The *Observer* called Charles Cookman, district superintendent for the Assemblies of God and a PTL board member. When Cookman said he had "very recently" heard the accusation but had been assured it was false, the newspaper continued to sit on the story.

From his headquarters in Lynchburg, Virginia, Jerry Falwell was taking a major interest in the action. Falwell had already been through what could be called a dress rehearsal for the PTL takeover. In Bangor, Maine, a preacher named Buddy Frankland had admitted adultery in 1985 but balked at leaving his pulpit; after the congregation had nearly disintegrated, Frankland invited Falwell to set things right. Falwell did just that to the satisfaction of all, providing a new pastor from his own Liberty University faculty, getting the church's finances in order, and then withdrawing gracefully from the Bangor scene.

The Frankland episode had earned Falwell high marks for statesmanship among his colleagues, but it also reinforced his fears of the damage a major scandal might do to the whole field. Now Falwell heard from D. James Kennedy, a prominent TV preacher in Fort Lauderdale, that Ankerberg had warned him off going to the PTL conference, and Falwell called Ankerberg to find out what he knew. Ankerberg sent copies of the Matthew 18 letter to Falwell and Swaggart on March 11, proposing that all three sign it and round up other signatures as well.

The letter was blunt. Ankerberg had recruited John Stewart to draft it for him, and Stewart wrote that there were "well-documented facts, plus additional allegations, involving Jim Bakker, PTL, and an unmarried woman from New York State." The woman had been paid more than $250,000 "as a result of certain sexual improprieties by Jim Bakker," the letter said. "Furthermore, it appears that these sums were paid by PTL and used to cover up the improprieties." The time had come, the letter said, "to seek a Biblical solution to this situation according to Matthew 18:15–20, including appropriate discipline, confession, repentance and forgiveness."

When Swaggart saw all that on paper, he got cold feet. After a long talk with his wife and principal adviser, Frances, he dictated a memo to Ankerberg warning that Bakker and his people would merely distort the letter and publicize selected parts, portraying it as a witch-hunt by preachers who had a grudge against PTL. "I know how the minds of Bakker and Dortch work," Swaggart wrote.

"Please believe me, there is absolutely no chance of Bakker and Dortch stepping down for any type of rehabilitation. First they will try to lie their way out of it, but the documentation should be irrefutable. Then they will pull out of the Assemblies of God. Their last step will be to institute a barrage, which has already begun, to elicit sympathy from the general public." The procedures of Matthew 18 had already been satisfied, Swaggart said: He had confronted Bakker's people, and they refused to admit any sin, let alone repent. Swaggart knew that the *Observer* was chasing the story and that the Assemblies of God was beginning to investigate the rumors, and any further action could be left to them. "The *Charlotte Observer* will do its part," he said. "The Assemblies of God has finally started to move on this, and they will do their part."

The wording of the dictated memo left room for interpretation, and in weeks to come, the promise that others "will do their part" would be cited again and again as the main "evidence" that Swaggart was plotting a hostile takeover of PTL. But in context Swaggart's meaning seemed clear enough.

Falwell maintained later that he felt just the way Swaggart did, and also that "In the event this thing blew, I didn't want to be within fourteen light-years of PTL." It is a bit difficult to reconcile that stance with his earlier eagerness to be in on the show and even harder to make it jibe with his next move. Without telling Swaggart or Ankerberg how he felt or what he planned to do, he sent three of his people in his private jet to show the Matthew 18 letter to Dortch, who was in Tampa for the weekend. There, on March 12, it was first suggested that Falwell should take over PTL. And after all the schemes, confusion, charges, countercharges, and maneuvers that were to follow, the fact remained that Falwell's takeover was precisely what happened. Whatever his motives, Falwell's moves from that point on were as swift and deft as those of any Wall Street takeover artist. Swaggart and Ankerberg didn't know it yet, but they had hatched the cuckoo's chick.

They weren't the first to make that mistake. In 1979, when a group of conservative political strategists headed by Paul Weyrich first saw the possibilities of the new Christian right, they chose Falwell as the right country preacher to front up an organization that Weyrich named Moral Majority, Inc. If they were looking for a biddable figurehead, they got the wrong parson. In a matter of months Falwell *was* Moral Majority, and soon after that he was taking loud and public credit for the Reagan landslide, as if Moral Majority were the whole New Right. Not only had the new organization registered four million new voters, he evangelized, but it had mobilized ten million more church members. "Church people are the secret ingredient that none of the pollsters counted on," he told the press. In the euphoria of Reagan's new dawn, the hyped numbers didn't seem to matter, and Falwell did it so ingenuously, with such zest and panache, that it was hard to resent.

Ronald Reagan aside, Jerry Falwell may be the most likable man in American public life. He is big, genial, and unaffected, with an easy laugh and a direct interest in anyone he talks to. A solid but not spellbinding preacher, he is best in small groups and one-to-one conversation. Around Lynchburg he is down-home unpretentious, taking a four-wheel-drive GMC Suburban on his ministerial rounds and personally conducting nearly all the services in his Thomas Road Baptist Church. His faith seems deep-rooted and pervasive, but he wears it comfortably. On one of his cross-country jaunts with a *Newsweek* reporter in his ministerial jet, he asked an aide to pray for a safe voyage. But there was no bowing of heads on the return flight: It was a round-trip prayer, he explained. First and foremost, he has insisted throughout his national exposure, he is a pastor: "I still hatch, match, patch, and dispatch."

He came to it the hard way. He was born in 1933, the son of a popular and hard-driving businessman and sometime bootlegger, Carey Falwell, who had been the central figure in a small-town epic of sin and retribution. Carey's younger brother Garland, a dissolute charmer, was his partner and nemesis. Addicted to drink and drugs and chronically in trouble with the police, Garland tried one night to kill his brother in a berserk rage; in self-defense Carey shot him dead. But he brooded about the fratricide for years, drinking harder and longer, his fortunes ebbing and flowing with the liquor; eventually he died of cirrhosis of the liver.

Carey Falwell found Christ on his deathbed, but Jerry's mother, Helen, had known Jesus all along. In his autobiography, *Strength for the Journey*, Jerry remembered years of Sunday breakfasts with Charles E. Fuller's "Old Fashioned Revival Hour," the most popular religious show of the time, playing on the radio. Jerry and his twin brother, Gene, would listen with half an ear each, too lazy to get up and shut it off. The message never sank in with Gene, but Jerry eventually got it.

Jerry was the bright one, skipping a grade in school and driving hard to be best at everything he did. In little Lynchburg, he just about was. He was good at baseball and was elected captain of the football team; he was editor in chief of the high school newspaper, and with a 98.6 average he was valedictorian of his class. But he was good at troublemaking, too. Like his father, Jerry was a prankster for years. He still loves practical jokes, but his early efforts sometimes got out of hand. He once put a large rat in a teacher's desk drawer, and he locked another teacher in a closet to keep her from giving a surprise test. In high school he and some friends tackled an unpopular gym teacher and locked him in the basement without his pants. That was all in fun, but in his senior year what started as a prank turned serious: Jerry discovered where the cafeteria tickets were kept and started handing them out to his friends. By the time the stunt was discovered, the school was out several thousand dollars, and Jerry wasn't permitted to give the valedictory address.

That was in 1950, just two years after his father had died. Falwell's autobiography shows no bitterness at his father's alcoholism; he tells admiringly how his mother treated her drunken husband with patience and sympathy, soothing his rages and welcoming him home whatever his condition. Falwell tells of finding his father one morning on the path from the barn, where he had passed out on the way home. His father repented before he died, but after his death Jerry ran with what, for Lynchburg, was a fairly wild bunch. His Wall Gang had fistfights with rivals, plotted ambushes and rumbles, and made adolescent mischief with no worse consequences than a few unauthorized bonfires and broken bones. The range of his sinning remains vague. Once, in a sermon called "My Testimony," he said he and his friend Jim Moon, now a copastor at the church, spent days and nights away from home, in "places it's not necessary to talk about, doing things it's not necessary to talk about." He has left it at that.

He was in his sophomore year at Lynchburg College, with the highest math average in school and active plans to be an engineer, when one of Fuller's Sunday morning sermons finally hit home. Jerry felt edgy and excited, he recalls, the way he felt before a storm;

he drifted through the day and that evening surprised both himself and his Wall Gang friends by leading two of them, Jim Moon and Otis Wright, to the Park Avenue Baptist Church. He found himself walking to the altar, where an old deacon named Garland Carey explained it to him: " 'The wages of sin is death,' but if you believe in Jesus in your heart, you will be saved." Jerry heard, and believed, and was saved. He hasn't doubted it, he says, to this day.

By that fall he was enrolled in Baptist Bible College in Springfield, Missouri. The school wasn't much more than a drab collection of Quonset huts run by the relatively small Baptist Bible Fellowship, a schismatic group that had organized itself only two years earlier. When Jerry was graduated in 1956, the Lord led him back to Lynchburg to start a church of his own. It was not a popular move; his first congregation was thirty-five dissident members of the Park Avenue church, and neither their pastor nor Jerry's mentors at Bible college blessed the enterprise. But he went ahead, with what turned out to be characteristic bullheadedness, feeling that God wanted it that way.

He rented an empty Donald Duck cola bottling plant on Thomas Road and scrubbed it relatively clean of syrup drippings; then he began recruiting a congregation. (Early members recall that if they stood in one place too long, their shoes would stick to the floor.) A week after his first church service, he started a half hour weekly radio broadcast. Later he went daily on the radio and began preaching on television on Sunday evenings. At the end of his first year, Thomas Road Baptist Church had 864 members. For the past few years its membership has hovered around 22,000, and in 1987 Falwell started raising funds for a new sanctuary to seat more than 11,000.

Falwell's ferocious energy is his most conspicuous asset. He acknowledges no limit to what can be done, and he sets out to do it. In the early days at Thomas Road, he was leading the volunteer carpenters who were fixing up the place, tending to his flock, giving four weekly sermons, publishing a weekly mimeographed newsletter, and personally knocking on a hundred doors a day, six days a week, to recruit new members. He also found time to woo the church pianist, Macel Pate, who eventually became his wife. Through years of growing membership and expanding building programs, he never stopped. Thomas Road is by far the biggest church in Lynchburg. It has a school, Lynchburg Christian Academy; a summer camp for children; a home for alcoholics; active programs tailored for children, unmarried mothers, prisoners, the deaf, and the poor; a family counseling center; a magazine with a circulation of fifty thousand; a twenty-four-hour Christian radio station; the cable television Liberty Broadcasting Network (LBN); the main show, the "Old Time Gospel Hour," and a spin-off, "The Pastor's Study"; and a number of miscellaneous ministries. Falwell takes a personal hand in all these, though some parishioners felt he was slacking off during his years of political activism.

Falwell decided early in his ministry that his heritage would be a great university, to keep his influence alive the way Thomas Jefferson still pervades the University of Virginia. "I foresee creating for political conservatism what Harvard has done for political liberalism," he said. He broke ground seventeen years ago for what became Liberty University, a school for the well-scrubbed sons and daughters of Christian families. It is now the fully accredited alma mater for seventy-four hundred students on campus and twenty-four hundred more in correspondence school, and has turned out more than a thousand evangelical ministers. It remains to be seen whether a college that teaches "creation science" rather than evolutionary theory can develop the academic prestige of a Harvard, but Falwell has no doubts: He aims for it to grow to fifty thousand students by the turn of the century. Nobody thinks that's realistic, but few would bet much against it.

Falwell's second great trait is ambition, paired with a tenaciousness that can be formidable. He is a man who puts his hand to anything that seems to want doing, on as big a stage as he can find. When Moral Majority propelled him into the national spotlight, he was ready, and he took to it with a combative edge that made him a national symbol of right-wing Christianity.

Until then, like most fundamentalists, Falwell had believed in a thorough separation of the ministry from politics. In 1965 he had preached that message, denouncing militant civil rights ministers and casually linking Martin Luther King, Jr., to leftist politics. (He now says he repents his inbred southern race prejudice, but critics say he still shows traces of that and an associated anti-Semitism.) In a major conversion in the mid-1970s, Falwell decided that it was his Christian duty to do something about the state of the nation. As he and other fundamentalists saw it, that condition was bad verging on parlous; the country was being morally corrupted by the evils of pornography, abortion, homosexuality, drugs, crime, divorce, and "secular humanism."

Moral Majority set out to fight those ills, and Falwell led the way with a stridency he now at least halfway regrets. His followers loved it when he denounced South Africa's Bishop Desmond Tutu as a "phony" and urged American businessmen to invest more in South Africa, when he called AIDS a "gay plague" and assailed what he called the National Organization of Witches. But he was getting negative poll ratings for both himself and his organization. In 1986 he folded Moral Majority into the broader Liberty Federation and said he would cut down on his own political activities. After the PTL fiasco, he resigned to spend all his time on his ministry.

"Moral Majority by necessity became the lightning rod of the conservative movement," Falwell explained. "We achieved what we wanted to do. We created a religious and social and political conscience for these millions of religious conservatives." But there is considerable evidence that Moral Majority was really more smoke than fire all along. In a study of the group's literature, sociologist Jeffrey Hadden and three associates maintained that its membership was probably never much more than the circulation of its newsletter, about 482,000, far short of the 2 to 3 million that Falwell regularly claimed. What's more, they found that the organization didn't organize a new constituency but merely linked existing like-minded groups, and that the activities it claimed to foster were mostly inconsequential. Moral Majority was not a grass-roots structure but a "facade," Hadden and his associates said; Falwell had done a masterful job of raising issues and consciousness but blundered by exaggerating his accomplishments. He had to kill Moral Majority, they concluded, because the truth was beginning to show.

Jerry Falwell's third driving force is his fundamentalist's certainty that he is in the right. He has indeed admitted error when that justifies what he wants to do next, as when he discovered that he had been mistaken to stay out of politics. Still, when it comes to right and wrong, he sees no room for pragmatism. "On spiritual matters, compromise is always the wrong route," he told his congregation in the thick of the PTL battle, and his idea of what is spiritual stretches well into the political sphere. He recalls "shaking with excitement" in his seminary days when he heard a preacher de-claim, "Hell will freeze over before the courts replace God's word as the ultimate, final, and only authority in this place. We will obey God and no other!" Falwell has himself had notable battles with Caesar—once when the SEC charged him with fraud in marketing some church bonds (he settled the case) and again when he refused to pay taxes on some property owned by the "Old Time Gospel Hour" that was not technically tax-exempt (he got the legislature to change the law).

The trouble with this certainty is that it lets him use dubious methods to achieve any cause he considers just. Falwell says he hates the sarcastic phrase *evangelistically speaking* and deplores lying of any kind. But he finds it hard to resist. In small matters he has practiced outright deception: He sent out recruiting brochures for what was then Lynchburg Baptist College with pictures of im-pressive buildings that weren't on its campus. He said often and loudly that his ministry's finances were strictly separated from his political activities, but in fact, he transferred $6.7 million in politi-cal contributions to the ministry. And in 1987 the "Old Time Gospel Hour" was found to have bought Bibles at inflated prices from Falwell's I Love America political action committee, creating an improper contribution of $28,000. Each group was fined $6,000.

When caught in a discrepancy, Falwell characteristically blusters his way out of it. He is adept at indignant talk show denials and practiced at falling back from one level of exaggeration to a lesser one that comes a bit closer to the strict truth. Sometimes, however, even this doesn't quiet the criticism. When Lynchburg's paper, the *News & Daily Advance,* reported that some contributions to Moral Majority had actually been used for the ministry, Falwell first said the donors didn't care and nobody had been misled. When the newspaper found a contributor, Beulah Himebaugh of St. Peters-burg, Florida, who said she had been deceived and cared deeply about it, Falwell said he had explained the whole thing to her on the phone and she had apologized for the misunderstanding. When Mrs. Himebaugh denied that, too, he called her again, and again insisted that she had apologized. If her line had changed, he said, it was because she was a Jim Bakker fan.

Falwell's critics have suggested that he simply has a dual-image problem: He has been slow to adjust from the fundamentalist pulpit in Lynchburg to a national stage. The expectations of the two audiences are surely different. In Lynchburg, Falwell must project the old-time religion with all its moral certainties intact, from the reality of the devil to the need for wives to submit to their husbands. Nationally, he plays to a constituency that wants statesmanship and compromise.

The two roles mix badly. In Chicago one day during the PTL fight, Falwell talked compassionately about Jessica Hahn as the "real casualty in all of this, and no one seems even to care about her." But back home just the night before, he had used her in a casually sexist joke for his congregation at prayer meeting: On a recent trip, he said, one of his aides had wanted to stick around where Jessica was, "but I saved him and brought him home"—the implication being that no man would be safe in her neighborhood. On another occasion, in Alaska, Falwell fabricated a conversation with then President Jimmy Carter and had to apologize for it. The discrepancy between national Jerry and Lynchburg Jerry "gets to be deception after a while," complains Rabbi Marc Tanenbaum of the American Jewish Committee. "People begin to say, 'Will the real Jerry Falwell please stand up?' "

In the PTL battle, as in his other lives, the real Jerry Falwell is hard to find. Was he just a good Samaritan, as he said, trying to fend off a national scandal, taking over PTL only when Jim Bakker resigned and asked for his help? Or did Falwell plot the takeover, promising to give the ministry back but determined from the outset that Bakker should never return?

It's possible that Falwell's version of the story is true: Bakker was under fire for the Jessica Hahn incident, expecting even worse accusations to follow, and was afraid of Swaggart, righteously closing in to get him defrocked, so he tried to park his ministry with Falwell until the scandal cooled and he could take it back. Naively, Falwell tried to help. It was only when he found out Bakker's true financial and moral depravity that he fought to prevent Jim's comeback and keep PTL.

But it's beyond dispute that Falwell's public statements didn't match some of the things he was saying in private, that his actions spoke louder than his words, and that even his public story changed. At the very least, it's clear that he never intended to keep his promise to let Jim Bakker back into the ministry at PTL, no matter how repentant Bakker might be. The likeliest explanation for Falwell's role is that at the outset, he saw in the scandal an opportunity to take a hand in PTL, with some evident risks and some possible rewards. At one extreme he might win kudos for statesmanship in rescuing a troubled ministry and easing the corrupt Bakker out of power; at the other he might come away with control of the entire empire, doubling his audience and the revenues at his disposal, and cementing his position at the top of the electronic church. So Falwell ditched Swaggart and Ankerberg, tricked Bakker into handing him the ministry, and almost brought off the takeover.

On the face of it, PTL seemed well worth fighting for, with assets pegged at $179 million and debts that ultimately climbed to $72 million. In theory, the owners could sell it all off, pay the debts, and walk away with more than $100 million. But that happy outcome was by no means sure. For one thing, there were gigantic claims for back taxes, and there might be other hidden liabilities in the ministry's tangled books. For another, the money sent in by the lifetime partners, entitling them to vacation time in the hotel, could be read as an additional liability, not a mere donation, and if so, the claim could amount to $160 million or more, wiping out PTL's net worth.

The legal hurdles were even worse. It would be almost impossible simply to take over and plunder any tax-exempt, nonprofit organization, and PTL had special wrinkles that made a takeover particularly iffy. Its charter stipulated that Jim Bakker would be chairman for life, and that its board would have to vote unanimously to change that rule. That meant that PTL couldn't be taken by force; Bakker and the entire board would have to be persuaded to give it up voluntarily. What's more, another party already had a claim of sorts to PTL: If Bakker were to leave the ministry without designating a new leader and the board were stalemated, the charter specified that PTL should be liquidated and the proceeds should revert to the national Assemblies of God. This "reversionary clause" was to crop up repeatedly as the holy war raged, but no two parties ever agreed on precisely what it meant.

Apart from these practical problems, there was another and bigger reason why Falwell would fear any involvement with PTL: As a fundamentalist Baptist, he would be in foreign territory if he tried to move into a charismatic ministry. "To one who follows these things, that's shocking," said Gary Gaddy, a journalism teacher at the University of Wisconsin and a student of religious broadcasting.

"It's like asking Zhou Enlai to sit in for Khrushchev." Not only would Falwell risk rebellion and loss of donations from Bakker's Pentecostal followers, but he would be in trouble with his own flock and his fundamentalist colleagues for associating with the charismatics. In the upshot, that's exactly what happened: Falwell found himself being preached against by Baptists across the country, and a resolution expressing "strong reservations about this entire, very precarious situation" came from his own Baptist Bible Fellowship. "It's like being turned out of your own family," said Ben Armstrong of the National Religious Broadcasters.

But for all these excellent reasons why Falwell shouldn't get involved, there was an overriding attraction: the PTL network. It was Jim Bakker's answer to the cost squeeze of buying television time, and together with Bakker's ability to fatten the average donation he was getting, it made his operation uniquely profitable. By the time the scandal erupted, PTL was losing ground in the Arbitron ratings, which don't include the cable audience, and was no longer among the top ten TV ministries. Yet its revenues were probably third highest of all, at $129 million. The leader, Jimmy Swaggart, with nearly five times PTL's Arbitron viewers, had revenues only $13 million higher than Bakker's. Falwell conspicuously lacked such an asset, and he was feeling the pinch.

Falwell came late to the network idea. It wasn't until early 1986 that he bought a small and failing southern cable operation, which he renamed the Liberty Broadcasting Network. But in contrast with the early days of cable, systems have now learned to charge networks for access to their subscribers, they have no lack of programming, and the FCC has all but eliminated their obligation to provide public-service broadcasting. What's more, LBN's transponder was on a satellite that got less traffic than PTL's, and many cable systems would have had to install costly new dish antennas to receive LBN even if they wanted the programming. So LBN reached no more than a million homes, lacked contracts with major cable systems, and had few prospects for expansion. The market might even shrink. Many cable systems recently have bumped televangelists in favor of more lucrative home shopping networks. Falwell's direct donations have been dropping, from fifty-three million to forty-four million dollars in four years. His political operations, nominally separate from the ministry, probably returned a little revenue, but Liberty University has been a major drain. His ministry's total revenues for 1986 came to eighty-four million dollars, but the operation as a whole badly needed new sources of funds.

After leaving PTL, Falwell said he was planning to expand LBN, fattening its programming with Southern Conference football games and family-oriented material including gospel music, Bible study, and family counseling. Recognizing that it was too late to re-create the early cable networks, he formed a plan to sign up large blocks of time on small, failing TV stations around the country. That would be an interesting gamble, but win or lose, TV experts said there was no question Falwell would have been better off if he could have kept control of PTL's Inspirational Network.

Throughout the battle, Falwell denied that he had any such designs. "We did not come in to steal the network or to do any of the other things that our critics are saying we planned to do," he told Ted Koppel on "Nightline." "I plan to take nothing with me anywhere." Still, it wasn't surprising that cynics all over America came to the opposite conclusion. "If Falwell can sell off the amusement park and get away with controlling the network, it's a substantial net gain," said Rice sociologist William Martin. "It certainly seems plausible. If he can, he comes away with a pretty good bargain from a fire sale." That theory was reinforced when one of Falwell's own PTL board members, the Baptist preacher Bailey Smith, publicly predicted in mid-May that the board could sell off the theme park and other assets, make the network more spiritually oriented, and come out $110 million to the good.

Falwell said Smith was speaking only for himself, and the sale of assets didn't materialize. But Falwell himself provided the most persuasive and damaging evidence of his intentions in a conversation with a Florida preacher, Dr. Bob Gray of Jacksonville, when Gray came to see him in Lynchburg to protest Falwell's new association with the Pentecostals.

As Gray recalled the conversation in a sermon to his flock on April 26, 1987, Falwell reassured him that he was not turning charismatic. But his private protestations only confirmed the impression that he was out to steal the network. Gray quoted him as saying, "Let me explain to you what my motive is. . . . When I received word that this was about to happen, I determined that if at all possible I would try to get the PTL network for the 'Old Time Gospel Hour,' and this is the only way that I felt like I could do it." Gray said he protested that Falwell was putting his friends in an indefensible position, but Falwell told him that there was more to the scandal, that he would soon be accusing Bakker of homosexual behavior. Gray said Falwell also predicted that PTL would go into bankruptcy—"the sooner the better," he said—and then the assets would be auctioned off, and Falwell could buy the network and go on from there. Gray concluded, more in sorrow than in anger, that he couldn't condone such tactics; although he still loved and respected Falwell, he told his congregation, he would call off any further association with him until he was out of PTL. Until then, he said, nobody should send Jerry any money either.

Gray's testimony was hard to explain away, but Falwell tried valiantly when the sermon came to public attention a month later. Gray had misunderstood, Falwell said. He had indeed warned that there would be homosexual charges against Bakker and that it was possible PTL might go into bankruptcy. But Falwell insisted that the only thing he told Gray about the network was: "That television network, Bob, is the last major Christian television cable network on this continent and may be the last one ever. It must not be allowed to go commercial. It must be kept what it is right now. We've been on that station for years with the 'Old Time Gospel Hour.' And you can trust me."

Then Falwell once again took to the telephone, explaining to Gray how he had got it wrong. Gray told reporters somewhat dryly, "I stand corrected." But he issued no new statement endorsing Falwell, and when asked if he thought Falwell wanted the network, Gray said, "I think if it comes up for grabs, he'd like to have it." It didn't help Falwell's case, either, that the action played out very nearly as Gray had predicted: Within days of that first conversation, Ankerberg was accusing Bakker of bisexual sins, and in June the bankruptcy papers were filed.

Falwell's motives and strategy were the subject of intense speculation in evangelical circles. As some saw it, Falwell's aim was to buy the network at auction, just as Bob Gray had said. Others theorized that he hoped to reorganize PTL and keep the whole thing going, theme park and all, under a board that he would name. In that scenario, Falwell might not profit directly from his raid any more than the chairman of General Motors benefits from a merger he maneuvers. But he would have enhanced prestige, a larger total operation, and effective control of the network even if it weren't in his own portfolio.

There was also money to be made. According to Billy Robinson, the court-appointed examiner in the bankruptcy case, Falwell's man Jerry Nims came up with a plan that could have brought in millions of dollars for him and the other executives Falwell had put in charge. This was a scheme to take part of PTL public as a profit-making venture and issue huge blocks of stock to the top executives. Robinson said he had proof. "They were all going to be immensely wealthy. They'd be fat and happy," he said. The Falwell side denied there was any such plan.

Even if PTL went under and the network was sold to a commercial operation, that, too, could be a benefit for Falwell: He could try to sign up its paying preachers and add at least some of its cable systems to his LBN network.

In the end, though, Falwell gave up the fight. Did that mean he didn't want the network?

More likely, he concluded that he wanted other things more, his good name among them. By the end game, Falwell's motives were so suspect that if he had captured the network, the case against him as a raider would have been universally taken as proved. By abandoning the effort, he could come away as Jeffrey Hadden predicted from the beginning: at least arguably "a real statesman," the one TV preacher with enough status, skills, and guts to try to heal a scandal that was hurting the whole tribe. Even if he had failed, he could claim some credit for trying. But after all the charges and countercharges, the network would no longer be a trophy. It would be a scarlet *G,* for "greed."

"As I was walking around the grounds, the thing that came to me is that Jerry Falwell is a wolf in sheep's clothing," said Andrew Zacharias, an electrical engineer from Indianapolis who was vacationing at Heritage in his Airstream. "That may or may not be God speaking to me; I don't know.

"Falwell is not a man who's just trying to preserve something. He's trying to shape something in his own beliefs instead of the beliefs of the people who built it. It's just sad."

Still, Zacharias gave a hundred dollars to Falwell's PTL. What mattered, he said, was to keep the ministry alive.

Chapter 7

White Knights, Trojan Horses, Judas Goats

When he explained to his astonished flock why he had resigned from PTL, Jim Bakker said it wasn't because of what had happened with Jessica Hahn; that was just a regrettable incident, and Tammy and God alike had long since forgiven him. He was leaving, he said, to forestall a "hostile takeover" of his ministry.

Given the warfare on Wall Street about then, it was a familiar idea. So was the form of Bakker's defense: Beset by an unwelcome suitor, he got a "white knight" to come to his rescue. And like many of his corporate colleagues, he decided later that his white knight had betrayed him. Jerry Falwell denied that, repeatedly and plausibly. To say that he stole Bakker's ministry, he protested, "is like accusing someone of stealing the *Titanic* just after it hit the iceberg."

The notion of a hostile takeover was silly, Falwell and his men argued. PTL wasn't like a public corporation, which could be taken over by someone buying up shares and making alliances with other big holders. Here there were no shares. There was a chief executive with lifetime tenure, set out in the PTL charter. Not only would Jim Bakker himself have to agree to be deposed, but his entire board of directors would have to approve any such change by a unanimous vote. How could any takeover artist hope to get over all those hurdles?

It was an excellent question, but in the event, that's precisely what Falwell did. And the key moves began when he sent three of his men to talk to Richard Dortch in Tampa on March 12, 1987.

The logic behind the mission was something Falwell never quite reconciled with what he said he was doing. As he told it, he was still fretting over the damage a major scandal could do to the electronic church as a whole and hoping that the looming *Observer* article could be stopped or defanged. But that didn't make much sense. If the whole story was a fabrication, there would be nothing to worry about. But if Jessica Hahn had been paid not to tell it, there was probably something to it, and in that case, how did he think the *Observer* could be silenced? If he really wanted to distance himself from the PTL mess, as he sometimes claimed, why had he called Ankerberg in the first place? And if he really agreed with Swaggart that Bakker couldn't be trusted to respond to the brotherly concern of the Matthew 18 letter, why talk to Dortch at all?

People don't always act logically, and it's possible that Falwell hadn't thought the whole thing through at that point. It's just as possible that he and his team had charted the whole scenario: that they knew Bakker was afraid of Swaggart and could be persuaded he needed a rescue, and that they planted a lawyer in his camp to help with the persuading. But the case is circumstantial, and no witness has confirmed any such plot. That's only the way it worked out.

Along with the Buddy Frankland case in Maine, there was another precedent for Falwell's involvement with Bakker. Falwell had come to PTL's defense a year before, when the *Observer* was on the attack about mishandling of funds and Bakker had made a persuasive rebuttal. On that occasion, Falwell used the "Old Time Gospel Hour" to say that while he and Bakker didn't agree on everything, he was ready to defend a brother who was being unfairly treated. PTL asked for a tape of that speech and played it repeatedly for the next week. Given that experience, said Falwell's personal assistant Mark DeMoss, Dortch "didn't think it strange that we would come to them and say 'Look, are you getting slammed again?' "

Swaggart and Ankerberg were still waiting for Falwell's response to the Matthew 18 letter, and they found his silence increasingly irritating. The rumors about Bakker were accelerating, and the *Observer* was said to be ready to run its story; but Falwell wouldn't return phone calls for more than a week—during which, as it turned out, he took over the brotherly mission and PTL as well. Afterward he apologized to both of them; according to him, they understood, and Ankerberg willingly enlisted in Falwell's camp. But Swaggart kept his distance after that. He told friends later that he still liked Falwell, but his wife, Frances, thought Falwell had used her husband and Ankerberg.

Falwell's first approach to PTL was made through Warren Marcus, an old hand at gospel TV who was then free-lancing as a producer for Falwell's LBN. Marcus had recently been interviewed for a job at PTL and got to know Dortch, who was running PTL in Bakker's absence. Jerry Nims, the Atlanta businessman who was running Falwell's television operation, suggested that Marcus call Dortch and sound him out on how serious the problem might be.

Marcus was flabbergasted. No sooner had the conversation started than Dortch volunteered Jessica Hahn's name and denied that she had been raped. Somebody was trying a takeover raid, Dortch told him. And considering the value of the network, Marcus said, the idea of a raid sounded plausible. At first Dortch said there was no need for any consultation, but as soon as Marcus mentioned the Matthew 18 letter, Dortch said, "Wait a minute. What document? You've got to come down. We'll fly you down. We'll pay for the fuel." The meeting was set for the next evening, March 12, with Marcus, Nims, and DeMoss representing Falwell.

In their telling, it was a dramatic scene. "I was dumbfounded," said Nims. Dortch was weeping. He sat sobbing uncontrollably at a conference table in the Tampa airport, his head in his manicured hands, describing Swaggart's scheme to take over PTL. Nims exchanged embarrassed glances with DeMoss and Marcus. Marcus stood up and patted Dortch's shoulder, saying, "Take it easy, brother." But Dortch plowed on, Falwell's men said. He didn't know why Swaggart hated him; he had been his good friend; perhaps he had inadvertently insulted Frances Swaggart. Dortch had worked for years for the Assemblies of God, he sobbed, and now they had turned on him. The *Charlotte Observer* was a demon, Satan himself, getting ready to smash PTL. Swaggart was vindictive, Dortch went on. He hated the idea of water parks and entertainment at Heritage USA and wanted to use the money for ministries instead. He had been plotting for months, Dortch said. He had even boasted that he had got Marvin Gorman ousted from his pulpit down in New Orleans but that was nothing compared with what he would do to PTL.

In the Bakker camp, the idea of a hostile takeover was anything but new. Former aides said Jim and Tammy had worried for years that someone might be plotting against them; they even said it on the air and mentioned it in their books. There had been talk that first one minister, then another might be on the prowl. And ever since the move on Marvin Gorman, Swaggart had been the center of suspicion. Swaggart "was in a mood of execution," Doug Oldham said. "He felt like he was God's right arm and he was doing surgery." As Don Hardister told it, Jim fretted that if Swaggart succeeded in driving Gorman out, "he'll get me next"—a fear that Hardister understood only after the Jessica Hahn affair became public. So Jim had defended Gorman on the PTL show, and in retaliation, Swaggart had stepped up his denunciations of PTL's water slides and prosperity theology. And in Tampa, as Dortch spelled out the takeover threat for Marcus, Nims, and DeMoss, it sounded bizarre but plausible. "This man has a wonderful persona—the white hair, the tan, the look-you-right-in-the-eye," said Nims. Nobody said it was a silly idea.

The meeting went on for nearly four hours, an exhausting session, with only some hamburgers by way of dinner. As Falwell's men told it, Dortch assailed Swaggart and the *Observer* over and over. He said the Hahn story wasn't true and denied any knowledge of a payoff to her; he implied that his signature might have been forged on letters and even checks. When he said Swaggart had turned the Assemblies against Bakker, Nims suggested that Falwell could be a neutral mediator: "He's not the charismatic terror that Swaggart is, and he's not the Assemblies of God." In the end, Dortch agreed to ask Bakker, still in California, if he wanted to meet with Falwell, Ankerberg, and Swaggart. And just as the session was breaking up, Dortch made an astonishing suggestion.

"We were getting ready to go downstairs," Nims said later. "Richard turned to me and said, 'Why don't you guys take the ministry?' I said: 'Say what? What?' He said: 'Well, you guys can pull it out. We're—we're in deep trouble, we can't make it, and we're going to leave the Assemblies of God. We're resigning. . . . They're going to pull our credentials anyway, so we're going to go before they do it. . . . So, you guys take it.' " Nims maintained that after the long meeting, the suggestion didn't really sink in; he brushed it off, treating it as if it hadn't been made. DeMoss said his reaction was that the idea would be a nonstarter since Falwell had already decided to curtail his political activity and focus on his own ministry and family. And when they told Falwell about it next morning,

Falwell said, he took the offer as merely another indication of the tension Dortch was feeling. Dortch called Lynchburg that day to say Bakker was willing to meet with Falwell but not with Swaggart or Ankerberg. Falwell said later he wasn't thinking about anything but the next dilemma: To go, and risk further involvement, or let the scandal fall out as it would?

There was another move at the Tampa meeting that turned out to be just as important: Nims suggested that Dortch hire Norman Roy Grutman as a libel lawyer to fend off the *Observer*. If Falwell were plotting a raid on Bakker, he couldn't have done it better. Bakker charged later that Grutman was Falwell's Trojan horse, planted to point the finger at Swaggart and distract attention from the real coup.

Grutman is a New Yorker, colorful, smart, and controversial, with a florid turn of rhetoric and a slash-and-burn style of litigation that has made him cordially detested by a good many adversaries. He has a talent for antagonizing people; in his undergraduate days at Yale he was blackballed from the honor society Phi Beta Kappa, and later he took a major law firm to arbitration when it failed to make him a partner. In Falwell, however, Grutman found an adversary who had been won over. Falwell sued *Penthouse* in 1981, saying he was damaged by its use of a free-lance interview with him without his permission. Grutman's defense of the magazine was so effective that Falwell decided he wanted the lawyer on his side in the future and hired him in several disputes, including a landmark lawsuit against *Hustler* magazine for a savage parody picturing Falwell as an incestuous drunk. Now, when Dortch talked about the threat of the *Observer*, Nims said Grutman's name just "popped into my mind," with no prior discussion. He recommended him to Dortch; the next day he called Grutman and put the two men in touch.

Dortch's story of the meeting is considerably different. As he told it to associates shortly afterward, it was Nims and DeMoss who convinced him of the Swaggart raid. He said they even showed him a copy of the dictated memo with the phrasing *they will do their part* as proof of the plot. If that happened, it would be strong evidence that Falwell was already planning his own raid. But his men denied showing the memo to Dortch; they argued that they didn't even have a copy then. Marcus first called Dortch on March 11, before Swaggart had reached his decision. But on the day of the

Tampa meeting, Ankerberg had received the memo and called Falwell's office to discuss it. And according to Dortch's associates, Dortch returned from the airport meeting talking about the Swaggart memo. Since it had been dictated only that day, it's hard to imagine how Dortch could have known about it if Marcus, Nims, or DeMoss hadn't brought it up.

Dortch also said Falwell's men told him that Swaggart had arranged for a group of disgruntled PTL partners to file a class-action suit against PTL after the *Observer*'s story appeared. And when Nims called him the next day, Dortch said, it was to say that Grutman had a letter to the *Observer* already prepared, "and all he needs is your permission" to send it and stop the story from being printed that weekend. Falwell's men denied all this, arguing, among other things, that Grutman couldn't have written the letter in advance since he didn't even know what PTL was until he talked to Dortch. They certainly hadn't originated the idea of a Swaggart takeover in Dortch's mind, they said; in fact, they found out later that Dortch had visited an attorney and described the scenario of the supposed Swaggart plot a full week earlier.

Dortch hired Grutman on March 13, the day after the meeting, and Grutman succeeded in getting the *Observer* to postpone its piece. In return, Grutman promised to deliver Bakker and Dortch for an interview about the Hahn charges on March 19. In the weeks to come, it was Grutman who led the charge against Swaggart, repeatedly talking about a hostile takeover and ultimately confirming that Swaggart was the preacher he was accusing. All the while, Falwell publicly doubted that Swaggart could be playing any such game, but he didn't rule it out. At first, Grutman claimed to represent Falwell, Bakker, Dortch, and PTL all at once, but when Bakker and Dortch both were ousted from PTL, Grutman stayed on as general counsel, working for PTL and Falwell. When Falwell finally left PTL, Grutman went with him.

All that was still to come. Bakker had agreed to meet Falwell the following Tuesday, March 17, and DeMoss set up the meeting. In Falwell's telling, he was still worried about going; if it got out that he was having private sessions with charismatics, he said, his constituency would be up in arms, and he spent several days discussing whether he could let this cup pass. But he would always prefer to get in trouble for having done something than for failing to act;

predictably, he decided to go. DeMoss, a brainy and efficient twenty-five-year-old who is the son of a major donor to Falwell's ministry, was hoping the meeting could be held in Chicago or some other neutral ground, to shorten the flying time. But Bakker's people pleaded that he was having an allergic reaction to a bee sting and couldn't travel. *That kind of stinks*, DeMoss thought, but it wasn't worth arguing about, so the date was made for Palm Springs.

Falwell, DeMoss, and Nims, accompanied by Dortch and Grutman, flew out on Monday afternoon, March 16, in the ministry's Westwind II. By then, Falwell said later, he was pretty well convinced that the scandal was serious, but he was still hoping that a deal could be made to delay or water down the *Observer*'s story. Dortch at one point offered Falwell a check for twenty-five thousand dollars, for expenses of the trip. "I was smart enough to give that back to him quickly," Falwell said—not that he was suspicious, just that he wasn't about to be beholden. Nims said he thought at the time, *Well, wait a minute; fuel doesn't cost that much.* Later, when he thought about it, Nims decided that Dortch "was trying to do a number on us"—to get them involved in the ministry's problems by giving them money. For whatever reason, somebody at PTL later had the check shredded and even the stub destroyed.

Grutman, born Jewish and converted to Christian Science, had fought several legal battles for evangelicals, but he was unfamiliar with PTL and its problems. So when Dortch tried to reassure Falwell on the plane that he had no fears of the outcome—"I honestly have a total peace . . . I will really trust in the Lord"—Grutman cut in: "Listen, Reverend Dortch, you are a dreamer, but this is the real world, and that sweet Jesus stuff won't cut it. I need some facts." The two spent more than an hour of the five-hour flight talking privately in the front of the eight-seat plane. Behind them, the conversation was desultory and guarded; with Dortch in the plane and the outcome uncertain, nobody was unbuttoned.

Still, Falwell later recalled a curious argument with Grutman. Before leaving Lynchburg, DeMoss had obtained a copy of Swaggart's cold-feet memo by telex from Ankerberg. On the plane, Falwell read it for the first time. "I remember asking Roy, 'Where is the takeover in this?'" Falwell said. Grutman had evidently seen or heard about the memo before and was already a convert to the takeover theory. He pointed to the key phrases, but Falwell scoffed:

"Come on now, come on now." Grutman would never be convinced that there wasn't a plot, Falwell said six months later, but he himself hadn't seen one then and still didn't.

In Palm Springs, the wagons were circled. Two weeks earlier, David Taggart had called Don Hardister to his room, warning him that he had serious news. When Hardister showed up, Taggart told him a bit primly, "Your boss has been a bad boy. He fooled around a little bit." He gave few details but warned that a media blitz could be expected; security would have to be beefed up. When Hardister said he would need more staff, more equipment, and perhaps twenty thousand dollars to cover the bill, Taggart replied, "Whatever you need." So Hardister brought in a consultant for expert guidance, then flew four more of his men to California.

Hardister worried about how much had been paid to Jessica Hahn, and by whom. When Taggart told him it was hundreds of thousands, not millions, and it had come from a close friend of Jim's, Hardister thought he knew the answer. Only Roe Messner, the contractor who had put up most of Heritage USA, had that kind of money readily available. If Messner had paid it, there were plenty of ways for PTL to make him whole.

The Oldhams, too, were hearing rumbles. Laura Lee had been with Tammy since the end of February, and Jim had called Doug to Palm Springs just the weekend before the meeting. "He was talking about a conspiracy," Doug recalled. Dortch had told Jim in a phone call about the Swaggart memo, heavily stressing the incriminating phrase *they will do their part.* Doug had also heard about the Jessica Hahn episode, including her twenty-three-page deposition, though not about the money she got. But nobody was expecting Jim's resignation.

Hardister had been told that Falwell was skittish about being seen in Palm Springs and that he should make arrangements to hide the Westwind II. When he greeted the travelers at the airport, he told them he had arranged to park it for the day at Thermal, twenty-five miles away. But the first thing Falwell's party had seen on landing was Jimmy Swaggart's plane (by pure coincidence, he was in Palm Springs for a revival that week). For whatever reason, they told Hardister not to bother trying to hide. Still, he drove a roundabout route to Maxim's Hotel and took them in through the basement entrance, bypassing the lobby on the way to their rooms. It was only nine o'clock in the evening, but the easterners' clocks were running three hours later. Nims and Grutman went to their rooms right away. After snacking on some sherbet, Falwell and DeMoss turned in, too.

Hardister drove Dortch to the Bakkers' compound, and it was four hours before he came out to be taken back to the hotel. "Be in prayer," he told Hardister. "Jim has to go along with my plans. He's just got to go along with my plans. You know we have real problems."

"Yes, I understand," Hardister said. But he didn't ask what plans Dortch was making; Hardister has an ex-cop's prickly sense of where lines get drawn, and the payoff question was still worrying him. "Reverend Dortch," he said, "if somebody paid this money for Jim, I don't have any problem with it. But if we paid it from PTL, I can't deal with that. It's wrong. I don't want to be a part of it." Dortch assured him, Hardister said, that the money couldn't be traced to PTL "because we didn't pay it."

The crucial meeting the next morning began at nine o'clock, when Jim and Tammy showed up at a suite in the hotel for an awkward round of introductions. Although Falwell had shaken hands with Bakker at some evangelical functions, they had never really talked, and on the one occasion when Falwell visited Heritage USA, it was a hurried fifteen-minute drive through the place, with Macel driving and the preacher lurking in the back of his van to avoid being seen on the alien ground.

Now the Bakkers explained that Tammy wouldn't stay, that she just wanted to meet everybody. She looked awful, Nims said, nervous and close to unstrung, wearing more makeup than he had ever seen for that time of day. "I felt desperately sorry for her," Nims said.

And it was then, he and Falwell reported, that Tammy launched into a strange speech, telling Falwell, "Jerry, you know, this is the third time this happened to us." What did she mean? "Jim and I started 'the 700 Club,' and we lost it. We started Trinity Broadcasting, and we lost it. And now we've lost PTL. Maybe God wants us to start ministries and give them to somebody else."

Why would she say that? On the face of it, it would seem she was talking about a prearranged deal, one she assumed he was in on. But six months later, Falwell said it proved only that she and Jim had already decided to ask him to take over. It was also evidence for his conviction that the Bakkers had known when they went west that they would never come back. They had by then been warned by their lawyers that they were breaking the law, he said, and had responded by firing the lawyers; they knew the ministry was losing three million dollars a month, yet they had plundered it for all they could take in salaries, bonuses, and expense money. Jim hadn't even flown back to give a single sermon in three months. "When he left, he felt he was getting out just ahead of the dam bursting," Falwell surmised. But that theory came later; when Tammy talked about losing PTL, Falwell said, he didn't know what she meant.

She left the men, Hardister driving her back to the compound, and the business meeting started. First there was an hourlong one-on-one talk between Falwell and Bakker in a bedroom of the suite, followed by a longer general session. Grutman met alone with Bakker for fifteen minutes or so, and then the two of them drove to the Bakkers' house to talk for an hour with Tammy. Finally the men joined again at the hotel for club sandwiches and another two hours of talk before the visitors left for the airport and the flight back to Lynchburg. For each part of the action, there were at least two versions of what happened and why. All told, it is a kaleidoscope of plots, motivations, and justifications, with each party twisting the story to arrange the pieces in the most favorable light.

As Falwell told it, his time alone with Bakker was no more or less than pastoral counseling—the confession of a troubled man purging an old sin. Falwell opened, he said, by saying he was there to help; if Jim didn't want to talk about it, he should just tell him to go home. "He began to tell me about the seven years of hell he had gone through, seven years of hell. 'And every morning I've gotten up looking over my shoulder, thinking this is the day that it all collapses on me.' Then he tells me the story."

The confession was along the lines of Jessica Hahn's deposition, Falwell said, except that "He said to me—by now he's weeping—he said, 'Jerry, I didn't rape her. If anything, she raped me. She undressed, she almost literally manhandled me. She knew all the ropes. I was so frightened that I could not get an erection.' And said, 'Fifteen minutes later I'm in the shower, crying out loud and screaming, "Oh, God, I've been with a whore." ' " Bakker explained that he was just trying to make Tammy jealous; he thought she had been having an affair with the singer Gary Paxton. Falwell said he asked about the hush money, and Bakker assured him it came from his own funds.

Then, Falwell said, Bakker started talking about Swaggart's campaign to discredit him with the Assemblies and asked about the infamous memo. "I showed him that letter and said, 'I don't think there's an ounce of takeover in this letter.' " But apart from that, Falwell said, there was no discussion of PTL or Jim's resignation; the talk "had nothing to do with management. It had to do with praying for him, had to do with spiritual help, totally and entirely. And he knew that. We left that meeting and came back into the next room."

In Falwell's version, it was well into that second session when Bakker disclosed that he and Dortch were about to be defrocked by the Assemblies of God and said they had decided to resign before being pushed. Then he asked Falwell to take over for him, explaining, "You're the only preacher I trust right now."

Falwell said later he was hesitant, adding: "There never was a time in my mind that I thought I would want that ministry or anything about it. My first thought was how impossible that would be, what my wife would say, and then what my constituency nationally and my local church members would perceive this to be. But I continued to believe that if this ministry exploded, ceased to exist over this horrible problem, the fallout would be absolutely devastating." In his own mind, Falwell told *Newsweek* later, he didn't really decide to accept until the following day, after talking it over with his wife and an old mentor. But he has also said he agreed on the spot. In either case, his doubts didn't show; the group assumed he would do it and went on to discuss who should be invited to join the new PTL board.

Falwell has consistently maintained that he was surprised by Bakker's offer, but the degree of astonishment has varied in his several tellings. Since Dortch had suggested his takeover fully five days earlier, as Falwell's own men said, and Tammy that morning appeared to think it a foregone conclusion, the idea could hardly have come as a bolt from the blue. Yet he told an interviewer from the Pentecostal magazine *Charisma* that Jim's offer at the meeting "was the first time I had ever heard of such a likelihood. I had never even thought about the possibility, much less suggested it. It came as a complete surprise."

He left similar room for doubt on another key point. Falwell's early accounts of the meeting stressed that "There was no discussion . . . at all" about whether Bakker might eventually return to PTL. Only later, when Bakker and his supporters furiously charged that Falwell had gone back on his word, did Falwell acknowledge that he had indeed made a promise. As he recounted it, it was carefully hedged: "I said, 'Jim, if everything you've told me is true —no intercourse, no hush money—[if] restoration occurs with the Assemblies and it is God's will for you to come back, I would not stand in your way.' "

Jim Bakker's story of what was said came from the opposite side of the kaleidoscope. "When they came to Palm Springs, they came to steal PTL," he said flatly three months later. The pretense, he said, was that Falwell and his people wanted to help save Jim from the Swaggart takeover plot. It was Falwell who used the term *hostile takeover* and who went on to say, "If I don't help you stop him, he will destroy me next." Falwell told Jim he had played along when Swaggart and Ankerberg first approached him with the Matthew 18 letter, pretending he would help in order to find out what they were up to. And he produced Swaggart's memo as the final proof.

Falwell introduced him to Grutman, Jim said, and "he gave me the idea this man was vicious, a very strong lawyer. He said he never wanted to sit across from him again, that he wanted him on his side." It was Grutman who told Bakker the details of Swaggart's plot. First, the lawyer said, the *Observer*'s story about Jessica Hahn would come out; then Ankerberg had thirteen PTL partners ready to file a class-action suit that would throw PTL into receivership. Next they would ask the South Carolina government to declare the lifetime partnerships illegal. The resulting tax claims would destroy PTL. What was left would fall into the hands of the Assemblies of God through the reversionary clause, and the Assemblies would naturally give the television ministry to Swaggart, its biggest contributor and already a national TV preacher.

Grutman told Jim the *Observer*'s story would destroy him, Jim said. But if he would resign first, Grutman said, Jessica's accusations would become secondary. Falwell would take over, but purely as a figurehead, to preserve credibility until it was time for Jim to take PTL back. "I will never touch your ministry," Jim said Falwell promised. "Jim, if I stole your ministry, it would destroy me." Dortch would stay on as president, hosting the show. Falwell said he wouldn't even be on the scene, and Jim could continue to run PTL from a distance, even picking the guests on the show. Jim could name his own board.

Jim was reluctant, but he was also frightened. Dortch was telling him this was the right thing to do, he said, and Doug and Laura Lee Oldham, who had worked for Falwell, had talked about him as a good man. Finally Jim agreed to the plan. But "Tammy's not going to go along with this," he warned.

"Just let me talk to her," Grutman said, and they drove to the house to talk to Tammy on the patio by the swimming pool.

"No, no, no, no," said Tammy.

But Grutman was persuasive, Jim said, and after running through all the other points, the lawyer threw in a kicker: "I'll make sure you and Jim have the written resignations of this new board of directors. The minute you nod your head, we'll just turn in those resignations. That will give you the protection to feel secure that these people aren't going to hurt you."

Tammy gave in, Jim said, but "still wasn't thrilled about it. She has a better intuition than I do." Those resignations never materialized, but Grutman wrote Jim's own resignation for him.

Which version of the meeting was closer to the truth? The subordinate players had their own views but generally tended to back their principals. Thus Grutman said that Tammy hadn't seemed at all surprised by the plan when he and Jim went to the house to tell her and that the business of the signed resignations was pure poppycock. "Mr. Bakker lied, lied. Mr. Falwell made it explicit that the board be controlled by him . . . this business that Bakker was going to get signed resignations is preposterous," said Grutman.

Dortch, on the other hand, told his staff when he returned from Palm Springs that Falwell had indeed promised to help them fend off the takeover and that Falwell's one-on-one with Jim hadn't been all spiritual. In fact, Dortch told his aides, Falwell emerged from the private meeting saying, "Jim has asked me to help him, so I will have to form a new board." Dortch also spelled out details of the treaty, including stipulations that Jim would be a PTL consultant during his exile, keeping his regular salary, and that the PTL show would carry periodic reports on Jim and Tammy's rehabilitation.

DeMoss and Nims hadn't heard any of Falwell's talk with Bakker; they had spent that first hour watching Swaggart on television. But

Nims said that in the second part of the meeting, Bakker was crest-fallen, contrite, and humble, a man who knew he had blown his chance. "He struck me as a sad little boy," Nims said.

There was one more witness, on the fringe of the action: Don Hardister. Short, tough, and intense, Hardister is a man of fierce loyalties, considerable intelligence, and a heavy twang in his speech; in what passed for affectionate jest, Jim Bakker called him the "resident redneck." Hardister said that after the poolside meeting with Grutman, Tammy drove off to go shopping, showing no undue signs of agitation—a point that tended to support Falwell and Grutman. But Hardister also said that as the visitors were leaving the hotel for the airport, Dortch put his hands on Jim's shoulders and told him, "Now, nothing's changed. Don't you worry about a thing. Don't even entertain any thoughts."

Jim replied, "Okay, okay. I trust you."

At the airport, Dortch told Hardister that Jim would brief him on what was happening.

Then Falwell walked over and said, "Don, you've been with Jim a long time. Well, there are going to be mighty rough days ahead. But hang in there. Everything's going to be okay."

When Hardister returned to the compound and asked Jim what was happening, Jim handed him the resignation statement and walked away. "This is going to sound crazy," Hardister said, "but I just fell right down on the floor and cried. He walked by me four or five times, but I just couldn't get myself together. He had passed the baton, and I knew it was over."

Finally Hardister told Jim he wished he could take the blame. The only remorse he ever saw in Jim, Hardister said, came in the reply: "Well, you know you can't do it. This is something I've got to face."

"But you didn't have to quit," Hardister said, and Jim said, "I know what I'm doing."

Hardister remained a faithful part of the entourage for many more weeks, until he became convinced of the truth of the charges about Jim's homosexuality. Then his allegiance switched to Falwell. But both before and after the switch, Hardister was convinced that Jim Bakker really believed that Falwell was saving him from Swaggart. The evidence for that was Bakker's sudden sense of betrayal when he heard Falwell change his line.

The first shock came when Falwell said at a press conference that he doubted Swaggart had been plotting a takeover. Bakker played the tape over and over, Hardister said, muttering, "He's betrayed me." Falwell was able to calm that storm, telling Jim he had to handle things his own way. But a few days later, Hardister said, Jim summoned him at three o'clock in the morning. "He stole it from me, he's lied to me," Jim said. Who? asked Hardister. "Jerry Falwell. Falwell told me he'd give it back."

Appearing on Ted Koppel's "Nightline," Falwell had said Bakker could never return to PTL. He might be rehabilitated and forgiven by God, but a pastor who had defaulted morally could not continue as a pastor. "The ministry of God is a great responsibility," Falwell had said. "You don't get two shots at it." It had to mean that Falwell was the real takeover artist.

For a while, Hardister thought so, too. But when he changed sides, Hardister decided that Falwell had had to renege on his promise when he found out Bakker wasn't telling the truth. There were some holes in that theory, the biggest being that when Falwell publicly ruled out Jim's return, he had no more solid evidence of wrongdoing than he'd had when he'd made the promise. That would have to mean that Falwell never meant to keep the promise at all. But Hardister preferred Falwell's version. He is a man who needs to believe in his leader.

Hardister never bought the idea of a takeover plot, he said. He thought Swaggart was an honorable man, and the business about the memo was no more than three men deciding to do something and then one of them backing out. However, he could imagine Swaggart trying to get Jim defrocked just as a matter of principle (it was no secret that Swaggart had never approved of Heritage USA). He could also see Jim demanding a promise that he could come back before he resigned and Falwell making that promise.

Maybe the key was Dortch, Hardister concluded. Dortch had said it was his plan, and he kept reassuring Jim, "Nothing will change." Maybe Dortch made Jim a lot of promises, all the time thinking *he* was going to be president, *he* was going to run the show, Falwell was going to keep out of it, and Jim wasn't coming back. Or maybe it was Falwell making promises and Dortch was his Judas goat—the animal that leads the trusting sheep down the ramp into the slaughterhouse. Anyway, after Falwell's "Nightline" show, Hardister said Jim was frantic. "He's calling David Taggart, calling Reverend

Dortch, saying, 'I'm going to come back. I'm not going to take this. I've made a mistake.' And Reverend Dortch is saying, 'No. You're not coming back. It's too soon. You're going to ruin the whole thing.' " Then Dortch called Hardister. Whatever you do, he told him, don't let Jim get on a plane and come back to Charlotte.

In his pose as reluctant dragon, Jerry Falwell said later that he was hoping right up to the vote that he might still have an out. The PTL directors would have to agree unanimously to accept Bakker's resignation, elect Falwell and a new board, and resign, and who ever heard of a church board voting anything unanimously? The directors met in emergency session on the evening of March 18, the day after the Palm Springs agreement, in the Heritage USA Presidential Suite. Bakker was waiting in Palm Springs to resign by telephone, and Falwell was sitting by a speakerphone in Lynchburg.

If he really had any doubts, Falwell needn't have worried. Dortch and Grutman were running the meeting, and it went like clockwork. In fact, two of the departing board members charged later that they had been railroaded. Both Evelyn Carter Spencer, an evangelical minister from Oakland, and Ernie Franzone, a Dallas hotel executive, said Dortch and Grutman warned the board about the Swaggart takeover and the threat of the class-action suit. In a letter to the Assemblies of God, Franzone said Grutman "stated that the board must resign because they were in a serious criminal situation that might involve the board members . . . [that] the board might be subject to legal action that might or might not be covered by insurance, and that somehow our resignation would make our situation better and stronger." Franzone said he felt "extreme pressure" to take actions he shouldn't have taken without legal advice. Moreover, in an affidavit to Bakker's lawyers, Spencer said Dortch and Grutman told the board, "If we loved and cared about the ministry and Jim Bakker, it was our duty to resign."

Dortch and Grutman also persuaded the board to withdraw PTL from its association with the Assemblies of God and to revoke the reversionary clause that might give ownership of PTL to the Assemblies. There was considerable debate afterward over this action. Some said the board voted it after resigning, so that the vote didn't count; others said the resignations weren't official until the new board met and accepted them, so the timing didn't matter; still others said the clause didn't mean anything anyway. For their part, the elders of the Assemblies professed not to care whether the clause had been deleted or not. But it would figure for months as evidence of plots on both sides. Grutman himself maintained that the whole operation was scrupulously correct and that "The suggestion that this was done surreptitiously by Jerry Falwell, by stealth, is buncombe." And Jerry Nims argued later that the operation was Dortch's doing, meant to pave the way for Bakker's comeback. "Richard told me about the clause and told me he was going to take it out when I saw him in Tampa," Nims said. "He said, 'There's a clause and we're leaving the Assemblies and we're going to take it out and screw them.' "

Falwell tried to cater to both doctrinal camps in his new role. He promised, "I do not own this ministry. . . . I have no intention of making PTL a Baptist campground or a Pentecostal campground. I plan to keep it open as a Christian outlet for the family of God." His new board was chosen to reinforce that pledge by including a charismatic bloc: Dortch, the aging televangelist Rex Humbard, and James Watt, the former U.S. secretary of the interior. Watt and Humbard had been suggested by Bakker, but his other nominees, the singer Pat Boone and Dale Evans, wife of movie cowboy Roy Rogers, weren't invited. Falwell also picked himself and Nims; Ben Armstrong of the NRB; a Christian publisher, Sam Moore of Nashville; and Charles Stanley, former president of the Southern Baptist Convention. Even if Dortch wouldn't support him, Falwell was assured of a solid fundamentalist majority. But the board was to be a sometime thing. Director Stanley didn't make it to the first meeting, and other seats changed hands rapidly. Soon the fundamentalist vote would be unanimous.

Grutman next had to deliver on his promise of an interview for the *Observer.* He didn't quite manage that, but nobody complained. It was another telephone conference session, with Grutman moderating and the *Observer*'s wary editors not knowing what to expect. First Bakker read his resignation from Palm Springs and hung up. Dortch said he and Bakker were leaving the Assemblies, and so was PTL. The stunned *Observer* staffers, already exulting over their coup, asked a few questions; they didn't quite realize that Falwell was also on the line until Grutman called on him.

It was a great triumph for the newspaper. The March 20 edition carried nine stories on the PTL upheaval and not much else on page one. But the paper couldn't keep its exclusive; the best it could do March 19 was tell the wire services that tomorrow's editions would carry the story, and for the fleeting few minutes it took to confirm the news, the wires ran it with the *Observer*'s credit.

That evening, as Macel and Jerry Falwell listened to a Bill Gaither Trio concert at Liberty University, the phones in DeMoss's office were ringing off the hook. By the next morning Falwell had done interviews with all three networks and fielded phone calls from numerous celebrities. Vice President George Bush advised him about riding tigers, he said, and Billy Graham offered to pray for him. Ronald Reagan didn't call, Falwell said later without self-consciousness, "but I'm sure it crossed his mind."

The next week was a circus. The Hahn story, still being billed as a "tryst," touched off the predictable media fire storm. Reporters mustered in squadrons in West Babylon and outside the Palm Springs compound. Jim and Tammy, who had until then registered only dimly on the national scope, sprang into focus as full-blown grotesques: a tiny preacher caught in adultery and his weepy, painted wife, praising God and streaking her makeup. At Heritage USA, the faithful gathered to show support and forgiveness. Most visitors stood with Colleen Brantley, a housewife from Charlotte: "We all love 'em, we'd love to have 'em back. If I don't forgive Jim Bakker, how can I forgive my sons for what they might do?" But a few, like Bill Sones, a retiree from DuBois, Pennsylvania, were disgusted. "Everything that's happened, well, it just left a bad taste in my mouth," he said.

The story gained resonance from the antics of Oral Roberts, ensconced that very week in his deathwatch Prayer Tower. And it really took off when Roy Grutman went public with his story of a hostile takeover plot, by a rival preacher whom Grutman wasn't yet naming. Peccadilloes are no big deal these days, wrote columnist William Safire, "but when you're talkin' hostile takeover, you're talkin' Sin."

Jim and Tammy fanned the flames. They appeared on a taped segment of what was still called "The Jim and Tammy TV Ministry Hour," speaking to their flock from Palm Springs. "We're very, very sorry" for the episode with Jessica, Jim said; it had been a mistake, an effort to make Tammy jealous and win her back. But that wasn't why he had resigned. The whole episode had been part of a "diabolical plot" by false friends, using Jessica to set him up for blackmail and engineer the hostile takeover of his ministry. Fortunately, the complete plans of the enemy—still unnamed—"fell into our hands," and "the only way to save PTL was for Jim Bakker to resign." The rest was pure Jim and Tammy, the darkest day yet in their unfolding saga. "We may be helpless, but we're not hopeless," Jim told the faithful. "We have God on our side. . . . We've felt the pain, the stabs in the back, the rejection, and the hurt. But God has let us feel his wonderful love." Through her tears, Tammy sang:

> The storm it's going to end,
> Your midnight's almost over . . .
> And the sun it's gonna shine again.

Shouting over a two-minute ovation from the studio audience, Dortch told the viewers, "Write Jim and Tammy, send the letter to us, and put in a generous offering." Anybody sending at least twenty-five dollars, he promised, would get an album.

With that, the holy war was on. At his base in Baton Rouge, Swaggart was fuming over Grutman's accusations, clearly aimed at him. He tried to call Falwell to find out what Grutman was up to, but Falwell wouldn't return his calls. Finally, after Swaggart's lawyer, William Treeby, had dictated a frosty letter to Falwell and made sure it was read to his office, Falwell called. But he said he couldn't really control Grutman or what he was saying, and Swaggart couldn't buy that. So Swaggart decided to go public. He confirmed that he was the preacher who had started the investigation of Jim's sins, but he denied angrily that he had any intention of stealing PTL, calling that the "most thoroughly absurd, ridiculous accusation that could ever be made."

Then Swaggart broadened his fire. He was no takeover artist, he said. He was only appalled as a churchman at what was going on. "I'm ashamed, I'm embarrassed," he said. "The Gospel of Jesus Christ has never sunk to such a level as it has today. We've got a dear brother in Tulsa, Oklahoma, perched up in a tower telling people that if they don't send money that God's going to kill him. Then we got this soap opera being carried out live down in South Carolina, all in the name of God."

Now Grutman confirmed that he was indeed talking about Swaggart. He insisted that the plot was real, that Swaggart had been feuding with Bakker ever since he'd been "bounced" from the PTL network and was out to get even. He thundered biblically at Swaggart: "You will bring down the pillars of the temple on your own head, like Samson." Grutman wasn't above using threats either: On "Nightline" he warned Swaggart not to try to push the takeover any farther, or "we're going to be compelled to show that there's smellier laundry in his hamper than the laundry he thought was in Reverend Bakker's."

Rival evangelists chose sides. Oral Roberts, addressing Swaggart rhetorically, accused him of "sowing discord among the brethren because somehow you think you're holier than thou. Somehow Satan has put something in your heart that you're better than anybody else." Oral told his listeners to "go to your checkbooks" for Jim and Tammy. John Ankerberg accused Bakker of trying to "cover up." Pat Robertson said God was cleaning house, and it was probably a good thing. Falwell, with Grutman carrying the takeover ball, was judicious. He said he didn't believe Swaggart had any designs on the ministry—but then again, Bakker might have proof.

More details of the scandal were unfolding. On Long Island, Jessica Hahn said she had got only a few dollars of the hush money. A few newsmen had her deposition, and hints were spreading that the episode might be gamier than a casual roll in the hay. In Charlotte, the *Observer* printed details of the settlement and the fees taken by Roper and Stewart. The newspaper also reported that the IRS and the state of South Carolina were claiming millions in back taxes from PTL.

Already there was talk of a comeback for Jim. Charles Cookman, district superintendent for the Assemblies of God, had resigned from the PTL board on March 16 to take over his church's investigation of his old friend, but it was clear his heart wasn't in it; now he said he had urged Jim to reconsider his resignation and begin the two-year process of restoration to the ministry. "It's not an open-and-shut case," Cookman said. "I fully believe and expect him to rise to the top again."

In Springfield, the elders of the church were less tolerant. "We do not believe there is any evidence of blackmail," said the general superintendent, G. Raymond Carlson. "To the contrary, the evidence seems to indicate that effort and money have been expended to cover moral failure."

The first meeting of PTL's new board was on March 26. Jerry Nims said later he was astonished that none of Bakker's directors had had second thoughts in the eight days since they had resigned. They could still have changed their minds, he said, and the fact that they hadn't was proof that Bakker was lying when he said later he had found out within a few hours that he had been duped into resigning. Now the board accepted all the resignations, making them official.

Falwell issued a stern rebuke to Grutman, ordering him to cease and desist from his clamor about Swaggart and the hostile takeover. But there wasn't much sting in the lecture; the board had already shown how much it disapproved by appointing Dortch president and Grutman general counsel of PTL. Falwell was playing the naive country preacher, believing good of all the world. When he was asked by the press if Grutman didn't have a conflict representing all those people, he said no, explaining that they weren't suing each other. Falwell also said Dortch would head the new board's investigation of Bakker's conduct of the ministry, and he saw no conflict in that either.

Falwell's call for a cease-fire in the holy wars caught Swaggart in mid-volley, saying he had heard Jessica's taped deposition and that while he preferred not to say what was in it, "Well, it would make you very angry." Swaggart also predicted that Dortch would soon be defrocked by the Assemblies. Falwell fired a shot of his own across Bakker's bow: PTL would continue to pay Jim and Tammy's salaries, he said, but if they tried to come back, the entire board would resign.

Meanwhile, Bakker's friend Jamie Buckingham was going after Jessica, charging that when she sinned with Jim, she was "very professional for 21 years of age; she knew all the tricks of the trade." And for viewers of the newly renamed PTL Club, Christian psychologist Fred Gross recounted for the faithful how Jim had long ago confessed and repented his sin. "He was sobbing," Gross said. "He was shaking so violently I had to hold him. In ten minutes, we were on the floor. His face was buried in the carpet. He was sobbing and kicking and screaming. . . . If there has ever been a release, that was a release."

The nation was gripped by a sort of morbid fascination. The story was front-page news in papers nearly everywhere and on the covers of *Newsweek* and *Time*; the networks reported it daily, and the leading characters spent hours on CNN with Larry King and "Nightline" with Ted Koppel. There were cartoons, bumper stickers, advertising parodies, greeting cards. There was a T-shirt with the smushy imprint of a made-up face and the legend "I ran into Tammy Faye at the mall." Johnny Carson practically built his nightly monologue around Jim and Tammy and Jerry. There was a country music song: "Would Jesus Wear a Rolex on His Television Show?" And in his down-home comic strip *Kudzu*, the *Observer*'s cartoonist Doug Marlette focused on the Reverend Will B. Dunn, who lost his television ministry when he confessed to the national scandal Mascarascam. He was the one, he told his flock, who first turned Tammy Faye on to cosmetics. Reverend Dunn was hounded off the air for that, but a Hollywood agent persuaded him to cash in on his disgrace, and he wound up with a talk show of his own. "Remember, brothers and sisters, keep the faith," he counseled. "Just send me the checks, and you can keep the faith."

All the predictions were coming true: It was a bad time for the electronic church, and worse was to come.

In Elizabethtown, Pennsylvania, Martha Cravener, fifty-two, a widow and a PTL contributor, was upset about Jimmy Swaggart's maneuvers. "Because somebody is down, you don't kick them and stomp them into the ground. You lift them up," she said.

"Jimmy Swaggart should know that if you have a calling to the Lord in your life, Satan is after you all the stronger. You are more susceptible to Satan's power because every day you're going to do the work of the Lord.

"I'm not saying he is the devil. But he's definitely letting the devil use him."

Chapter 8
The Ashes of Sodom

Tammy was going stir-crazy. She had been in the compound at Palm Springs for two days since the meeting with Falwell, and it was like an armed camp under siege, with Hardister's men in a trailer by the big wooden gate and dozens of reporters camped outside.

"Nobody wanted Tammy to go out," said Laura Lee Oldham. "They didn't want anybody to go out except the people who went for groceries. We were not to talk to the press. She was a wreck; she couldn't stand it." The house was full of telegrams and flowers from their backers, and it felt funereal. Jim had gone all broody. Hardister told the reporters that he was spending six hours a day praying and reading the Bible, but the truth was he had become a recluse. So on the third day, Laura Lee said, Tammy put on a disguise: tight black pants and boots, a leopardskin top, a long black wig, dark makeup, and sunglasses. She scrunched down in the back seat of the car, and they simply drove past the reporters, who shrugged off the driver and Laura Lee as nobodies. But when they got to the flea market and Tammy got out, Laura Lee said, "Everybody thought she was Tina Turner. She got so much attention—people coming up and talking to her, people hollering, people looking—it raised such a ruckus that when we finally came home, she took off all that and said, 'To heck with it. I'm going as me.'"

Some days, Tammy and Laura Lee sent the driver out alone, then walked through the backyard and a neighbor's driveway to meet him. But most often they drove past the media mob with Tammy lying on the back seat. When other shoppers recognized her, Laura Lee said, they were usually supportive and pleasant, sometimes even more so than in the glory days. Just once, in a restaurant, Tammy heard a man in the next booth calling Jim Bakker a hypocrite. She grabbed his arm and told him firmly, "My husband is not a hypocrite." The man backed down, surprised and embarrassed; sorry, he said, I only know what I read in the papers.

Another time, when a reporter recognized them out on the town and started chasing them, they hid in the back of a bookstore. Laura Lee went out to negotiate with him, but he wouldn't leave them alone; she thought she had a deal—Tammy would give him just one flashing smile—but Tammy said, "Not a chance." The people in the store sneaked them out the back door, but the reporter had figured that out and came racing around to meet them, so they ducked into a dress shop and hid in a dressing room. Finally the owner's husband drove them back to where their car was parked. Laura Lee was ready to go home, but Tammy was howling with laughter at the adventure. "We've given him the slip. Let's shop," she said.

If Tammy didn't much enjoy life in the compound, that was understandable. "She couldn't figure out how Jim could just give it all away," said Laura Lee. "It would just make her so mad. She would really go after him about that." And she didn't see why they were stuck there. "When they were king and queen, they had two thousand serfs running to solve everything instantly. So she couldn't believe that in two or three days' time it wouldn't be okay just to turn around and go back now. She just couldn't get it in her mind that this was going to take time." In fact, Jim and Tammy both talked sometimes about how Tammy hadn't resigned from anything, so she could just go back and be on the show and put things right.

The mood flickered from optimism to despair. Some days, Hardister said, Jim would tell everybody that God would deliver them and they would come out stronger than ever; then he would slump into a mood of "It's over; we'll never minister again; we'll never again be on TV." They started having little prayer meetings in the evenings, first with just the family and close retainers, then with a growing group of guests. The message was always the same, Hardister said: "What God was saying to us was that Jim was right and Jerry was wrong."

Jim was also starting to have doubts about Richard Dortch. Dortch had been cementing his position at PTL for a long time; he had brought in his own executive group, and several people, Doug Oldham among them, had been told that Dortch was keeping a thick dossier on Jim as job insurance. Now, as Jim worked the phone to PTL and watched the show with Dortch as host, he got to feeling uneasy, Doug said. "He thought that maybe Richard was trying to usurp the throne." Finally Jim sent Doug back east to keep an eye on things. Even so, Doug didn't find out till later that Dortch had given orders to the people on the show not to talk about Jim and Tammy. "Let me handle everything that has to be said," he told them. "Doug and I will take care of that." But he never told Doug that, knowing well that the word would go straight to California. Doug found out later he was on the list to be fired, but Dortch wasn't ready for the showdown with Jim. "I don't think Richard ever expected Jim to come back," said Doug.

What none of them knew was that the next wave of the scandal was about to smash over them. Falwell was ready to go public with the long-simmering charge that Jim was guilty not just of adultery but of homosexuality, too.

After the seven-day media orgy of Jim's resignation and Falwell's takeover, the headlines cooled down. The *Charlotte Observer* was still following the hometown story; but TV coverage had died, and the national press ran only occasional updating pieces. Behind the scenes, though, there was feverish activity. The holy war had gone underground; preachers were choosing sides and changing them, with public character assassination and private backstabbing that rivaled the intrigues of the Borgias.

The first moves after the takeover were made by Roy Grutman, who was now wearing the hat of a lawyer for Falwell's PTL and apparently was trying to find out just how much Swaggart knew about Bakker. The day after the March 18 board meeting, Grutman tried repeatedly to get Swaggart to meet him. As one of Swaggart's associates recalled it, "He was very mysterious about what he was going to say, but there was this attitude of you-scratch-my-back, I'll-scratch-yours." Swaggart didn't refuse, but he wanted Falwell to be present at any such meeting or conference call. They were still negotiating when Grutman suddenly lost interest. "Maybe it's not that important after all,'' he said, and then he began his public campaign accusing Swaggart of the takeover plot.

Swaggart and Ankerberg still hadn't heard from Falwell, and they met again on March 20 in Palm Springs, at Ankerberg's urging, to hear the tape recording of Jessica's deposition. Stewart and Roper were there, and as the two evangelists listened to the tearful woman and her pathetic story, they were thoroughly convinced that she was telling the truth. Ankerberg said Jim Bakker was getting off too lightly, that all the charges should be made public to clear the air and force genuine repentance. But Swaggart still didn't want to get involved. Ankerberg could carry the ball, he said; if he could help, he would.

So Ankerberg started pressing Falwell and his men, telling them the problems at PTL ran deeper than they knew. They just had to meet with him, he insisted, and hear the evidence. "Frankly, our feeling was, so what?" said Falwell's assistant Mark DeMoss. "The damage had been done. We didn't want to get tied down in gory detail. But he was persistent. He really believed that there was a deeper problem."

This air of reluctance on Falwell's part was almost surely exaggerated. By then he was already saying Bakker could not return to PTL—if he tried, Falwell warned, the new board would quit immediately—and hard evidence to keep him away would have been welcome. Although the subject hadn't yet been publicly raised, testimony supporting the old rumors of homosexual activity would be ideal for that purpose. In a case of simple adultery, which was all that had yet been established against Bakker, the Assemblies of God would permit restoration of a minister after a two-year period of repentance, but there is no restoration after proof of homosexuality.

As it turned out, Falwell not only consented to listen to Ankerberg but brought some of his new directors along as well. However, he brought only the fundamentalist board members; the charismatics charged later that this was really a secret board meeting to load the dice against Bakker.

The hottest protest came from the former secretary of the interior, James Watt. He had been invited to hear the sex charges but said he didn't want to sit around and listen to such things. Jerry Nims had called Watt to say the meeting was canceled. Then, Nims said later, the activists had persuaded Falwell that it should go on. The

Falwell side maintained that since Watt had already said he didn't want to come, it wasn't necessary to tell him that the meeting had been reinstated. Watt agreed that he had told Falwell he was "totally repulsed by the homosexual thing" but said he would surely have wanted to be there if he had realized that Falwell was holding what amounted to a secret board meeting. It was a grievance that festered.

The Falwell team met with Ankerberg, the Swaggarts, and Roper on April 11 at Nashville's Sheraton Music City Hotel, and Falwell recalled later that he opened by saying it was not a board meeting. Then there was a general mending of relations. Swaggart used the occasion to ask whether Falwell or anyone else still thought he had been plotting a takeover and got assurances that no one did. Swaggart was also miffed that as he saw it, Falwell hadn't been zealous enough in defending him, and Falwell said Swaggart must have missed a couple of his statements (later DeMoss sent the complete file of clippings to Swaggart). Swaggart and Ankerberg asked why Falwell had made his move on Bakker without consulting them, and Falwell explained that Bakker wouldn't agree to talk to either of them, so he'd had to decide whether to act alone. It was another of Falwell's trick answers: His key move had been to send his delegation to talk to Dortch on March 12, and he'd done that before he had any inkling that Bakker wouldn't talk to Swaggart and Ankerberg. But he slid over that, and at this meeting, they didn't protest.

Jessica's tape was played, almost interminably as far as Falwell and his men were concerned. It went on for more than an hour, telling them what they had already read in the newspapers, and Falwell finally said, "Hey, I'll tell you what. I'll take your word for it. Can we go on to something else?" That started a general discussion of good guys and bad guys at PTL. Swaggart in particular was urging that Falwell get rid of Dortch and a long list of other executives. Swaggart was so persistent, Falwell said, that he broke in: "I said, 'Hey, Jimmy, you want [PTL]?' And that was: 'No, sir, you got it.' I said okay. Then we got right back to it. Everybody had suggestions on what to do."

Falwell portrayed this later as a serious offer to give the ministry to Swaggart, saying he had a quorum of the board in the room and would have turned over PTL on the spot if Swaggart had agreed. Presumably that would have made it a board meeting after all. But as others told it, it sounded more like a bluff-calling gambit to shut off the gratuitous advice.

In the California sun, Jim and Tammy said they loved their enemies and wouldn't fight to stay at PTL anymore.

As young marrieds and with their CBN puppets. After a storybook beginning, the Bakkers had to travel a long, hard road.

PTL's royal family in 1977.

Togged out for rejoicing, Tammy helped celebrate her twenty-fifth wedding anniversary. The matching doll sold for $675—but later, with the word *Forgiven* stitched in its heart, it fetched $800.

The Presidential Suite had gold-plated swan faucets, ninety-two throw cushions, and a fifty-foot-wide walk-in closet for Tammy.

Doug and Laura Lee Oldham, the Bakkers' "Best Friends."

Don Hardister, the faithful friend and bodyguard.

Just before the fall, Tammy and Jim with Jamie Charles and Tammy Sue.

The air-conditioned doghouse became a symbol of PTL's wretched excesses.

After the return to Tega Cay, there was more than ever cause to cry.

The Bible Belle, Jessica Hahn, in her first tabloid photo, scandalized the faithful, and later, so did the Playmate.

Jimmy Swaggart took a particular interest in preachers with sexual problems.

Oral Roberts said God was going to "call me home" if the money didn't come.

John Ankerberg went public with the sex stories.

The water park was supposed to make Heritage USA a place for
Christian families to play and pray together. Critics said there was
entirely too much playing.

In song, story, and billboards, the royal family became a personality cult.

For PTL's partners, an indoor baptism crowned a visit to Heritage USA.

Under a plaster sky, a place for the faithful after Tammy's own heart.

A healing service in the Upper Room, a scene too hot for the cool medium.

Norman Roy Grutman played high-stakes poker all the way.

Was Jerry Falwell the good Samaritan, or did he plot the takeover?

Falwell's board prayed for Jim and Tammy. From the left: Rex Humbard, Richard Dortch, Falwell, Ben Armstrong, James Watt, Jerry Nims, Sam Moore.

Richard Dortch was all smiles.

Falwell takes the slide.

When the going got rough, Melvin Belli said Jim was his kind of preacher.

David Taggart (right) and his brother James found heaven at PTL.

Jerry Nims was Falwell's man to find the dirt at PTL.

William Robinson didn't play Falwell's kind of game.

Judge Rufus W. Reynolds aimed to spread the pain.

"THAT'S RIGHT — JIM AND TAMMY WERE EXPELLED FROM PARADISE AND LEFT ME IN CHARGE!"

Doug Marlette's Pulitzer Prizewinning work for the *Charlotte Observer.*

The meeting didn't get very far on the question of Bakker's homosexuality; nobody there had more than gossip to go on. The gossip was intriguing, and Falwell wasn't ready to drop the subject; but the next major move on that front came from the Assemblies of God, whose elders may have been having misgivings about turning over their investigation of Bakker and Dortch to Bakker's friend Charles Cookman. Even before Cookman and his district board had their first meeting on the scandal, the national presbyters in Springfield were beginning their own inquiry into the old rumors of homosexuality at PTL. In the first week of April, they called Gary Smith, the former operating chief of PTL, to come to Missouri and tell what he knew. That proved to be mostly secondhand evidence, but Smith, who had become a management consultant in Houston, named several other potential witnesses who could testify about Bakker. Sometime after that, someone at the Assemblies passed Smith's name to Ankerberg.

Smith is a rambly and fidgety man, wary of questions and somewhat self-important. He pictures himself as angry and frustrated at the misbehavior that went on while he was at the helm of PTL in 1979 and 1980, and he certainly parted company with Bakker with no love lost. When Ankerberg called him early in April, Smith enlisted eagerly in the campaign to discredit Bakker, actually rounding up witnesses and taking their statements. There were four or five, he said a month later, and some of them had their lawyers with them; the statements weren't formal depositions, but all the witnesses said they would be willing to testify if necessary. Yet another meeting was arranged in Nashville on April 23 for Falwell and Ankerberg to meet the witnesses and hear their stories.

April 23 was to be a crucial day in the PTL drama, with several plot strands coming together. There were two separate meetings in Nashville that day, and they were to give rise to public charges that Falwell had conspired to bring off the original takeover and was now plotting to blacken Bakker's name. It was also on April 23 that Falwell had the conversation with the Florida preacher Bob Gray, who told his flock that weekend that Falwell was really out to get the network. Rumors were circulating that Bakker was planning some sort of comeback. Falwell's men were finding out that PTL's financial problems were truly horrendous. And Falwell, secretly maneuvering to get rid of Richard Dortch, was publicly threatening to drop the whole hot potato called PTL.

In California, Jim Bakker had probably heard of the new round of charges about to be thrown at him. In a desperate effort to head them off, he sent a telex trying to persuade Falwell to leave PTL and threatening to escalate the holy war if Falwell persisted. Then, just as he had taken to his bed in lesser crises, Bakker holed up in a mountain cabin.

In his telex, Bakker didn't explicitly demand to be reinstated, but he asked that Jim Watt be made chairman of a new charismatic board, with Rex Humbard and Dortch remaining as members. The columnist Jamie Buckingham told reporters that Jim planned "to go off for a time of personal healing" and come back when the new board agreed he was ready. Bakker's telex said he would not fight if Falwell refused to step down, "but I must let you know that what you are embarking on will truly start what the press has labeled a 'holy war.' "

The telex didn't come as a total surprise to Falwell; Watt had shown up in Lynchburg the day before, offering to form a new board if Falwell should choose to leave. Watt had been soothed about the April 11 "secret meeting" at a real board meeting six days later; but he was clearly veering away from Falwell, and it was a cagey conversation on both sides, neither man telling what he knew about Bakker's plans. Falwell wasn't ready to declare open war; he was now hoping to fire Dortch at the next board meeting on April 28, and he thought he might need Watt's vote. Falwell warned Watt about the next day's meeting and the new accusations about Bakker, and as he wrote in his autobiography, "It was easy to understand why Jim Watt didn't want to hear any new charges about his friend Jim Bakker's sexual or financial misconduct."

They parted with Watt assuring Falwell of his continued loyalty if Falwell stayed on and with Falwell promising to let Watt know if he decided to leave. But from then on, Falwell treated Watt as part of the enemy camp, and in the Falwell fashion, he often referred to Watt after that with a gushy compliment—"I consider Jim Watt to be a Christian gentleman of impeccable integrity. My wife and I have for years believed that he was one of the best and greatest assets in the Reagan administration"—closely followed by a zinger: "His son Eric, as you know, has been an aide to Reverend Dortch. Eric is a fine young minister."

The two meetings in Nashville that day were held back to back in the same room of the Sheraton Music City Hotel. There were four distinct focal points to the meetings and the debate that followed: the accusations of homosexuality; the charge that Falwell and Ankerberg had conspired to make sure they became public; the growing evidence of financial chaos at PTL; and the curious red herring called the reversionary clause, with its value as evidence of Falwell's intentions.

Falwell met first with the national elders of the Assemblies of God, headed by its general superintendent, G. Raymond Carlson. As Falwell told it later, his purpose was to be reassured that the Assemblies approved of what he was doing with PTL, that the church disapproved of Bakker's prosperity theology as much as he did, and that it, too, was concerned about the homosexuality charges. He said the elders told him they were still hearing witnesses to those charges but couldn't share the evidence with him and couldn't tell him in advance whether Bakker and Dortch would be defrocked. Still, "I heard enough to know where it was headed," Falwell said.

But that was his agenda, and there was another at the table as well. Mike Evans, a preacher from Fort Worth, Texas, who described himself as "a tadpole evangelist" with a weekly TV show then running on the PTL network, had interjected himself in the scandal ostensibly on behalf of his parent Assemblies, which he felt had been damaged by Dortch and Grutman's removal of the reversionary clause. Evans said later he had set up the meeting and paid for the room specifically to discuss that issue. He was certainly more preoccupied with the clause than the Assemblies' officials themselves; Joseph Flower, secretary of the Assemblies, said later that the elders hadn't objected to its removal and "are not in any position [to object] because we had nothing to do with it being placed there in the first place." But Evans said Falwell had promised to restore the clause to the PTL charter and even said he would bring along a letter to Carlson making that promise formal. He hadn't kept either promise.

The reversionary clause was first added to PTL's charter in 1980, mainly for tax reasons. At the time, the ministry's claim to tax exemption was shaky at best: Bakker had performed some weddings and had presided at a few funerals, but PTL was only dubiously a church; there wasn't even a congregation. Both county and state authorities were challenging the tax status, and it was mainly on a lawyer's advice that Bakker affiliated his ministry with the Assemblies, a recognized denomination. The lawyer also advised that in order for PTL to keep the federal tax exemption as what the tax code calls a 501(c)(3) organization, its charter should include a clause bequeathing the ministry's assets to another religious order if it were ever dissolved. The upshot was that the board passed two resolutions, one giving Bakker the presidency for life and the power to appoint his successor and the second stipulating that if Bakker died and a "stalemate" developed on the board, PTL would be liquidated and the proceeds turned over to the Assemblies.

But the wording was vague, and Grutman argued later that the clause didn't mean anything. It certainly didn't apply in this case, he said, since there was anything but a deadlock on the board, which had unanimously accepted Bakker's resignation and approved Falwell as his successor. In that case, why had Grutman pushed so hard to remove it? He said that had been Dortch's idea, but Evelyn Spencer and Ernie Franzone described Grutman as the prime mover. In any case, Evans argued later, the rush to remove the clause proved that Falwell was afraid PTL might revert to the Assemblies when Bakker was gone and had ordered Grutman to have it nullified as quickly as possible.

Falwell said that he had tried to keep his promise to Evans and persuade his new board to restore the reversionary clause but didn't have the votes to do it. Later, after Evans had joined the enemy camp, Falwell's men said that what Evans had really wanted was to be the new host of the PTL show. At the April 23 meeting, Falwell had casually asked Evans who should succeed Dortch as host, and the next day Evans sent Falwell a five-page letter spelling out his qualifications in embarrassingly eager terms.

He had mentioned the search for a host to his wife, Evans wrote, and "Carolyn looked at me and smiled and said, 'Honey, the best possible person for that job is you, but I would never agree to it.' " He assured Falwell that even though he belonged to the Assemblies of God, "I am not a wild-eyed Pentecostal," so there was no reason he couldn't run the show without embarrassing Falwell or promoting his own beliefs. If Falwell wanted him, he thought the two of them might persuade Carolyn to give up her opposition.

The letter came in handy. When it became clear that Evans's hope was in vain and he took the lead in charging Falwell with conspiring to steal PTL, Falwell's men could show Evans's own words to the press to discredit him.

The first meeting on April 23 lasted four hours, ending at 2:00 P.M., and it was only after Evans and the elders of the Assemblies had taken their leave that Falwell and Ankerberg invited the witnesses into the conference room to take up the question of Bakker's corruption. The talk began with management abuses at PTL, but after listening politely for a while, Falwell put the blunt question "Do you know anything about homosexuality?" Then, according to one man present who lined up with neither side, Falwell added a line that suggested he was planning to use the evidence in a smear campaign: "We keep hearing all these rumors, but we can't go on the air and say anything about it."

What the witnesses knew, however, was pretty wispy. The best evidence at this meeting was provided by Gary Smith, who said that he had once confronted a frequent guest on the show who was showing up drunk and was rumored to be bisexual. Smith said the man graphically described some homosexual acts and blustered that if he chose to perform them on his own time, that was his business, and so was the booze. Maybe so, Smith said, but you're fired. At that point, the guest sneeringly defied him.

"You don't understand," he said. "I've been with Jim Bakker on his houseboat." Well, said Smith, so had he, and so had his wife and children. The man said it again, with heavy emphasis: "You don't understand. I've *been with* Jim." Smith said he went to Bakker and told him he was firing the man, and Bakker said okay—only to call Smith at four o'clock the next morning and countermand the order.

Smith also said that Bakker had once made a pass at him when the show was still being broadcast from Heritage Village in Charlotte. Bakker asked if Smith would like to go for a swim in the indoor pool at the end of the day. Bakker came out of the shower nude and gave him a suggestively inviting look, Smith said; Falwell was to quote Smith often, in slightly varying language, as saying "he knew now the awful feeling that a woman must experience when she's being seduced by a man. It was terrible." Smith said only the unexpected appearance of another staffer and his wife saved the situation, forcing Bakker to retreat and put on his swimming trunks. The story seemed thin gruel indeed when it eventually appeared in print, and Bakker's defenders talked sarcastically about what a "homosexual look" might be. But the newspapers primly chose not to print one key detail: In Smith's story, Bakker was unmistakably tumescent.

In the weeks to come, better evidence emerged. Some witnesses told their stories to the Assemblies of God; others, to Falwell's people and the media.

A former PTL executive who attended the April 23 meeting later told of being asked to meet Bakker in Bakker's house to discuss the PTL operation. He found Jim in bed, he said, not an unusual occurrence, and in the course of the conversation Jim asked him to rub his back. The executive complied, a bit awkwardly, and Jim asked if he could unkink a calf muscle for him.

"I realize he's not wearing anything, but he's lying on his stomach," the man told *Newsweek*. "So I sit down on the bed. I'm semiuncomfortable, still talking a mile a minute, 'Boy, I've got an idea for the hotel!' He takes my hand and pulls it and plants it on his organ. I just freaked, honestly freaked. I had no idea. I broke into an absolute cold sweat. I stood up, and he reached for my zipper."

The executive, whose name wasn't linked to the story because it would have endangered his subsequent job, said he had been trained to anticipate the unexpected, but "That was not a contingency I had ever put into the system." He staggered away from the bed, he said, shocked and tongue-tied. Then Bakker told him, "You can close the curtains."

"I've got to go," he replied, babbling ridiculously that his wife had dinner ready.

The executive bolted out, and said nothing about the incident to anyone; he stayed on for a while at PTL but never talked to Bakker about it either. He volunteered his evidence to Ankerberg only after hearing the other witnesses at the April 23 meeting, and hearing Ankerberg worry that some of them might recant.

The most dramatic story came later from Austin Miles, the one-time preacher and frequent guest on the PTL show who later became disillusioned, stopped preaching, and returned to his career as a circus ringmaster. Miles is a vivid, fast-talking, and theatrical personality. As he told his story to *Newsweek*, it was both unpleasant and pathetic, with Tammy Faye Bakker in a frantic and helpless walk-on role.

Miles said he was visiting PTL on January 13, 1977, when he was invited to use the health club at Heritage Village. After the taping

of the show, he fell asleep. When he woke up, he decided to see if
the health club was still open and walked in at an odd hour of the
evening. What he found was a semiorgy: four men, including Jim
Bakker, cavorting in the nude around a massage table. One of the
men lay on it as Bakker massaged his leg, working up toward the
thigh; as Miles watched, he said, he saw hands and mouths where
they shouldn't have been. Again, the men had erections.

After a long minute or so, Bakker realized someone was watching.
He grabbed a towel and wrapped it around his waist. Then he
chattered at Miles with what sounded like a veiled offer to keep him
quiet: "That was a real good show today, Austin. You'll have to
come back." And turning to another of the men, Jim said, "Be sure
to book Austin once a month."

"Yeah, Jim. See you," Miles said he muttered, and he backed out
of the room. He wandered down the corridor and stopped, he said,
shaken and revulsed. Then he heard a clatter of heels and looked
up to see Tammy Faye, banging determinedly on the door he had
just closed.

"Jim Bakker, you come out of there!" she yelled. "I mean it! I
know you're in there; now come out of there!" There was no response. As Tammy pounded the door, one of her eyelashes fell off.
"Dammit," she yelled. "Goddammit." She leaned against the door
and began to sob, Miles said. Tears and mascara streamed down her
cheeks. Then a woman who worked on the show walked up and
put her arm around Tammy's shoulder. "What am I going to
do?" Tammy implored her. Saying nothing, the woman gently led
Tammy away.

As one name led to another, more witnesses came forward. At one
point, Falwell casually told a press conference that there was evidence that Bakker's homosexual life went as far back as 1956, when
he was only sixteen. And a television man, who was still working
at PTL, told the presbyters of the Assemblies of God that he had
several times had sex with Jim Bakker. According to the story he
told *Newsweek*, he wasn't homosexual by choice but had simply
succumbed to one of Jim's abrupt passes, out of fear for his job and
deference to Jim's charisma. He said Jim sometimes invited him to
his studio office after the show and sometimes called him to the
Bakker house late at night when Tammy wasn't home. Jim was
looking for relief from tension, not for an emotional affair, he said;
oddly enough, Jim seemed to think homosexuality wasn't cheating

as much as adultery would be. But as the man put it, "He didn't like to talk about it much. We just did it."

The man said he often asked himself why he put up with Jim's sexual harassment. "But who do you tell? Who would believe me?" he said. If he were told such a story, "I'm not even sure I would have believed myself." Finally, he said, "I just realized I didn't have to do this," and he refused. Jim made one more pass at him, he said, and he refused again. Two days later he was demoted.

Falwell's men found other evidence as they sifted through the files at PTL. Falwell said they had come across five photo albums, pasted up by Bakker himself after he and Tammy had taken a vacation in Hawaii with several other couples. The photos were of the vacationers; some of them were bordering on obscene, Falwell said, and Jim had furnished them with captions apparently clipped from men's magazines to suggest the off-color fun they had been having. The caption given one couple who had apparently drawn a line was: "Mr. and Mrs. Moral Majority."

Falwell's preacherly sensibility may have been overly offended; by other accounts, the photos were merely suggestive. But "It was embarrassing to my wife, to me," Falwell said. "Those pictures are the kind that I could sell Hugh Hefner. I could get more for those five books than Jessica Hahn got for her interview." The albums had been left behind by the departing Bakker troops, he said, along with an exotic gift to Jim from one of his executives, a pair of silky black underpants—"I would give them to my wife," said Falwell, "but they were for men."

But the most vivid and persuasive stories about Jim were still untold when the April 23 meeting at Nashville broke up, and Falwell was fretting that the evidence might not be conclusive. He and others at the meeting were also worried about being sued when the charges against Bakker came out. They agreed to chip in to a fund for legal fees, to be used to defend lawsuits against any of them; Smith said the agreement would set a ceiling of $450,000 to indemnify each man in what they called the "Ankerberg group." And Falwell asked Smith and Ankerberg to convene the witnesses again four days later to take formal, legal depositions that could be cited to the PTL board—or used in court if it came to that.

According to two of the men present, Falwell said he had another aim as well: to convince Jim Watt that Bakker was indeed homosexual and thus to win his vote for the firing of Dortch. The depositions would be taken on April 27 in Atlanta, and Falwell said he would be there with Watt. Falwell later denied the story, but as Smith and another witness told it, Falwell laid out an elaborate scenario: Watt would be persuaded by the witnesses, then flown to Lynchburg in Falwell's plane for dinner with the fundamentalist directors. That would keep him safely out of touch with Dortch and his allies until the crucial board meeting next day.

After the Nashville meetings, the former executive who had bolted from Jim's room decided to volunteer his own testimony in Atlanta—mainly, he said later, because he was impressed by Ankerberg's sincerity in pursuing moral wrongdoing. So after calling his wife to tell her for the first time what had happened, he repeated the story of Jim's pass at him to Grutman and a tape recorder. He was promised that his identity would be protected, but within days he got a blustery call from Bakker himself. How dare he tell that story? Bakker demanded. Then he threatened: "I'll put my hand on a Bible and swear you touched me first." The episode left a bad taste about Falwell and his group, the witness said: "I think they play the loosest with the rules of anybody I've had to deal with, including Dortch and Bakker."

To everyone's surprise, when the witnesses got to Atlanta, neither Falwell nor Watt appeared; they were represented by Grutman and Nims. Nims said later that the reason was simply that Falwell had no business running around the country listening to stories about homosexuality. After the Nashville meeting, he said, Falwell said disgustedly, "Ah, this is terrible stuff," and they all wanted to take showers. But there may have been another reason as well: By that time, Falwell had probably given up Watt's vote as lost anyway. In any case, Gary Smith, who was beginning to be upset with his unpredictable ally, was unhappy when Falwell didn't arrive. Smith had persuaded John Wesley Fletcher to be a key added witness, and Fletcher had come to Atlanta from a revival he was conducting just 250 miles away in Tupelo, Mississippi. Smith had him hidden in the Marriott Marquis Hotel so Fletcher could give his deposition without running into other witnesses. But at the last minute, Smith said, Nims met him in the lobby and told him Fletcher wouldn't be needed after all since Grutman had now enlisted in the anti-Dortch movement and would recommend the firing.

Nims denies saying any such thing, and in any case he and Grutman apparently tried to get Fletcher to testify later. But Fletcher remained in hiding. At one point, somebody tried to flush him out. The hotel's fire alarm was set off twice in rapid succession, but Fletcher didn't appear, and nobody would admit to the stunt. "When the fire alarm went off, I started looking," Nims recalled innocently. "I thought I was going to see John Wesley Fletcher, but I didn't."

After the depositions had been taken, Grutman sent Smith off in Falwell's plane to see Fletcher again. He wanted Fletcher to tell his story to PTL's board next day, but Fletcher refused. That evening, Fletcher called Falwell in Lynchburg while the fundamentalist board members were having dinner, and they talked for nearly an hour. Falwell said later that Fletcher wanted to tell his story, but not just then.

By that time, still another bomb planted at the April 23 meeting in Nashville had exploded. John Ankerberg appeared on the TV talk shows on April 24 to charge that Jim Bakker was guilty of a lot more than adultery. Gary Smith and Mike Evans said later that Ankerberg and Falwell had plotted that move to make sure the accusation was on the public record before the crucial board meeting.

As Smith told it, Falwell complained during the second meeting in the Sheraton Music City Hotel that the media weren't responding to the rumors about Bakker's homosexuality. "The press will take the financial stuff and run with it, but the press won't take the other stuff and run with it," Smith quoted him. Both Smith and Al Cress, Richard Dortch's secretary and representative at the meeting, said that Falwell asked Ankerberg about appearing on the CNN talk show "Larry King Live." Smith later told the story many times, and the words varied; but the gist was the same: "John, when are you going on the Larry King show?" Falwell asked.

"I *could* go on tonight," Ankerberg supposedly replied.

Falwell said, "Good."

Ankerberg flatly denied the story. He said he had decided to pick up a standing invitation to appear on the King show and "Nightline" only because he knew Bakker was plotting a comeback before the April 28 board meeting. Ankerberg said he had confirmation from the Assemblies of God that Bakker had asked the elders to support his return. Even though the Assemblies turned down the request, Ankerberg said, there was real danger that Bakker might sweep back into his empire with a mob of supporters and simply take over. If that happened, Ankerberg reasoned, the new board would resign, and the second wave of charges against Bakker would come too late to accomplish anything except more damaging scandals and controversy. So he made his move to head off the coup.

As for plotting his television appearances, Ankerberg said the question never came up. He argued that Falwell couldn't have known in advance about the shows since he himself didn't know until the next morning that he would appear on the King show and "Nightline" on the night of April 24. "I did not check with Jerry Falwell," he said. "He did not know at all that I was going to be on either of those programs."

The denial was not persuasive. For one thing, Ankerberg had been quietly trying for some time to interest reporters in the gamier charges against Bakker. Then, too, Falwell's assistant Mark DeMoss told Mike Evans that Ankerberg asked Falwell during the meeting, "Well, then, is it all right for me to go on 'Larry King' and 'Nightline'? Because they're both calling me." As DeMoss told the story in a phone call that Evans taped, Falwell "evidently didn't hear" the question, "and that was the last we heard from Ankerberg." Perhaps the most telling case for a conspiracy was that on Saturday, April 25, the day after the two shows and long before the question of his motives had been raised, King's producer, Tammy Haddad, told the *Washington Post* that Ankerberg had called her Thursday night, after the Nashville meeting, and said, "I'm ready to talk." She said she had tried to book him for the following Monday night, April 27, but he said he was available only the next day, Friday, so she bumped two other scheduled guests. By that testimony, Ankerberg was lying when he said he didn't know about the shows until the next morning.

Falwell's own memory of what he said is interesting, if only to show his creative powers of reconstruction and the impossibility of pinning him down. He has given several versions of his remarks about the press at that meeting. In one of them he said, "Someone from the group with Gary Smith asked the question 'Why will the *Charlotte Observer*, which does have this information on homosexuality, why will they not print it?' I said that in my opinion, the *Charlotte Observer* feels that the personal orientation and practices of the Bakkers are not the issue at stake, that financial and fiscal irresponsibility is the issue. I said, 'You need not expect the *Char-*

lotte Observer to print that kind of information.' " In a later version, he dressed the same idea in less formal language and added the revealing thought that "cold, hard facts" would be needed to enlist the *Observer*. Then, he recalled, "Someone said, 'Well'—maybe it was Ankerberg, maybe it was somebody [else]—'maybe Larry King would do it. Maybe so-and-so would get it out.' All that discussion. And I said, 'Well, let's hope it doesn't get out.' "

It is a baffling sequence. First Ankerberg's version: The question was never asked. Then DeMoss's: It was asked but went unheard. Then Falwell's high-mindedness, with its casual afterthought of "All that discussion," followed by a pious hope that further scandal might be avoided. After the bombshell, Falwell said Ankerberg had done a service to the church in telling the story, but he continued to deny that he knew Ankerberg was going to do it. It may be technically true that Falwell didn't know that Ankerberg's appearance was signed and sealed, but it is a fair conclusion that there were two minds with a common purpose in Nashville that afternoon.

In any case, Ankerberg's gambit worked. Once again the PTL story exploded. There were tabloid headlines (REV. SAYS JIM HAD GAY OL' TIME, said New York's *Daily News)* and patches on the network roundups; the morning talk shows scrambled for follow-ups to Ankerberg's revelations on the King show and "Nightline." His themes: "We have heard taped statements by individuals who ought to know, who have stated that Reverend Bakker has been involved in episodes with prostitutes, and he's also been involved in homosexual incidents. We have reason to believe that those statements are true . . . [that] there were specific instances where there was wife swapping on the staff. . . ." And to bolster Falwell's other agenda, Ankerberg laid heavy stress on the notion that Richard Dortch had known about the scandals since he arrived and hadn't done anything about them. In fact, Ankerberg charged, Dortch had covered them up.

The story of the prostitutes traced back to an exposé by Charlotte's ABC television affiliate, WSOC-TV, which reported on the day of Bakker's resignation that it had found a local massage parlor hostess who said Bakker had visited her three times at forty dollars each session. He was disguised in a blond wig and wasn't very friendly, she said; it wasn't until after he left the first time that her snickering colleagues told her who he was. True or not, nobody pursued that tale very hard. As for the wife swapping, old-timers at

PTL confirmed that there had been one such incident on the staff back in the 1970s. But after the first day's headlines, that part of the story faded quickly, too.

What mattered was the charge of homosexuality, and in his own talk show comments on the story, Falwell drove the point home. "You know, the Assemblies of God . . . will restore a pastor for about every possible imaginable failure, except homosexuality," he told Larry King. Jim should have a chance to confront his accusers, Falwell said; but "very frankly" he personally had found the witnesses credible, and if the story was true, well, God asks more of ministers than he does of other people. Jim might be forgiven but not restored. Down deep in his heart, Falwell said, Jim Bakker had to know that his return to PTL "would be the death knell to the ministry."

The rumors about Jim Bakker had been circulating for years, but he apparently never confronted them head-on; whatever Tammy knew or suspected that day Austin Miles saw her pounding on the health club door, her friends the Oldhams were convinced that she didn't know the truth. "Apparently he has lied to her so successfully she believes him," said Laura Lee. "Well, if she didn't, the whole world would know. She's not going to keep it to herself. I mean, she *cannot* keep it to herself."

Tammy told Laura Lee everything. "Sometimes she'd tell me a thing that Jim told her not to," Laura Lee said. "She'd tell you a little bit, then sit and worry on it and have a piece of pie, and then she'd tell you the rest. And if she got on the trail of somebody double-dealing or something against her, buddy, if she got on to that, she'd dig until she found it. And then she'd tell." So, Laura Lee decided, if Jim were truly hiding such a sin, "he would lie to her to keep her from ever knowing." And when the secret threatened to come out, Jim ran away and hid from Tammy and nearly everybody else.

He took Jamie Charles and a single bodyguard and drove three hours into the California mountains to a small cabin near the Big Bear resort. It was totally unlike Jim, the Oldhams said; even more than Tammy, Jim liked his creature comforts and the reassuring presence of the entourage, and there he was without so much as a telephone. "He said he took Jamie Charles fishing, but when we went up there, they hadn't even been out of the cabin," said Laura

Lee. "He didn't even know where the lake was. They had rented some awful videos—Jamie Charles–type videos—and they had gone to the grocery and stocked up on some bachelor-type stuff. They had to go to a 7-Eleven to call once a day. We had no idea how to get in touch with them. We had to drive up there and see them."

Tammy was in Palm Springs, trying to hold things together and fielding the phone calls Jim usually took. At one point, their old friend Vestal Goodman called from Tega Cay to say that it was the last chance to save the ministry, that she and Oral Roberts's son, Richard, were going to fly to California and bring Jim back. Tammy didn't know what to do. Why would Jim go away and leave her with this mess? She was finding out things she hadn't known, Laura Lee said: "There were fifty things that came through the phone that she was just wild over." But the one that got to her was the tip that the stories about Jim's homosexuality were about to come out. "She had brushed that subject a time or two, but always in a laughing way," Laura Lee recalled. "Whatever she heard panicked her enough that we got in the car and drove three hours to find him."

"Aw, don't worry," Jim told Tammy and Laura Lee. "It's going to be all right." Whatever he felt inside, the preacher could still carry an audience. "He made her feel okay, so we turned around and drove home," said Laura Lee.

But nothing was all right. Jim stayed brooding in the mountains and left Tammy to defend his honor. She telephoned Larry King at home after Ankerberg's bombshell, complaining that Ankerberg had been given airtime. King told her that she should respond, but she could only waver: "Larry, they're ganging up on me. This is not true." Instead, she handed the reporters at the gate a written statement from Jim: "I have never been to a prostitute and I am not or have ever been a homosexual."

As a rebuttal, it was short of overwhelming.

Outside the Palm Springs compound, a neighbor who didn't want to give her name stood among the tourists and reporters. "It's kind of been like a funeral parlor around here lately, complete with circling vultures," she said. "I feel kind of sorry for them. But I don't mean to imply that I approve of what he did. And I do believe he did it—all of it."

Chapter 9

The Loose Canon

Richard Dortch was everybody's favorite villain in the PTL drama. Some thought he was conspiring with Jim Bakker to hand the hot potato to Jerry Falwell until it cooled down a bit, when they could snatch it back. Others said Falwell had lured Dortch into his own takeover plot with promises of sharing the power, then dumped him after Bakker had been tricked into leaving. And still others believed that Dortch hoped to deceive both Bakker and Falwell, scheming to wind up with the ministry all to himself.

Richard Dortch hasn't said. For months after Falwell finally fired him, Dortch kept quiet about what had happened; he went to ground in Largo, Florida, awaiting a grand jury indictment and letting his lawyer, Bill Diehl, speak for him. When he finally surfaced, it was only to say he had paid off Jessica Hahn under threat of violence. As the lawyer portrayed him, Richard Dortch was a greatly maligned and misunderstood man. When he joined PTL in 1983, Diehl said, Dortch was bringing his churchly prestige and executive talent to the aid of a ministry badly in need of both, under fire not only from the *Observer* but from the IRS. And as the crisis grew, the lawyer argued, Dortch was trying only to save the ministry. If he had it to do over, he might not do all the same things, Diehl conceded, "but he was doing the best he could to keep the damn thing afloat. And I think Falwell knew that."

In fact, Falwell takes what he has called the charitable view of Dortch: "I think his chief crime was intense loyalty to a very bad

157

man." Falwell's men are less generous. As they portray Dortch, in the month after Falwell had made him president of PTL as "a transition person" to help the ministry through its ordeal, his true colors showed in three separate sets of sins: hiding his role in the Jessica Hahn payoff; trying to cover up the depth of the ministry's financial crisis; and finally, when he saw the net closing around him, conspiring to restore Jim Bakker to the throne.

From his first days at PTL, Richard Dortch got mixed reviews. Roger Flessing, the television executive, recalled that Dortch arrived with all the right credentials, having been a preacher himself, a national presbyter of the Assemblies of God for ten years, and a leading candidate to be the denomination's general superintendent. Dortch also made all the right promises to straighten out the problems Bakker had caused with his slipshod management. He said he would cut spending, impose strict budgeting, and curb Bakker's impulsive drive to expand.

None of that happened. Instead, a salary structure that had been carefully worked out was scrapped, with top officials suddenly getting huge wages. "They didn't control spending," said Flessing. "They spent more money in the three years after Dortch came than we had spent in the previous ten. Dortch was always out trying to find a big loan. He did exactly the opposite of what he said." Flessing decided that Dortch couldn't be trusted when a friend of his, still at PTL, told him Dortch was hinting that Flessing was the leak to the *Observer.* Flessing said he tried to confront Dortch about that, but Dortch ducked the issue.

As insiders and visitors alike told the story, Dortch set anything but a frugal example for the workers at PTL. The bodyguard Mike Richardson wrote that Dortch arrived with his wife, his divorced daughter Deanna Collins, and her young son, and moved into one of the PTL houses at Tega Cay after a remodeling job that was rumored to cost five hundred thousand dollars. He drove one of the ministry's Cadillacs and, just as Jim Bakker had done, bought a houseboat. His son went on the payroll as finance director, and for a while Deanna was cast as Tammy's companion. That association would clearly have been useful to Dortch, but Deanna couldn't keep up with the mercurial Tammy. She wound up as a producer on the show.

Amiable, courtly, and smiling, Dortch "was like a grandfather. Anything he said you would believe," said Warren Marcus, president of Falwell's LBN. But the appearance was deceptive, he added. When Marcus visited Heritage USA for a job interview in December 1986, the experience left him uneasy. A converted Jew, he thinks Christians should strive for Christ-like humility. He and his wife and daughter were treated lavishly, he said; they were given expensive gifts and handed $270 in cash to pay for expenses they weren't running up, since they were being taken to all their meals, too.

By the third day the atmosphere was stifling, Marcus said. "My wife said it felt like some kind of armed camp." The family felt watched and guarded all the time, with some parts of the place clearly off limits—including Kevin's House, the supposed home for handicapped children. "We don't want to disturb the kids," Dortch explained, not bothering to add that there were only two. And when Marcus asked Dortch if he should account for the $270 and turn back what he hadn't spent, Dortch told him, "This is for you. Don't worry about it. We do this all the time." Jim and Tammy were affable and charming when Marcus met them, but he was repelled by the blatant hawking of merchandise, and he knew he didn't want the job after one look at the Presidential Suite with its lush carpets, six bathrooms, and gold-plated faucets.

Marcus particularly remembered a chat with Dortch in the new Mercedes that Dortch had just been given. That was a special arrangement, Dortch explained, a tradeout with a local Mercedes dealer. Marcus was skeptical; what kind of tradeout could there be, he asked himself, if PTL didn't carry commercials and didn't give airtime to sponsors? He tabled the question, but then Dortch boasted about how he had gotten the *Observer* off PTL's back. He said he had hired a private investigator to follow the paper's executives around, and one of them turned out to be seeing women. So, Dortch told Marcus, he set up a meeting with the *Observer* people and told them he would spread the story if they didn't lay off, and they did. Dortch told him the newspaper people had protested that it was blackmail, but he told them, tough and cool, "No, that's survival." At the time, Marcus didn't know that story wasn't true, and he said it bothered him. It seemed a far cry from the Christian idea of ethical behavior.

When Jerry Falwell came to explain to the reporters why Dortch had to leave PTL, the main reason he gave was Dortch's role in the Jessica Hahn payoff. It had been a "tearful, heartrending" board meeting, he said, but as Grutman solemnly explained, "Mr. Dortch was involved in the [Hahn] transaction." Board member DeWitt Braud, a Baton Rouge businessman, compared the affair to the Watergate scandal and asked rhetorically, "Could Nixon have stayed?"

But as Dortch's lawyer, Bill Diehl, remarked later, his role in the scandal could hardly have come as that much of a surprise. As far back as March 22, the *Observer* had spelled out Dortch's connection with John Wesley Fletcher, his two meetings with Jessica Hahn in New York, his attempts to persuade her to repudiate her story, and his trip to meet her champion, Paul Roper, in California in February 1985. The story described the payment of $115,000, saying PTL officials refused to say where it had come from, and reported that an additional trust fund for Jessica had been discussed. The *Observer* even quoted from a letter in which Scott Furstman, a lawyer hired by Dortch, told him: "I would appreciate you contacting me at your earliest convenience so we can discuss who to designate as the Trustor of the Jessica Hahn Trust. . . . I believe the trust agreement can be structured whereas the purpose is to discharge an obligation or a debt as opposed to a gift . . . [so] there will be no gift tax consequences."

That story had been widely picked up by the time Falwell chose Dortch as his "transition person," Diehl argued, and Falwell should have known everything in it, including the damaging disclosure that Dortch had lied to board member J. Don George when George asked him about the Hahn story. So what was the real reason for firing him?

Falwell and his men denied that they had known all that. They said Dortch denied in Tampa on March 12 that he had anything to do with the payoff or even knew that it had been made. "He said it as clearly and slowly as he could," DeMoss recalled. "Quote, 'If there ever was a Jessica Hahn trust fund, I know nothing about it.' " But Diehl said Dortch had certainly told Grutman all about the fund and his role in it on the plane ride to Palm Springs on March 16, since at the time he believed Grutman was his lawyer. And "as it turns out," Diehl said dryly, "that would be like talking to Falwell, Nims, and the others."

Falwell insisted, however, that Dortch's role in the case wasn't clear until shortly before the crucial board meeting. The contractor, Roe Messner, had told the board previously that he had advanced the $115,000 check for the payoff and then billed PTL for the money with a phony invoice, written for work on the Heritage USA amphitheater. On the invoice Messner had scrawled: "Per Richard Dortch instructions." But "when the issue became provocative later," Falwell said, the invoice was nowhere to be found; it had disappeared from Dortch's files.

At that point, Messner took a personal hand in the action. A tall, rangy Kansan, Messner claims to have built about twelve hundred churches and synagogues, more than anyone else in the United States. He had been PTL's chief builder since 1983 and became its biggest single creditor, with claims totaling more than fourteen million dollars. He, too, was soon to fall out with Falwell; but now he was still in camp, and as Falwell recalled it, Messner's secretary reminded him that he had sent a copy of the invoice to Bakker. "Without alerting anyone," Falwell said, "Roe Messner said he went to Jim Bakker's office. No one there had been instructed to destroy the invoice. And so he found the invoice in Jim Bakker's file."

Falwell said Messner told him only later, riding in a car after the crucial board meeting, that Dortch had tried that very morning to enlist him in another cover-up. In one of his virtuoso recollections of verbatim dialogue once removed, Falwell said Messner told him: "I received a call from Pastor Dortch this morning, very early. He said, 'Roe, we've got to get a story together that will fly with the new board.' I said, 'What do you mean, get a story together?' He said, 'I've got to be able to explain that faked invoice for the amphitheater.' I told Richard, 'The invoice stands. I'll be no part of a cover-up.'"

But for all the fanfare, Dortch's involvement in the payoff was just an excuse, and the invoice was merely a handy smoking gun, to be pulled out and used when the time came for Dortch's dismissal. What was really bothering Falwell and his men went a good deal deeper: Despite Dortch's energetic foot-dragging, they were beginning to find out the real depth of PTL's financial and legal problems —and the fact that Dortch himself was part of them.

The point man in rooting out the facts was Jerry Nims, the Atlanta businessman Falwell had brought in to be chairman of PTL's executive committee. A fast-talking preacher's son with an urchin's rubbery face and a dramatic, elliptical turn of speech, Nims had had a controversial career as a talent agent, a music publisher, and an entrepreneur before hitching up with Falwell. A college dropout who went back for a degree in social sciences at the age of thirty-two, Nims was later given an honorary doctorate by a small religious college in Texas to which his father-in-law is a major donor. He is often referred to as "Dr. Nims" in interviews and press releases.

At one point Nims marketed a 3-D camera called Nimslo, with a company whose stock traded as high as $4.81 a share in 1982. By the spring of 1987 it had plunged to 16 cents; after a successful test marketing, the camera ran into technical and production problems. Like many another entrepreneur whose deals have gone sour, Nims has been sued by business associates; one such suit, claiming fraud, was settled—to save the expense of litigation, he explained. After the collapse of Falwell's PTL operation, Nims found another berth when Falwell named him his successor as head of the political Liberty Federation, which had taken over the better-known Moral Majority.

When Falwell and his new board first met on March 26, Nims said, "Dortch gave us a speech and said everything is wonderful. He went on the record saying financial shape couldn't be better, everything is great, money is up, great to have you. It made an impression on me. I'm sitting there as a new director, a fiduciary."

It may very well have sounded reassuring. There had indeed been periodic reports of financial trouble at PTL; but that was standard among TV ministries, and Bakker especially was known for his dramatic veering from crisis one week to expansion the next. It would be hard for any outsider to judge the health of a TV ministry.

Still, there was hard evidence available to the new board that things at PTL had been deteriorating for some time. Just two days before that board meeting, the *Observer* had printed an exhaustive story based on PTL's financial statement for 1985, which had been released only a week earlier—almost two years after that fiscal year had ended. It showed clearly that spending had outrun revenues that year by $17.5 million. That would explain why the ministry had slowed construction in the fall of 1986, scaled back other activities, and announced hundreds of layoffs from a payroll that had reached twenty-eight hundred employees. But the *Observer* also disclosed that the IRS and the state of South Carolina were claiming millions in back taxes, that IRS auditors were still probing the ministry's tangled books, and that PTL's own auditors, Laventhol & Horwath, had qualified their endorsement of the financial statement. The story was a clear signal of major trouble.

One point at issue with the IRS was whether the Bakkers and other officials of PTL were being paid more than what was "reasonable" for their services—a standard set by the agency as a trade-off for tax exemption. On taking over PTL, Falwell had said Jim and Tammy's pay would be continued, though he didn't yet know how much it was; it wouldn't be Christian, he explained, to cut off the founders of the ministry while they were in a family crisis. It was more than two weeks before the salary and bonus figures were compiled, and it turned out that they didn't include the personal perks, credit card advances, and other casual benefits the Bakkers had been taking. Another, more complicated question was whether the ministry was properly dividing its profit-making enterprises from its ministerial functions and whether ministerial deductions were being used to cut taxes on commercial business. The IRS might frown, for instance, if wave-making machines for the water park had been billed to the ministry.

Such tax disputes might be regarded as routine, but the *Observer* had clearly flagged two more areas that would be major problems. The first was the lifetime partnerships, entitling thousand-dollar donors to three free nights each year, for the rest of their lives, in the Heritage Grand Hotel or the still-unfinished Towers Hotel. Conservative accounting required the revenues from lifetime partnerships to be amortized over many years, with reserves set aside for the future liabilities. Instead, Bakker had simply spent the money as it had come in, using it to cover operating expenses as well as construction. In addition, the state tax office was contending that sixty-six million dollars raised for the two hotels by selling partnerships in 1984 and 1985 would be subject to hotel occupancy taxes —a claim that would cost at least four million dollars for those two years. It might open further claims for 1986 and 1987 and raise the possibility of federal taxes, too.

Even worse, the *Observer* hinted at criminal liabilities. Its story said the IRS was challenging the way PTL had bought property, paying for part of some plots not with money but with receipts for donations to the ministry that hadn't been made. Such receipts would be worth about half their face value in tax deductions for the sellers, but they might also be evidence of tax fraud. The new directors could not be held liable for crimes committed by their predecessors, but if any of them had read the story or learned the facts from PTL's files, they should have seen a bright red warning light.

But such questions weren't asked at that first meeting, and as Nims recalled, it became apparent only over the next two weeks that "Dortch was stonewalling us." Facts and documents were promised but not delivered to the new team, he said. "None of the staff would talk to us. We would suggest they do things, they wouldn't do anything. So for a month that place just ran itself straight ahead." Nims himself went to California for a visit with his father, who was ill, and while he was there, he began getting hints that things at PTL were not what they seemed. The transcript of his interview with *Newsweek* gives both the sense of gathering trouble and the characteristic Nims style:

"I got a phone call from Jim Bakker's old law firm. The guy said: Hi, I was the law firm and I quit, um, a year ago. And I quit because —and, um, do you have any questions. I said: Well—I mean I'll never forget this one, I was sitting out on the beach, looking out at the ocean, said: Well, yeah, um, what's going on? What's happening? And he said, um, he said: Well, I wrote a very clear letter on why we quit. I said: Would you send me a copy of that?

"And they sent me the documents they'd sent to Jim two years before. They sent me their letter of resignation. Chapel, Wilkinson, Riggs & Abney. And they had resigned September ninth, 1986.

"The guy went on to say to Jim, um: Hey, Jim, you're going to blow it. You're not doing what you should do. He goes through and defines here how Bakker's strategy was to always shift lawyers and never give anybody all the facts. And this is a well-respected law firm there. It was very—a pretty strong letter.

"Then I called him back, and I said: Oh, now you're saying in this letter that he segmented his law business and switched and nobody knew what was going on legally? The guy said: That's right, that's exactly what I said in my letter, friend. And I thanked him for it. And as I was sitting on the West Coast, I started getting a bit of a queasy feeling."

Nims's new friend also pointed him to an accountant who had recently stopped working for PTL, and that led to another phone call involving words like *irregularities* and *tremendous financial problems.* So Nims cut short his visit and went back east, calling in a consultant, Harry Hargrave, a Dallas businessman with expertise in theme parks. That led to a confrontation with Dortch, Jim Watt, and Rex Humbard, the three charismatic board members, at a meeting of Nims's executive committee. While Nims was out of the room, he said, "Watt threw Harry out of the meeting. And there was a whole lot of words that: If you don't trust the staff, who can you trust? And Watt's quote to me was, Well, what are you doing with this swimming pool operator in here? And I said: What? Harry does theme parks. But they were quite upset. Dortch was saying: Well, if you don't trust me, and, What'll our staff say if a consultant shows up? That was the wrong thing to say. The flag came up."

Like Warren Marcus before him, Nims was getting spooked by the atmosphere around Heritage USA. "I looked at all the guards around the place with walkie-talkies," he said. "I noticed some of them were packing heat—pistols." One night, when he decided to wander around the place, a guard suggested he might want to go back to his room, "and I noticed another guy about twenty feet away with a walkie-talkie watching this guy. The last time I felt that way was in East Germany. I thought: *Well, look at this guy. Now, I don't think I'm going to argue with this guy. This is the strangest Christian environment I've seen in my life.*"

Dortch was also keeping close tabs on his contacts with staffers, Nims said, but he managed to sneak in a private consultation with another outside lawyer, from Baker & McKenzie, which had been working on PTL's defense in the IRS claims. Against Dortch's orders, he said, the lawyer showed him some documents in the case. Among other things, Nims said, he saw in an IRS work sheet that Jim Bakker had taken undocumented expenses totaling $860,000 in 1985. He flew to Lynchburg that night to give a copy to Falwell: "Jerry, you better read this document I got here, 'cause I read it on the plane, and I don't feel good at all."

Back at PTL the next day Nims found out that a basic strategy in the tax case was to establish that PTL was part of the Assemblies of God and thus indisputably a church. Now that PTL was leaving the Assemblies, he asked, what does that do to the case? "That's not good," he was told. Finally Nims brought up what would be the most serious issue of all: Were the lifetime partnerships really a time-sharing ownership plan, similar to the purchase of rights to a few days a year in a vacation condominium? That was a question that hadn't been raised, he was told. Find out, he said.

With that, Nims's questions to Dortch and his team grew more pointed. In a grilling of the outside auditor who supervised PTL's books, he said, he discovered that the man was getting paid extra for "consulting" and that he claimed to have developed some "innovative auditing procedures" for the account. "Then he said to me: Jerry, I don't believe in conspiracy and I'm an honest man," said Nims. "When an auditor tells me he's an honest man, I get real nervous, so I went through this whole checklist with him." That led to Nims's finding a secret payroll account, which was supervised only by the auditor and from which Bakker had been paid more than one million dollars. "Was this approved by the board?" Nims asked, and the auditor said, "Well, it—it must have been." "Oh," said Nims, "I see." The auditor left the session sweating profusely, Nims said. "And I said to myself: Ooh, phooey, phooey."

At least once Nims recognized a dialogue, well rehearsed for his benefit, that he was supposed to believe was spontaneous. At Dortch's say-so, Falwell had announced that PTL was negotiating a fifty-million-dollar loan in Europe to consolidate short-term debt and permit orderly payments, and now one of Dortch's men walked up while he was talking to Nims and announced brightly that the loan had come through.

There was much congratulation. "They did this little ratty-tat with each other," said Nims. "Chee, isn't that great? Well, yes, this really is terrific." But when he homed in on the subject, saying he had good contacts in Europe and might be able to help, the financial man couldn't tell him which investment banker in England had arranged the loan or which Swiss bank it was coming from. *Well, there goes the fifty-million-dollar loan,* Nims thought. *Takes care of that one.* He talked to Dortch for several hours, he said. Then he flew back to Lynchburg and announced: "Jerry, we in deep water, buddy. I can't tell you where it is, but there is something very, very wrong in that whole place."

Now that the issue of the lifetime partnerships had been raised, Baker & McKenzie decided that they were indeed time shares. The implications were serious. For more than a year, more than half of all the donations to PTL had been lifetime partnerships. Setting up reserves to cover the future liabilities would make chaos of what was already a financial mess. But that wasn't the worst: As time shares the partnerships would not be donations at all but technically purchases of securities. Selling them without issuing a prospectus and going through other legal formalities might be securities fraud in federal court and in more than twenty states as well. With donations lagging as a result of the scandal, Dortch was pushing hard to begin another telethon promoting the lifetime partnerships. If the new board were to approve, the directors would have to worry about their own criminal liability.

Nims said Dortch pooh-poohed his concerns. He insisted that the partnerships had been vetted and approved by a former lawyer for the state of South Carolina, Ken Hagreen, who had been PTL's consultant on the matter. Nims told Dortch to document that case and bring it to the next board meeting on April 17, only days away. But by now Nims was checking on everything Dortch had told him, and he tracked down Hagreen to confirm the story. Hagreen not only denied having approved the sales but said he had warned Dortch he was in deep water and told him he would not work for him again.

So Nims set a trap for Dortch. "I said: Ken, would you be willing to say this on the telephone to our directors? Ken said: Hey, I'd be glad to." The board meeting was held on Good Friday at the Airport Hilton in Palm Beach, Florida, since several members were in the area. It opened on a sour note, with a belligerent Jim Watt complaining loudly about the "secret meeting" in Nashville six days earlier to hear Ankerberg and the witnesses. It took nearly an hour, Falwell said, to clear the air, going over all the business of Nims's invitation, Watt's refusal, and the cancellation and reinstating of the meeting. Finally Watt subsided, and they got to Dortch's proposal to start a new telethon.

Dortch began, Nims said, by reading a telex from David McDonald, a senior partner at Baker & McKenzie, saying that the sale of partnerships would be no problem after all. But Nims had already found out from McDonald that the telex was a sham: Dortch had asked McDonald to send a message restating Dortch's own argument that the sale would be legal. Dortch then read it to the board, Nims said, as if it were the firm's opinion. He went on to argue that the lifetime partnerships were the only way PTL could survive since revenues were falling short by perhaps three million dollars a month. Finally Dortch invoked Ken Hagreen, the former South Carolina attorney, saying he had endorsed the whole deal.

Watt jumped into the argument, Nims said, berating Nims for raising the potential problem with Baker & McKenzie, and the two got into a distinctly unchurchly spat. "I said: Jim, why don't you wait for a while? He said: Well, you dirty rat! I said, Jim, don't mess with me, okay? So there was a little excitement going on." Then Nims sprang his trap. "I said: Okay now, I've just talked to Ken Hagreen. Dortch went schwoooo; his face was pasty." Then Nims spelled out the situation: Hagreen said the partnerships were time shares; selling them required prior permission from securities commissions in twenty-five states; without a prospectus, an auditor's statement, and full disclosure, it would be securities fraud on a massive scale, and all the directors would be liable. There was a kind of collective gasp in the room. Nims said that Roy Grutman, who until then had backed Dortch and wanted to keep him as president, "leaned over to me and said: Richard Dortch is an unmitigated liar. I said: That's right, you got it, guy. Richard just shut up, and then he said: Well, you know, I've never trusted Ken Hagreen."

To drive it home, Nims placed his call to Hagreen and gave the receiver to Falwell, who put the question: Who's quoting you right? Falwell repeated Hagreen's words for the benefit of the other directors: "In my opinion, and I have maintained it from the beginning, what you are doing may in fact be in violation of the law." If further advice was needed, Hagreen added it: Stop selling those things.

Nims wanted to fire Dortch then and there, but the other directors balked at such abrupt treatment of a fellow minister and put off any action until the next meeting, April 28. They did, however, vote down any further sales of lifetime partnerships, and Nims said he read Dortch the riot act: "Richard, you could have put every one of these guys against the wall. You could have gotten us, every man here, dirty. What are you doing? Come on, even if you're in trouble —maybe we can help you, but you can't do that stuff, man. You just cannot do it." He said Dortch's reply was just "mumbling to himself."

Dortch's side of that story remains untold. But the case may not have been as open-and-shut as Nims drew it. In fact, it could be argued that Nims was stirring up a lot more trouble than he had to. Neither the federal government nor any of the states had actually challenged the lifetime partnerships as time shares, and there was at least an arguable case that they weren't. Why was Nims so eager to be prosecutor, judge, and jury, shutting off half of PTL's revenues?

It sounded a lot like what the preacher Bob Gray said Jerry Falwell had told him: that PTL would soon be in bankruptcy, "the sooner the better." And for what it's worth, Bakker himself told *Newsweek* that the scenario matched what Falwell and Grutman had warned him about as Swaggart's plan. At the Palm Springs meeting, he said, Falwell and Grutman had said Swaggart would "file with the state government to declare the lifetime memberships illegal, which would throw a horrendous tax burden on PTL, financially sink it." If Bakker was telling the truth, Nims's "discovery" had been prefabricated.

But even if Nims had made matters worse by his intervention, there was no denying that PTL's affairs were in horrendous condition. As Falwell's men dug into the books and a tangle of forty-seven separate bank accounts, more debts kept turning up, and the operating surplus sank into deficit. Ultimately the debts totaled nearly seventy-two million dollars, with twenty-three million dollars overdue. The fifty-million-dollar consolidation loan never materialized.

And the bad news multiplied. The day after the Good Friday board meeting, the *Observer* printed the story that Jim and Tammy Bakker had drawn a total of $4.8 million in wages and bonuses since the start of 1984, while Dortch and David Taggart had each been paid more than $600,000 in 1986 and 1987. The pace of bonuses accelerated sharply in the first part of 1987. Falwell said later that proved the Bakkers knew the game was up: "In previous years they had raided the till in the last quarter, always around Christmas. But in early '87 they had paid themselves more than [they got] the entire previous year."

Coincidentally or not, the *Observer*'s story was well timed for the Falwell forces: It eclipsed the news two days earlier that former board member Ernie Franzone, the Texas hotel executive, had complained to the Assemblies of God about being railroaded into resigning by Grutman and Dortch. And in the days before the crucial April 28 meeting, the newspaper carried a string of well-leaked stories bolstering Falwell's case. First came word that the old PTL board had been bullied and suborned by the Bakker management. The *Observer* quoted Franzone and two preachers, A. T. Lawing of Charlotte and J. Don George of Irving, Texas, as saying they didn't know how much basic salary the Bakkers were paid, what bonuses they got, or even why the figures were secret. They said they weren't aware that any bonuses at all had been given in 1987, that they weren't allowed to take papers home and weren't even given minutes of their meetings. "I completely trusted Jim Bakker," said Franzone. "I completely trusted Reverend Dortch. If you want to call it a blind trust, I guess you could say it was."

The *Observer* also ran a detailed story about the lifetime partnerships, disclosing that the Bakker regime had vastly oversold them in relation to the capacity of the two hotels. At that point, the newspaper thought that 114,000 partnerships had been sold. If both hotels used half their rooms every night to honor the promise of a free three-night visit for each partner, the paper said, there would be room for only 60,000 partners a year. It turned out later that PTL had actually sold 160,904 lifetime partnerships in all; as Falwell said later, there would be no room at the inn forever if they all turned up. Even at the lower figure, the story was enough to raise public doubts about the partnerships before the board meeting.

Doubts became fears when the *Observer* disclosed that the IRS was threatening to revoke PTL's tax exemption for the years 1981–1983 because "a substantial portion of PTL's net earnings" had gone to benefit Bakker, his relatives, and other officials of the ministry. If that happened, PTL would have to pay millions in back taxes and donors could no longer deduct their contributions; it would be a deathblow. The long-threatened class-action lawsuit also materialized, filed in Columbus, Ohio, by two brothers and a sister asking $601 million in damages on behalf of all the 507,000 PTL partners, on the ground that their money had been used for immoral purposes.

After the news of the huge salaries and bonuses came out, Dortch tried to ease the impact with a grandstand play: He told the flock on the PTL show that he had decided to forgo any salary for the next twelve months. He said he would continue to occupy his "parsonage" at Tega Cay but wouldn't take any pension or other benefits. "God has spoken to my heart, and he will provide for my needs," he said. Bill Diehl maintained later that Dortch hadn't been involved in plundering PTL; most of the money Dortch drew in 1987 consisted of salary or bonuses earned but not taken the previous year, the lawyer said, adding that Dortch had not been involved in any of the credit card advances. Whatever Dortch promised, however, he continued to draw his $13,500 monthly paycheck.

Coincidentally or not, as Dortch's relations with the Falwell regime cooled, the atmosphere at PTL showed a sudden warming trend toward Jim and Tammy. The staff had actually welcomed the Falwell regime, giving him a standing ovation at their first meeting, and the archivist Ellen Baker was to say later that the *Observer*'s story of huge salaries and bonuses had profoundly embittered many loyal workers. But as the April 28 board meeting approached, Dortch launched a campaign of rehabilitation.

FORGIVEN was the watchword, and it bloomed everywhere at Heritage USA: on gift shop T-shirts and baseball caps; stitched in the heart of the $675 Tammy Faye doll; blazoned across the lawn in a floral display. Dortch preached a sermon on Jonah—God had given him a second chance, he said—and he sent a message with Don Hardister to Jim in California: "Tell him I've opened the doors as wide as I can for him to come back." He sent along a tape of his sermon, to show Jim how hard he was trying.

Falwell was having some well-publicized doubts about staying on at PTL. He had decided there was no choice but to fire Dortch, he said later, but he wasn't sure he could carry his board: "I did not know where the vote was on Dortch, and over that weekend I was fluctuating. My wife was saying it's a good time to get out." The rumors of a Bakker comeback were also circulating, so Falwell appeared on CBS-TV's "Face the Nation" to warn that Bakker's return "would guarantee, in my opinion, the doom of the ministry." But he also said he was praying hard over his own involvement in the mess.

In fact, Falwell said after the climactic board meeting on April 28 that he hadn't decided to stay until the meeting had been going on for a full hour. Jim Watt disputed that, saying that Falwell made the announcement right after the opening prayer. Falwell explained that the board had been milling around and chatting for an hour before the meeting officially began. Perhaps more to the point, Watt argued that Falwell had clearly decided what he was going to do the night before, when he and the fundamentalist directors had dinner in Lynchburg.

That dinner, Watt charged, amounted to yet another secret meeting of Falwell's fundamentalist faction of the board. Watt said he and Humbard were in Charlotte that night for the next day's meeting, and he was surprised that the fundamentalist director Sam Moore wasn't there, too, because he had thought they were having dinner together. It was Watt's wife who found out from Moore's wife that the Lynchburg dinner was going on, Watt said, and after that, the actual meeting was no more than a charade. He said Falwell had decided then to carry out the full takeover; the board discussed what to do if Bakker tried to sweep back through the gates during the board meeting, and special Pinkerton guards had been hired to handle the situation in case Hardister's men chose the Bakker side. During the formal meeting the next day, according to Watt, the other directors were irritated when he kept asking questions. "The only thing I contributed," he said, "was to delay the press conference about two and a half hours. It was a railroad job of the first order."

Sham or not, that meeting was surely a dramatic scene. As Falwell recalled it, Grutman read a report accusing Dortch of passing PTL money to Jessica Hahn. Dortch denied it, and Watt came fiercely to his aid; but Grutman dramatically pulled out the telltale invoice and demanded, "Is that your name, Reverend?" Dortch might well have said, "What if it is?" It wasn't a signature; it was no more than Messner's accusation that the payoff had been made "Per Richard Dortch instructions." But Falwell said Dortch caved in, meekly admitting that he had given the order.

Even so, the board argued for two hours about whether or not Dortch should be fired. Sam Moore, the religious publisher, had said Dortch was indispensable, but in the final vote Moore abstained, saying he had a conflict of interest because he was handling one of Dortch's books. Ben Armstrong of the NRB also abstained. Humbard, Watt's fellow Pentecostal, resigned; looking ashen and saying nothing to the mob of nearly three hundred waiting reporters, he stalked out of the meeting and left town. In the end, only Nims, DeWitt Braud, and Bailey Smith voted with Falwell.

Watt was the lone dissenter. "Jim Watt allowed friendship and his heart—and he has a big heart—in this instance to run beyond his head," Falwell explained later. He added: "Eric Watt was receiving two thousand dollars a month, which helped finance his education at Yale Divinity School, from PTL per Richard Dortch's instructions."

Watt also resigned two days later, wiring Falwell that it was "a matter of conscience, personal integrity and management philosophy." Or, as he told a reporter, "I could no longer tell the good guys from the bad guys." Before that, however, he joined Armstrong and Moore in a car for the short drive to the press conference Falwell was holding. He said both of them agreed that firing Dortch had been a mistake, but there was nothing they could do.

"It was all decided last night. There was no use objecting. That was why I abstained," Moore told him. "You should have been man enough to speak up," Watt replied.

For the press, Falwell was all resolution. Dortch and David Taggart were out, he said; Harry Hargrave would be PTL's new operating head. The board was calling a halt to the sale of lifetime partnerships and bringing in new outside accountants, Arthur Andersen & Company, to make sense of the books. PTL wasn't out of the woods, he said—"I would be lying to you if I said that members of this board are not concerned about the future of this ministry"—but Jim Bakker was history now, and the "Forgiven" campaign was coming to a fast stop. "His ministry here has ceased, and that is a unanimous feeling," Falwell said. "You're looking at the leaders right now, and we have no intention of stepping aside. . . . I am going to lovingly and scripturally lead on until God says, 'Get out of there.' "

There were a couple of loose ends, and Falwell tied them up. Pay for the Bakkers would be stopped, he said; so would any further payments to Jessica Hahn. Roy Grutman made a dutiful half apology to Jimmy Swaggart. He "may have been mistaken" in accusing Swaggart of planning a takeover, Grutman said, and he called Swaggart the "Laurence Olivier of TV evangelists." Swaggart accepted the olive branch, calling Grutman "a whale of a lawyer." And with that pas de deux, the takeover was complete. Falwell had full control of PTL, lock, stock, and network.

Don Hardister got to the cabin at Big Bear on Monday morning, April 27, the day before the board meeting. He played Jim the tape of Dortch's sermon—there was no cassette player in the place, so they had to sit in Jim's Mercedes—but Jim wasn't impressed. Dortch wasn't anything like strong enough in defending him, he told Hardister. Don said he had heard that Dortch and Taggart were going to be fired at the next day's meeting, but Jim was scornful. "No way," he said. Don repeated the warning and urged Jim to come down the mountain and take a hand. Unh-unh, said Bakker, and again, "no way" were Dortch and Taggart getting fired.

The next day Hardister got the news of the meeting when he called the Palm Springs compound from a local pizza joint. When he drove back to the cabin, Jim was in front of the television set, staring ahead, almost comatose. "You've heard," said Don, and Jim started to cry, becoming nearly hysterical. "You've got to get out of here," Don told him. "You've got to do something." Jim said he had met an elderly couple on nearby Tinker Bell Lane, longtime PTL supporters; maybe he could use their phone. So Hardister drove over there, and Jim called Tammy. The old folks were excited that Jim Bakker himself was in their house, and trying to comfort him, they put on one of Tammy's tapes. She was singing something to the effect that God isn't finished with you yet, and Jim broke into uncontrollable sobs again. "Tammy's song was ministering to him," Hardister said. "It was really a wonderful moment, kind of tender. He was starting to get a spark of faith back."

But the arguments weren't finished. Hardister wanted to leave for Palm Springs immediately and had a plane standing by, but Jim didn't like the way Hardister flew and wasn't covered by insurance to make that kind of flight anyway. Finally he agreed to make the long drive back, but then they couldn't find the keys to Jim's car. After a long, frustrating hunt, Hardister went back to Tinker Bell Lane and found them beside the telephone, where Jim had put them down. The elderly couple led them on a shortcut down the mountain to the freeway for Palm Springs, but they got there too late to make the evening news.

It seemed to be the end, with no way left to get back into PTL, and in the next few days the mood inside the compound was open despair. "It's about as tough as it can get right now," Hardister confided. "I think he is in shock." Finally, on May 1, Jim and Tammy walked out to meet the reporters together. They said they were tired and sad and hoped to be forgiven; they didn't plan to fight for their empire. They hoped meekly that they might still collect eight or nine million dollars in royalties for books and records that PTL owed them, and Tammy wept a bit over the puppies and kittens left behind at Tega Cay. They denied all of Ankerberg's charges: the prostitutes; the wife swapping; the homosexuality. "But that's not important," Jim said. "We've been accused of so many things that we've just decided to let our accusers do what they like. We're just going to forgive them. We're going to go on, and we're going to love." It was all over, he conceded at last: "Without a miracle of God, we will never minister again."

Six days later, on May 6, 1987, what seemed like the last nail was driven into the coffin. Citing the Jessica Hahn affair and "alleged misconduct involving bisexual activity," the Assemblies of God defrocked Jim Bakker.

"We feel we were had. We feel he just took advantage of us," said Lilli Marzliker, sixty-five. She and her husband, a retired accountant, lived just two blocks from the Bakkers' house in Palm Springs; since 1970, she said, they had given PTL about $25,000. "He took advantage of many people and had his lavish cars and his million and a half each year. . . . He lives so high. I think they had the best thing going and they really goofed. . . .

"I feel sorry for Tammy. I always did think she was a real lady. I think she'll come back to the ministry. She's a sweetheart, there's no doubt about it."

Chapter 10

The Plots of Spring

A dozen people were crowded into the living room of a suite in the Marriott Hotel in Anaheim, California. Jim and Tammy were standing on a coffee table; the others stood around them, holding hands, gazing up at them, and promising, over and over, that they would reign again. "People have looked down on you long enough," said one apostle. "God's going to restore you," said another. "People are going to look up to you again," the others chimed in. "You're going to be elevated. God's going to restore you."

"It sounds kind of weird, but it wasn't really," said Don Hardister, who watched the scene. "It was very dramatic." It was also meant to be practical: The apostles wanted Jim and Tammy psyched up to go to a major revival, where they would receive communion and Jim would preach. Then the backers would announce that he was healed and fit for the pulpit again. They were going to set up a new ministry, with enough TV equipment to make it big-time. Then Jim and Tammy could win back their loyal flock from Falwell's PTL.

That was just one of the shadowy plots and counterplots of spring 1987, a season of feverish maneuvering, shifting allegiances, and gathering crisis. But May Day brought no outward signs of trouble at PTL. To all appearances, the holy war was over and Falwell's sway was unchallenged.

The lush spring of the Carolinas was bursting into flower, and business had never been better at the Heritage USA mall. The handmade Tammy Faye doll was in such demand that the price was raised, from $675 to $800. The Heritage Grand Hotel was said to be fully booked for the summer. The faithful were coming in droves to show the flag, rallying against the forces of Satan, and squadrons of reporters were descending on the scene to take the pulse of PTL and incidentally buy a few souvenirs. Gift shop manager Jerry Knode said sales for April had soared by 26 percent over the 1986 level. The crowds were snapping up Tammy Faye's album, *Enough Is Enough,* but the reporters were especially intrigued by Jim's cassette, *The Church's Greatest Thieves,* selling for ten dollars. (They were disappointed. The "thieves" Jim was preaching against were allegorical characters representing unchristian traits that steal God's power—such sins as spite, defeatism, and gossip.)

Yet, through the dogwood season, there was an undercurrent of tension. The staff and many residents were increasingly disillusioned about Jim and Tammy, disgusted by the charges of homosexuality and embittered by the stories of personal plunder. At least some of the visitors were coming to share that view, but there were two groups that wouldn't accept the new regime. Some PTL partners remained loyal to the Bakkers, hoping against hope for a comeback. Others, holding no brief for Jim and Tammy, nonetheless came to suspect Falwell's motives and tried to assert their own rights in the ministry. In uneasy alliance, these two factions started a grass-roots movement, and as time went on, they got help from a few preachers and a growing number of defectors from the Falwell camp. Falwell in turn heaped discredit on the Bakkers and anyone who opposed him, all the while playing out the *Perils of Pauline* on the financial front. Hairbreadth rescues and new crises followed each other in dizzying succession.

At the outset, the idea that PTL's humble partners might have a voice in what happened to the ministry seemed ludicrous. There were 507,000 in all, more than 250,000 of them making regular contributions; of those, 114,000 had bought one or more thousand-dollar lifetime partnerships. But they had never had any forum to speak their minds or press their views on the ministry's leaders. From the Bakkers' point of view they were there to praise God and send money, and there was no sign that Falwell and his people felt otherwise. To the end Jerry Nims called the critics a "small fanatic minority" of the partners.

The revolt began with a husky, mild-mannered schoolteacher from Marquette, Michigan. Don Lee, a PTL partner who taught criminal justice at Northern Michigan University, was honeymooning at Heritage USA early in May; he and his bride both had been married before, and they decided to get off on the right foot by attending an "inner healing" workshop to help them shed any leftover emotional baggage. But after the first day, the leader of their counseling session said she wouldn't be there tomorrow; she was one of more than two hundred PTL employees laid off by Nims and Hargrave to help deal with the financial mess Bakker and Dortch had left behind. June Nichols, the workshop leader, told Lee that the session leader and other counselors had offered to finish their three-day groups without pay, simply because they were dedicated to the work, and the next day the laid-off counselors sat in Main Street USA to prove they meant it. As Lee saw it, the volunteers should have been allowed to serve. "They never set policy," he said, "they never set bonuses; they never contributed to a hush fund. And they offered to finish it free, so it couldn't have been an economic issue."

Instead, pastors were assigned to replace the counselors. They were dedicated and well meaning, Lee said, but they weren't trained as counselors. Toward the end of the three days, one of them began sobbing uncontrollably in frustration. "Here you have a hundred and seventy-five people, some of them really strung out and in need of counseling," Lee said, "and there's the pastor up there bawling her eyes out. That was the straw that broke my back." It was a callous and heavy-handed intrusion on the ministry, he felt; something was seriously wrong under Falwell, and it was time the faithful stood up and said so. So he helped found the Association of PTL Partners, operating at first out of his room at the Heritage Grand Hotel, working telephones and copiers to reach out to a rapidly growing network of PTL partners who might be disenchanted with Falwell.

Lee recognized from the first that to be effective, the new group would have to be seen not as pro-Bakker but as pro-PTL. Thus he argued that his organization didn't want Jim restored to the throne. Jim probably shouldn't come back at all, Lee said, unless it was just to be some kind of host for the show. Lee's quarrel was with Falwell: "There's all kinds of corruption. There's the kind Jim Bakker has, and there's other forms. We're highly suspicious that the Falwell organization has a hidden agenda."

No matter what Falwell said about not making PTL a Baptist ministry, Lee and other charismatics argued that he was trying to do just that. Falwell had begun to run his own show, "The Pastor's Study," on the PTL network. While Lee conceded that Falwell was paying full rates for both that show and the "Old Time Gospel Hour," which had been on the network in Bakker's day, he said Falwell couldn't have bought the added time if he hadn't been in the driver's seat. Lee also saw mischief in the fact that PTL had broadcast a service of Falwell's Thomas Road Baptist Church rather than the first meeting of the Heritage Village Church under its new pastor, Sam Johnson. Even if it was true, as Falwell argued, that Johnson was a charismatic preacher and himself had wanted the first meeting with his new congregation to be private, the network could have used a taped show instead of Falwell's service. Similarly, one of the daily PTL shows was preempted to show the graduation ceremony at Falwell's Liberty University. Falwell was intruding on the Heritage USA scene, too: He banned bikini swimsuits at the water park and said he would set a dress code for the whole campground—"not prudish, but modest."

Those intrusions were only the tip of the Falwell iceberg. Lee's basic suspicion was that Falwell meant to bankrupt PTL, sell its assets, and "go home with our mailing list and satellite in his hip pocket." A key move in that game might be splitting off the network as a separate entity, which seemed to be in the works when Falwell sent PTL executives to Las Vegas to tell the National Cable Television Association that the network's name would be changed: It was dropping PTL and becoming simply the Inspirational Network. John McEntee, director of cable marketing, also told the convention that the network would separate its finances from those of the ministry, and the ministry might have to begin paying for the time used by the PTL show. All this was presented as a reassuring move. "The cable industry feels that if the PTL ministry should fold, that the cable network will fold also, and that's not true," said McEntee. "I do not think this ministry is going to go anywhere but upward, but if anything should happen, the industry will know the network is standing on its own." Just so, said Don Lee.

Lee also saw Falwell's move to block sales of lifetime partnerships as a step toward deliberate ruin. "If you run a business and cut off all the income, what can you expect?" he demanded. "He deliberately cut fund-raising off when he knew exactly the consequences." In mid-May, suspicion hardened into certainty when Falwell's friend and new PTL director Bailey Smith called a news conference and suggested that the board could soon start selling the ministry's assets, beginning with the theme park. Smith had already gloated that Falwell's takeover of PTL was a historic step, "the first time in history that a Pentecostal ministry has been put in the hands of Baptists." Now he was boasting about what the Baptists would do with it. "Christians can go to Disney World" rather than Heritage, Smith said, and the TV ministry itself was going to have more gospel and "less of the glamour, less of the Hollywood for Jesus." When the assets were sold and the bills paid, Smith said, "[We] could have $110 million left over."

Falwell insisted that he had no plans to sell anything, that Smith wasn't speaking for him. "Jerry Falwell's singular goal is to salvage this ministry and keep it there till Jesus comes back," he said.

But to Lee and his colleagues, Smith's prediction simply proved the plot. "This is blatant robber-baron activity," Lee said angrily. "Essentially, you've got the T. Boone Pickens of the gospel world here. . . . It's a basic question of honesty. PTL's charismatic partners paid for the ministry. We have to protect our assets so they don't wind up in Lynchburg."

Lee's fledgling group swung into action. Within weeks, the partners had filed a notice of impending suit in federal court in South Carolina to block any sale of assets from the ministry. The group also announced a poll of all PTL partners to find out how many wanted charismatic leadership. When he couldn't get the mailing list from Falwell, Lee called for telephone votes on a WATS line instead. Lee and the titular president of the group, Joe Haviland, a campground consultant from Marietta, Georgia, claimed membership of five thousand to ten thousand. That wasn't an impressive number—no more than 2 percent of the total partnership—and the group's legal standing was shaky at best. But Haviland's argument had the logic of an old-time shareholders' rebellion: "We basically own this place, but we've been left out in left field."

The effect was like a swarm of gnats around Falwell's ears, drawing pinpricks of blood. But the strains within the partners' movement were clear from the start. As one of Lee's group explained to the *Observer*, there were three main factions: "One says, 'Let's just pray for PTL.' Another says, 'Bring the Bakkers back.' And the third says, 'Get rid of Jerry Falwell, any way you can. Kill him if you have to; just get rid of him.' " When Lee's group put up a sign at a rented house near the Heritage USA gate, ASSOCIATION OF PARTNERS INFORMATION CENTER, some of the pro-Bakker faction added a twenty-five-foot billboard across the yard: WELCOME HOME JIM AND TAMMY. As many as several hundred people a day visited the house, and there were occasional angry confrontations as partners from rival factions hurled Bible verses at each other or shouted, "Repent!"

Eventually the organization splintered. The outright Bakkerites mustered as the Bring Bakkers Back club, headed by Vickie Goodman Meadows; she was the daughter of Howard and Vestal Goodman, singers on the PTL show and old friends and neighbors of Jim and Tammy at Tega Cay. Somewhat implausibly, Meadows claimed membership of ninety thousand lifetime partners. A third group, the PTL Partner Majority, Inc., disagreed with Lee's anti-Falwell line. It tried to persuade donors to stop giving to the ministry and instead to contribute to a trust fund to buy what remained when PTL went under.

In the end, the partners proved to be a crucial factor in the battle for PTL, but that seemed less their own doing than the result of Falwell's blunders and a little help from a judge with a quixotic sense of equity. Meanwhile, the partners provided a kind of chorus for the PTL drama, a presence consisting of billboards, a few marches and demonstrations, some angry confrontations around the Heritage Grand Hotel, and an undercurrent of lament for Jim and Tammy.

A second front in the guerrilla campaign against Falwell was opened by Mike Evans, the Fort Worth preacher. Evans had been in on the action from the start: He was listening when Ankerberg first told Swaggart about the trouble at PTL. Evans had then tried to get Falwell to restore the reversionary clause in favor of the Assemblies of God. Now he charged Falwell with breaking his word and joined the opposition, telephoning preachers around the nation to mobilize Falwell's critics. He compiled a twenty-page single-spaced dossier of complaints—a jumble of facts, conjectural questions, and mostly secondhand testimony—and used it to stir up the media and promote Lee's group and its proposed survey of partners.

Evans claimed to be a reluctant adversary, motivated only by revulsion at what he saw as Falwell's trickery. "I'm convinced that Jerry Falwell has taken over PTL," he said. "It looks to me like the good Samaritan has run off with the boy's britches and wallet." He said he was driven by concern for PTL and righteous indignation that a fundamentalist Baptist had usurped a charismatic ministry. At the least, he said, the partners should be allowed to vote on it: "If they want him, let them say so."

To Falwell's men, that seemed a red herring at best. Evans was just a disgruntled meddler, they said, resentful because Falwell wouldn't let him host the PTL show. His five-page job application seemed to tip his hand, and the Falwell group didn't hesitate to rub it in. "Mike Evans is capable of saying anything," said Jerry Nims.

Falwell himself took a shot at Evans, telling a press conference: "There's one dear brother, an evangelist. He's one of fifty who've asked me to become a host on this show. I did not feel he was the person to do it, and suddenly he's joined with this group and offered his eight hundred number, really attacking us. I love him. He's a great preacher. I'm going to be his friend, whether he's my friend or not."

Falwell showed the depth of his affection when he dropped Evans's weekly show from the PTL network, ostensibly because Evans was nineteen thousand dollars behind in payments. It was only a pretext, Evans charged. "I'm just a tadpole evangelist, and the show wasn't that good anyway," he said, in the best Texas aw-shucks style. "But if they got rid of everybody who was nineteen thousand dollars behind, there wouldn't be a preacher left on the air—including Jerry Falwell."

Evans was joined in the crusade by another defector from Falwell's camp: Gary Smith, the former PTL operating head who had taken the lead in assembling witnesses to Bakker's sexual misbehavior. He suddenly turned up as a self-proclaimed spokesman for Lee's Association of PTL Partners, gravely questioning whether Bakker had given up his ministry or Falwell had taken it from him. "Jerry Falwell is trying to fundamentalize PTL," Smith said. "The question is not Jim Bakker's immorality or financial indiscretions; it's what is Jerry Falwell's intent and purpose." And he insisted that he had heard Falwell and Ankerberg conspiring at the April 23 meeting in Nashville to leak the second tier of sex charges against Bakker.

It was an odd collection of challengers. So far Jim Bakker himself had made no public accusations against Falwell, and neither had Dortch. They were waiting, their friends explained later, for someone with more credibility to fire the first shot. But for the most part, the media weren't reacting to the charges being made. Lee's group of partners was still small and disorganized, with dubious standing. Evans's "evidence" against Falwell was mostly conjectural, as was Smith's. Some TV producers talked to Lee, Evans, and Smith, but backed off; their evidence didn't seem strong enough to challenge Falwell. But *Newsweek* talked to Jim Watt, whose status as a former cabinet member would carry weight, and Watt was ready to go public with at least some of his complaints.

As *Newsweek* went about reporting its story, the Falwell camp lighted a backfire, warning in advance that "a major magazine" had joined the enemy and was preparing a hatchet job. "Their goal, in my opinion, is to start what they call a holy war," Falwell warned on the PTL show. But the war was clearly raging already, no matter who reported it, and Watt's new accusations merely escalated it. He complained that he hadn't been invited to "secret meetings" of Falwell's board and said he had come to believe Evans's accusation that Falwell had meant from the start to hang on to PTL. "It's embarrassing how naive I was," he said. *Newsweek* concluded that "a new battle" was raging in the war, this time to oust Falwell.

With that, Bakker and his champions went public with their own accusations. Even Jimmy Swaggart, who had kept his head down after the opening shots in the war, now seemed to be turning on Falwell. After talking to Bakker, Swaggart told the *Washington Post* that Jim obviously had a credibility problem, "but his story is very convincing. . . . I don't want to prejudge Jerry, but I do know there are a lot of situations that look very bad."

Jerry Falwell had problems enough already. He was under heavy doctrinal fire both from his own Baptists and his foster Pentecostals; by his own calculations, his Thomas Road ministry had lost two million dollars in donations because of his controversial new role at PTL. His motives were under constant scrutiny, and he was embroiled in managing PTL, from the financial crisis to the thorny question of who should host the show now that Dortch was gone. He got involved in a comic opera standoff with Pat Boone, the aging charismatic crooner who was the clear choice of the Bakker faction.

Boone's name kept being dropped by people like Don Lee and James Watt, and the singer himself coyly told the press that he could contribute a lot to PTL, but he hadn't been asked. Braced about that on one of the talk shows, Falwell allowed that Boone was one of the major talents in the nation, and he could have the job anytime he wanted to call Lynchburg. It was an adroit way of saying the offer wouldn't be made short of hell freezing over, and nothing further was heard from Boone.

What was worse, Falwell was finally beginning to understand the financial disaster he had walked into. In Dortch's report to the new board at the outset, it had looked rosy enough: a comfortable operating surplus, $172 million in assets, and debts of only $42 million. Even if there was a temporary cash problem, it should be easy enough to fix, or if the hidden agenda was indeed bankruptcy and liquidation, there could be a tidy pot of leftover assets, just as Bailey Smith so indiscreetly had predicted. Then came the claim for hotel occupancy taxes, which could open new federal tax liabilities and force the ministry to set aside enormous reserves. When sales of the lifetime partnerships were stopped, more than half the ministry's income stopped with them. And in the welter of checking accounts, secret funds, and hidden liabilities, new debts turned up nearly every day.

The books were "a mess," Harry Hargrave announced after his first look at them. But from now on, PTL would be oriented to ministering, not to bricks and mortar. The new regime would sell the "extraneous" assets—such fripperies as boats, limousines, and the five luxurious houses whimsically known as "parsonages" at Tega Cay. Austerity was to be the watchword: Credit cards would be curtailed; executives would drive their own cars; people would fly coach rather than first class. And Falwell, who had quipped only months earlier that he hadn't issued any financial statements for two years because "I got ornery," solemnly declared those days over. The time had come for all the nation's sixteen hundred TV preachers and four hundred thousand pastors to be accountable. "Let's tell everything," he said. It was probably good advice, but Falwell himself found it as hard to take as ever.

The first layoffs came within a week, cutting more than 200 people from a payroll that turned out to be 1,480—well short of the 2,000 that PTL had been claiming. The layoffs gave the new regime a chance to purge some of the diehard Bakkerites, including Vi Azvedo, the Goodmans, Deanna Dortch Collins, and Jim's executive secretary, Shirley Fulbright, who had handled the delicate salaries and bonuses and was herself paid $209,881 for her secretarial labors in her last sixteen months.

But it was clear that worse was to come. The new auditors were mystified by the books; at one point, Nims announced that $92 million had vanished "into a black hole." That was a considerable dramatization: The money wasn't missing, just untraced, and the figure was to dwindle rapidly, first to $12 million and then to near zero. Still, donations were down, and the red ink was getting deeper.

In mid-month Falwell declared the "May emergency." The ministry needed $7 million by the first of June and another $25 million by Labor Day. "We are on very thin ice," he said. Lee and his PTL partners were calling for a referendum, but "This is the referendum," Falwell said. If the faithful didn't pay up, there would be no more PTL.

What followed was a classic evangelical tease. First Falwell said the response was wonderful, so good that he was going to raise the target: not just $7 million but $10 million in May. Five days later all was gloom again; the drive was falling short, and "This is not crying wolf." PTL owed $8 million to television stations for running the show, Falwell said; twenty stations had already canceled, and forty more were threatening. How could the word of God be heard? Then, on June 1, he declared victory. The May emergency had turned into a May miracle.

But no sooner had the hallelujahs died away than the revision came out. The real contribution for May was $8.5 million, well short of the revised $10 million target. Worse, when past receipts for the lifetime partnerships were properly accounted as reserves, it turned out that the ministry had been losing $3 million a month for the past nine months. PTL was going to need $4.5 million a month for the indefinite future; every partner should send at least $50 immediately. The only constant in Falwell's financial follies was the inexorable growth of the total debt figure: first $42 million, then $50 million, then $65 million, then $70 million. It would wind up at $72 million, with assets at $179 million. And $23 million of the debt was past due.

The biggest single holder of that debt was Roe Messner, the

church builder who had rung up $14.7 million in bills for building Heritage USA. Messner was an old friend of Jim Bakker's, but his relations with the new regime started out on a cordial note. Falwell took pains to say that Messner had been duped into channeling the payoff to Jessica Hahn and that the money owed him was specified as one of the ministry's chief obligations. But as time wore on, relations soured, and Messner became yet another of Falwell's former friends.

Messner said later that he had no inkling that his claim was disputed until he heard Grutman denouncing him at a press conference. "I almost fell out of this chair," Messner said. But the Falwell men said their misgivings had begun when Messner repeatedly failed to produce invoices to support his bills. Then came the stab in the back, said Nims: Messner, who had offered to set up an informal creditors' committee to work out an overall settlement, instead filed a mechanic's lien and a $14 million lawsuit against the ministry without giving any warning at all. Construction halted, and the half-finished Heritage Grand Towers Hotel was boarded up. And Falwell delivered one of his barbed tributes to Messner: "I just thought he was such a warm, wonderful, sincere guy. But every time he'd agree to something, it never happened."

If the fiscal mess was bad and getting worse, it did serve one useful purpose: It was a continuing public reminder of just how profligate Jim and Tammy had been, and Falwell lost few chances to rub that in. As the weeks passed, the details of lavish living flowed in a steady dribble of leaks to the press: the Gucci briefcases; $11,399 for a chartered jet to visit a marriage counselor; $67,000 worth of women's clothing; a restaurant tip for 119 percent of the bill. The Bakkers' plunder for 1986 grew in the latest accounting by $300,000, to $1.9 million.

"Funds were raised apparently under false pretenses," said Falwell. The word was passed that the IRS was investigating PTL; that it was challenging $1.3 million in what seemed to be personal expenses for the Bakkers; that the U.S. attorney's office was looking into criminal charges of mail fraud, tax fraud, wire fraud, and extortion. Hundreds of thousands of dollars had been paid to "consultants" who did no work, Hargrave said; "We had people to hold hats for people who held hats." Somebody had bugged the corporate offices.

It was ostensibly to raise money that PTL announced an auction of some of the gaudiest Bakker artifacts—among them the notorious doghouse, a 1927 Franklin car, some gold-plated bathroom fixtures, two executive desks imported from Italy, and the seven-foot brass giraffe. But the TV footage of the artifacts eclipsed the actual income: Bids totaled only $200,000, far short of the targeted $500,000. A well-wisher bought the doghouse for $4,500, then gave it back to be sold again. That time it fetched only $600.

The most spectacular reminder of lush living came when Nims and Hargrave took the press on a tour of the Presidential Suite—three thousand square feet of ostentation, from the gold-plated swan faucets and ninety-two throw pillows to wall-to-wall mirrors and Tammy's fifty-foot-long walk-in closet, lit by crystal chandeliers. It was "early Imelda Marcos," somebody quipped, and if Tammy's spendthrift image hadn't yet been set in concrete, that did it. Sadly for the photographers, the shoes had already been stripped from their long racks.

In California, Jim and Tammy were still riding the cycles of hope and despair. Flowers and encouraging words from well-wishers alternated with grim news from back east: At Heritage USA, their presence was fading quickly from the scene. Their books, tapes, and autographed gewgaws were still on display, but the giant heads on the entry billboard had been painted over, and they were no longer mentioned on the guided tour. On top of everything else, seventeen-year-old Tammy Sue eloped with twenty-four-year-old Doug Chapman, a lifeguard at the water park, and friends said Jim and Tammy were no happier about that than any other parents would be.

Throughout the spring, there were flurries of reports about new opportunities for them. The new Fox TV network had just dropped Joan Rivers as the host of a talk show, and Tammy let it be known that she and Jim had been asked to replace her. But Fox denied it, and it turned out that the invitation was for one night. The Ohio preacher Leroy Jenkins said he had offered Jim and Tammy $175,000 a year to host a Christian television show, to be sent by satellite to cable systems with fully two hundred million subscribers. Since that number was more than twice the number of TV homes in America, it sounded a little suspect. But, then, so did Jenkins. The *Washington Post* reported he had spent more than three years in prison for conspiring to commit arson and assault.

Jim was veering between angry determination and something like inert hopelessness. It may have been the jeering press tour of the Presidential Suite that triggered his phone call to Falwell on May 17. The tour was certainly one of the things he complained about; it was "totally out of order," Falwell quoted him later. Falwell replied blandly that Hargrave and Nims didn't mean to embarrass him, that "They were simply following through with a commitment to openness and full disclosure." And when Jim said it was preposterous to accuse him of stealing ninety-two million dollars from the ministry, Falwell said nobody had accused Jim personally of stealing anything like that much.

Jim's real purpose in calling was to demand the return of his ministry. You promised I could have it back, he told Falwell; the time has come. Until then, Falwell had denied even discussing any comeback, but now he judged he would have to acknowledge the promise and justify reneging on it. So he did, brilliantly and at some length. Falwell said later he had taped that call, and he recited many times what he said. His accounts varied in the tellings; what follows is a composite from several interviews and press conferences:

"I said, 'Jim, here's what I want to say to you. When I was there March seventeenth and confronted you with the story I had heard, that you raped some girl in the Florida hotel, you advised me in a private meeting that you did not rape anyone, that in fact, your wife at that time was in love with another man and you were trying to win her love back and hoping to make her jealous.

" 'John Wesley Fletcher, per your request, brought a nineteen-year-old [sic] girl down from New York named Jessica Hahn. You told me that when the door was closed and you and Jessica were in that room, that "I did not rape her. If anything, she raped me. I could not even manage an erection. Fifteen minutes later I was taking a shower, crying and saying, 'Oh, God, I've been with a whore.' " Jim, that is the story you told me.

" 'We came back into the room where several people were. . . . You said to me, "Jerry, I want you to take the ministry." And I asked you the question "Why do you want me to take it?" You said, "You're the only preacher I trust right now." . . . After I had agreed, [you] asked the question "Do you think I can ever come back to PTL?" '

" 'I told you, "Jim, I understand the Assemblies of God are about to defrock you. However, I understand they also have a restoration plan. If they can, in the next year or two years, restore you, and all that happens—if you're truly forgiven—if what you told me is true, no intercourse, no hush money—" ' He broke in and said, 'Well, I didn't—I didn't say no intercourse.' I said, 'You said you could not get an erection. I think I arrived at the correct assumption.' So he stopped. ' "There's no reason why the Assemblies of God should not restore you to the ministry. And I want to tell you that if God wants you back at PTL, I will not stand in your way." '

"I said, 'Jim, since that time I have learned that not only did you have sex with Jessica Hahn, so did your associate John Wesley Fletcher. And a third person, a member of your team, went in with the intention of having sex with her. And she was prostrate and on the floor, unable to respond, and could not accommodate him. And I've learned, Jim, that two weeks after that, in Hawaii, you went to that person and asked the question "Did you get her, too?" Jim, that made my blood boil.

" 'Now, Jim, I've also heard the homosexual stories, and I must tell you I believe them.' I didn't give him Gary Smith's name, but since Gary's decided to go public, Gary was one of them. I said, 'There have been four of them, Jim, that I know about. One of them told me about your attempts to have sex with him. He refused, but he told me about it. And when I mentioned his name somewhere, that name was taken out of that board meeting and carried to you. You then called this person at home—because he passed this information along to one of our people since then—and you, Jim, said to him, "Why did you tell that? You were as much guilty as I." '

"Jim did not respond, perhaps because there were others in the room, perhaps Tammy Faye, I don't know. I said, 'Jim, I've heard the stories. I now know the financial situation. And I must tell you now that you cannot return. I would do a disservice to God—as much as I love you and care for you—I would be doing a disservice to God and the church at large to allow you to come back, now or ever.' "

It was a remarkable performance—at least as much in the retelling as in the original speech.

As it happened, Tammy Faye was not in the room with her husband during the call. She was sitting in a room near the swimming pool with Don Hardister; she had asked him to listen to the conversation on an extension phone, hoping that Falwell would admit that he had indeed promised to give the ministry back and that Hardister would be a witness to the admission.

Hardister later confirmed the gist of the long talk as Falwell reported it. But he heard something else that was to shatter his stubborn faith in Jim Bakker, a line that Falwell omitted from his tailored public account. When Falwell brought up the charges of homosexuality, Hardister said, Bakker replied: "Well, that's ridiculous. You know that's not true." Falwell said, "You never made a pass at ——— ———?" naming the former executive who told of bolting from Bakker's bedroom. That was a man Hardister knew and liked, and Bakker's silence in response to the question stunned him; he had put no credence in Smith or the other witnesses whose names he had heard before, he said, but this was one man whose word he would take. He walked out of the room like a zombie, and Tammy told Jim that he had been listening. "What did you hear?" Jim said, looking a bit strained. "Then you heard him say he'd give it back?" Hardister confirmed that, and Jim and Tammy began exulting: "We've got a witness now!"

Hardister walked away, feeling only turmoil. The next morning he turned over the command to another guard, got on a plane, and flew back home to Tega Cay. He told his wife, Pam, what he had heard, but nobody else, and he brooded for a week until he got a call from Falwell himself, wanting to know what was wrong. Hardister told him he had been listening in on the phone call and was having problems with the homosexual business. It couldn't be true. "It's just crazy," he said.

He thought that would be the end of his job, but Falwell was sympathetic. "Don, you've been with him a long time, and I'm not going to get mad with you. But you're wrong. You need to check it out."

It was only then that Hardister called his old friend the former executive. "I'm not talking to the media," Don said, "but I've got to know, because I look like an absolute idiot." Yes, said his friend, you do, "and I understand, because I worked for him for years before it happened to me."

Hardister cried at that. Later he got increasingly angry at the thought that he might have been unwittingly guarding the door during some of Jim's frolics; they were having jokes at his expense, he said once, knowing he was the perfect cover since nobody would suspect him of any such leanings. But he is a man with a deep need for a leader, and he was already switching his fealty to Falwell. Falwell had asked him to stay with Jim, so he went back to California. He wasn't any kind of spy for Falwell, he said, and he still considered himself part of the Bakker household. But never again was he really comfortable with Jim.

The guerrilla war against Falwell was still mostly underground, with no important allies lined up with Lee, Evans, and Smith. Oral Roberts and his son, Richard, had been on Bakker's side from the start, even inviting Jim and Tammy to appear on Oral's TV show, but Oral wasn't attacking Falwell. Swaggart wasn't outright hostile either, but he was rumbling like a stirring volcano: "If [Falwell] promised that thing back to Bakker, he owes it back to Bakker. It's not right to get something under false pretenses." James Watt had left Falwell's board, but hadn't yet gone public with his complaints; in fact, he seemed to be playing a double game, trying to get information on Falwell's moves. He wrote Grutman a conciliatory letter in mid-May, assuring him that he hadn't talked to the press and wanted to be helpful to Falwell. As Falwell later quoted the letter, "Please give me a call and update me." Jim and Tammy had kept their peace. When they finally decided to attack Falwell in public, they chose a national forum: Ted Koppel's "Nightline."

The *Newsweek* article detailing the circumstantial case against Falwell had hit the newsstands on May 25, and it set off the new round of fighting. Koppel followed up the story the next night with a telephone conversation with Jim and a long, sometimes heated argument between Mike Evans and Gary Smith on the attack and Roy Grutman and Mark DeMoss defending Falwell. The big news was Jim's flat statement from Palm Springs: "I'm convinced they came here with the motive to steal Heritage USA and my ministry. I'm convinced of that, yeah." Smith and Evans backed that case, with modifications; Smith said that Falwell had admitted at the April 23 meeting that he had indeed promised to return the ministry. But after that, Smith said, Falwell added that he had found such financial and moral misbehavior that "There was no way he would give the ministry back to Jim Bakker. He would run it in the ground first."

The next night, Jim and Tammy made their own case on-screen with Koppel—a virtuoso display of injured innocence, qualified repentance, and Christian charity for their enemies. It was a measure of how the story was gripping the nation that this "Nightline" interview got the highest ratings in the show's records, eclipsing Koppel's discussions of such national crises as the Iran/contra scandal, the U.S. bombing of Libya, and the space shuttle disaster. The PTL saga, Koppel began, had "taken on the irresistible dimensions of a national soap opera. . . . It has revealed the hypocrisy that is buried just beneath the surface in most of us, claiming to be incensed, even outraged by what we hear, all the while clamoring for more."

More was what he got. "I think we've made a lot of mistakes, and I'm very sorry about it," said Jim. But he was hardly forthcoming about what those mistakes could have been, beyond allowing a grateful board of directors to pay him and Tammy huge bonuses. "We're a tad flamboyant," Jim conceded, and he said he was sad "that I've been part of something to bring this much, you know, pain and sorrow to the body of Christ." Apart from that, he insisted that Jessica Hahn's story of near rape was a lie, that he was not homosexual, that the stories being put out about their salaries were fantasies, and that Falwell had betrayed them and stolen their ministry. Jim said he believed in miracles, so he and Tammy still hoped to be restored to PTL, but if God and the partners didn't want that, he wouldn't fight. "If God cannot deliver us and restore our ministry, then we really wouldn't want it back anyway," he said. He could dream of starting another ministry, perhaps in California, "and I dream about maybe going back on television someday. And I'd like the people to write me if they want me to."

Koppel had started the interview on a hard line, and he stuck to it manfully at first: "While everyone is talking about love and forgiveness, you [and Falwell are] sticking knives in one another's ribs. It is, in a sense, a really disgusting display. I mean, on both sides."

But Jim wouldn't be provoked. "Yes, I agree," he said, "and I don't want to be a part of that."

The soft answer turned away wrath, and for the last ten minutes of the show Koppel seemed nearly stupefied as Jim and Tammy bathed him in bathos. He tried to raise the subject of the doghouse, but Tammy took the occasion to apologize moistly to the dogs for the loss of their quarters. "I'm sorry, Snuggles," she said.

Jim drove home the lesson. "We've made a lot of mistakes, but we have been forgiven, thank God," he concluded. "There is hope in Jesus Christ, and there is forgiveness. . . . God loves you. He really does."

"He really, really does," said Tammy.

"Bye-bye," said Jim.

Helplessly, Koppel thanked them and cut it off.

It took Jerry Falwell to deal with that tidal wave of treacle, and he started his counterattack as soon as Bakker opened fire. Even before Jim and Tammy appeared on "Nightline," Falwell assured his share of the headlines by responding to their telephoned accusation in a no-holds-barred, ninety-minute press conference. Falwell said Bakker "either has a terrible memory, or is very dishonest, or is emotionally ill." And he said it again: He had not stolen Jim Bakker's ministry.

Falwell did acknowledge that he had told Bakker he would return PTL someday, but he admitted it by rehashing the May 17 phone call, underlining the newly uncovered sins that made restoration impossible. Bakker would have to "come clean about Jessica Hahn and repent," Falwell said sternly. "That little girl was injured for life by that terrible incident." Bakker would also have to repent "homosexual problems dating from 1956 to the present time," Falwell said, and this account of the phone call stressed an inconclusive argument over whether Jim would confront the witnesses. As Falwell told it, Jim told him grudgingly to set up such a meeting, but nothing more was heard about that. Finally, said Falwell, Bakker "needs to return the millions of dollars that have been taken from the coffers of this ministry at the cost of widows and supporters." If Jim did all that, Falwell said sternly, he could be forgiven his sins. But even then he could not return to the PTL ministry.

Falwell had been saving a special store of ammunition for just this occasion. Nearly a month earlier, while Jim still believed in Falwell and his friend Roe Messner was still on Falwell's side, Falwell asked Messner to visit Palm Springs to negotiate with Jim and Tammy over their finances. As Falwell told the story, Messner was to ask what could be done to help them, but in Messner's version, Falwell asked him to find out " 'what it would take to keep their mouths shut.' That's a direct quote." Messner flew to Palm Springs and found the Bakkers in a receptive and undemanding mood. Falwell himself had suggested most of the items on the resulting list, Messner said; he wrote them down himself on a sheet of Tammy's pale yellow stationery, with a cover note to Falwell: "Jim and Tammy gave me this list of things they would like to receive. Jim said they would accept whatever you decide. They both looked great and had very good attitudes. Jim said he would not do anything to hurt you or the PTL partners. His desire is that the ministry will succeed. Jim is skeptical of Roy Grutman.''

That hardly sounded like a set of unconditional demands, and Jim and Tammy insisted later that they thought of the requests as a starting point for bargaining. "It was sort of like a Sears and Roebuck wish book,'' Jim said. But the list was impressive: Jim and Tammy wanted their salaries paid for life, three hundred thousand dollars a year for him, one hundred thousand for her. They asked for hospitalization insurance, rights to their books and records, secretarial help and telephone service for a year, security protection, two cars, the house at Tega Cay with its furniture, and attorneys' fees for their legal troubles.

When Messner read Falwell the list from the Palm Springs airport, Falwell was so excited that he wanted it sent by express delivery, not mailed. Messner understood why when Falwell used it as the biggest gun in his counterattack on Jim. He read the list to the news conference with a withering denunciation: "I don't see any repentance here. I see the greed, the self-centeredness, and the avarice that brought them down.'' It made a nice sound bite for the evening news, and Falwell held up the list long enough to make sure the cameras got that, too.

So two days later, Jim and Tammy called a truce. "If this be a holy war, I am declaring a ceasefire,'' Jim said in a statement handed to the press outside the Palm Springs compound. "The Lord did not call the shepherds to cause dissension among the sheep. . . . Tammy and I are going to minister . . . we want to preach the Gospel of Jesus Christ to hurting people, and that's what we're going to do.'' They may have made a mistake by talking to Koppel, he said; people he trusted had urged him to tell his side of the story, but the war seemed to have escalated as a result. He should have listened to the verse from 2 Chronicles (20:15) that so many well-wishers had sent him: "Don't be afraid! Don't be paralyzed by this mighty army! For the battle is not yours, but God's!'' So God bless Jerry Falwell, Jim said; let him have PTL. Tammy broke in: "We wouldn't want to be there if God wants Jerry Falwell there.''

It was time to think about the future, Jim went on. He had been offered many pastorships and TV ministries, though he wouldn't say where. But he and Tammy were planning their own ministry in California. "We are being forced to," he said, "by the volume of mail coming in," up to four hundred letters a day. The important thing would be workshops for hurting people, and if funds could be raised, there might be television, too. There wasn't much money, he said. He had about fifty thousand dollars left, and his daughter about the same, "and when that's gone, that's gone." If God wanted Jim and Tammy at PTL, he would put them back. But the war was over. They weren't going to scream and yell and fight anymore. And he added, "If we have to, we'll hold up a white flag and say we surrender."

The idea of starting over had real appeal. It was near the end of May when an old friend from Atlanta, a preacher named Earl Paulk, showed up in Palm Springs with a couple of friends, and while he was there, the workshop leader June Nichols called from Heritage to say she was talking with a California preacher, Ty Beason, who said it was really time to get Jim restored now. Paulk and Beason got excited about the idea; they agreed with Kenneth Copeland, an evangelist from Fort Worth, Texas, to meet with some friends a week later in Anaheim at a Believers' Convention. Jim and Tammy went, too, all expenses paid, and the plot gathered steam. There was going to be a larger prayer meeting, a Believers' Conference, at Oral Roberts University in Tulsa on June 22. Jim would preach there and be restored to the ministry, with Oral's blessings, as a step toward starting the new television ministry in California. Jim started calling it the New Covenant Partners. And to give him faith in it, the apostles perched him and Tammy on the coffee table and reassured them, over and over: "God's going to restore you."

Jim and Tammy seemed willing enough to think so, but Don Hardister was having problems. It was all very well to talk about restoration, but the homosexual issue was still open. Hardister had tried to tell Ty Beason about it on the phone that first day, but Beason said they would take care of that in Anaheim. Hardister thought that meant somebody would take Jim aside and confront him, but that didn't seem to be happening. So Don went to Beason and told him what his friend the witness had reported about Jim's attempt to seduce him. "There is some stuff to this homosexuality stuff," Hardister warned uncomfortably. "I'm not gonna go that far to say that it's full-blown, but there's something." But Beason and his friends just shushed him. Hardister tried to discuss it with Vi Azvedo, back in Heritage, but she put him off, too. Jim would talk to him, she said, and everything was going to be all right.

Hardister had the feeling that Jim was blowing hot and cold on him anyway. At one point, when Jim was impressed by the way Don negotiated a deal, he said Hardister would be his main man in the New Covenant Partners. "Don, I give you my word," he said, "I will not hire one person unless I talk to you first." That was probably unrealistic from the start, since Jim had always been impulsive, but within a week he had announced the appointment of a man Hardister just could not stand. Don decided the time had come to quit, but he meant to do it right; he figured to stay on through the Believers' Conference in Tulsa, three weeks off, and leave when everyone was feeling as good as possible. Meanwhile, he suggested to Jim and Tammy it would be a good time to go back to Tega Cay, pack up their belongings there, and get ready for the new start in California.

On June 10, they went back. It wasn't like thieves in the night —Jim, Tammy, and Jamie Charles flew first class from Palm Springs on a commercial airline, stopping over in Dallas—but it was far from the triumphal return they had long hoped for. No matter how they insisted that the fight was over and tried to scale back their ambitions just to starting fresh, they kept flirting with the notion that a miracle might happen, that God might sweep them back through the gates to the PTL throne. As the sociologist Jeffrey Hadden recalled, Jim had quoted a poignant question from Jamie Charles when they were first banished: "Daddy, will I be able to go back and get my toys?" He was really asking his father's question, Hadden said, and Jim was still seeking the answer.

The *Observer*, tipped in advance by Hardister, had a photographer waiting to meet Jim and Tammy in Dallas. They were chatty and affable with their old adversary. Jim said he was considering five separate offers for new ministries; he hoped to be on the air within a month but hadn't got all the cameras yet. "We're pretty good at starting over," he said. They would preach on the street if necessary, but they wanted most to found a healing center for people in crisis. "That's what the church is all about. We're to be our brother's keeper," he said.

They arrived to a celebrity welcome in Charlotte, Tammy carrying her high heels down the landing ramp, followed by Jamie Charles lugging a skateboard. When the limo arrived at the Tega Cay house, she knelt and kissed the driveway, and they went in to find twenty-five friends who had gathered for an impromptu welcome-home party at one o'clock in the morning. Tammy's mother, Rachel Grover, was there; so were Jim's parents, Raleigh and Furnia, along with Vi Azvedo and her husband, Ed, Howard and Vestal Goodman, and Tammy Sue. It was a loyalist gathering, and the talk was predictably hotheaded. According to the *Observer*, several of the friends counseled Jim and Tammy to "march in there and take it back."

For that evening, at least, they held to their peacemaking line. But the Bring Bakkers Back faction kept a swirl of rumors going all next day among the true believers packing the plaza in front of the hotel. Jim and Tammy were coming any moment; they would take control; they would march into the studio and take over the taping of the daily show; no, they would just sit in the front row of the audience; no, Falwell had banned them from the grounds. Six miles away at Tega Cay, more than fifty reporters stood watch outside a barricade, manned by the local police. One of the neighbors, concerned for the health of his shrubbery, rented a Porta-John.

Jim kept kicking around the idea of going over to Heritage, just to say good-bye. Hardister didn't like it. He knew Jim was at least halfway thinking of a coup; Jim had talked several times about appearing on the show and announcing, "I'm back." Hardister wanted no part of that, but finally he got Jim's word that it would be just a drive-through, a private visit with nobody stepping out of the car. "If you get out, I'm going to quit," Don said; when Jim promised not to, Hardister called Hargrave's people to warn them about the visit. They ducked the press by riding a speedboat to Hardister's house, a cove or two away on Lake Wylie, where the Goodmans' son Rick was waiting with a Mercedes. "We just have to go back and see if we can turn it loose," Jim told him.

By then, somebody had phoned for Bakkerite reinforcements at Heritage, and word was spreading in the hotel and along the mall. When the Mercedes arrived in front of the hotel, there was a crowd of several hundred of the faithful. Some cheered; some prayed; some spoke in tongues.

Whatever Hardister had promised, the car stopped. "Jim got caught up in the emotion," Hardister said later. "We had a serious arguing match in the car." Jim and Tammy got out, to be mobbed ecstatically. "We love you," Tammy screamed; she embraced everyone she could reach, leaving lipstick smears on a dozen cheeks.

But nothing more happened. It was the high-water mark of the return from exile. There was no plan of action, no loyal troops waiting for the coup; no angels with trumpets appeared to lead the mob in a march on the studio. In fact, there were some angry faces in the crowd. Jim realized, Hardister said later, that there was going to be a fight if he tried to come back. In two minutes, Jim and Tammy climbed back into the car. Tammy appeared in public once more, at an evening prayer meeting, but there was no more talk of taking over. To the microphones jabbed through the window of the departing Mercedes, Jim explained: "We just wanted to say good-bye to it all."

Was this really good-bye? "Maybe," Tammy said, and she giggled.

But Jim had the last word: "If Jerry Falwell lets us, we'll come back, but otherwise we're going to start a new ministry." They went back to Tega Cay, where Falwell had already made his position clear by giving notice that they were to vacate the place by June 15.

Things deteriorated after that. Don Hardister was furious that Jim had broken his word; he tried to resign, only to be talked out of it by Harry Hargrave. There was a strained reconciliation with Jim, but Don was feeling a distinct chill between him and the Bakkers. Perhaps, he said later, Vi Azvedo had told Jim that he had been talking about the homosexual business. Whatever it was, "I wasn't welcome in the house like I once was." Rick Goodman was there all the time now, and Jim was starting to take advice from him.

Jim's plans were up in the air, too. The restoration ceremony at Oral Roberts University had been looking shaky. Oral's son, Richard, had always been cordial and supportive during the exile; several times he had told Hardister, "Don't you go without anything. If you need anything, you call me—airplanes or whatever." But when Hardister asked Richard whether Oral's Falcon would be available for the flight east, Richard hung back. "If you want me to pursue it," he said, "I will talk to Dad, but I will only do it after you tell me you have prayed about it considerably." Hardister didn't know what had changed, but he figured that meant no.

And on the Sunday after the visit to Heritage, Oral and Richard called Jim to tell him flatly that he wouldn't be welcome in Tulsa.

Hardister heard only Jim's end of that conversation, but he said Oral seemed to be put off by the reports of the Bakkers' salaries and bonuses. "Jim said, 'Oral, you know, I raised thirty million dollars in one week. What do you pay a man who can do that?'" Hardister recalled. Roberts replied something like "You've missed the whole point. There's no need in us even talking about it. You've made more money in one year than I've made in twenty." Jim said "Okay, fine." But he was stung, Hardister said: "He got right up and went to bed, which was his escape, always. He was very depressed. It hurt him bad."

By then, PTL was in bankruptcy.

It didn't mean that the organization was out of business, Falwell's people protested. PTL was merely seeking the protection of the court from its creditors while working out a plan to reorganize. "We can turn the ship around and move it to a responsible course," Hargrave promised. "We're not going to miss a step. This is not an embarrassment. This is a new start." The staff applauded, but this time the hallelujahs came in whispers. No matter how many times people were reminded that Chrysler, Penn Central, Texaco, and Continental Airlines all had emerged successfully from bankruptcy, the word had an ominous ring. To the ordinary Joe, Hardister fretted, "It says 'gone under.'"

Falwell's men insisted that it would be business as usual for PTL, that they still hoped to pay the creditors in full and emerge from bankruptcy within a year. But they were also making sure the blame for the mess fell on the right head. Don Lee, among others, reacted to the move by saying it was only what Falwell had intended all along. But Roy Grutman denied that Falwell was in any way to blame. "Jim Bakker can say whatever Jim Bakker wants to say," Grutman orated to a packed news conference. "He can come here and kiss the ground. He can kiss the Blarney stone. The reality, the fact is in the numbers. The numbers don't lie; they don't forget; they don't go away. They may be hidden for a while, but we are finding them. Those numbers show that the deplorable situation which brought us to this problem was created by Jim Bakker and his administration, not by us. And we're going to solve it, honestly, correctly, and quickly."

Grutman also tossed a grenade in Roe Messner's direction. One reason for going into bankruptcy, he said, was to protect PTL from lawsuits, both current and prospective—including the fourteen-million-dollar suit Messner had filed. Almost incidentally, Grutman allowed that the real debt to Messner might be "drastically smaller" than that. And Jerry Nims added that the bankruptcy filing would also prevent the lifetime partners from suing to claim an ownership interest in PTL.

The Falwell regime had been careful never to acknowledge the partners' claim, since that would concede a huge new layer of debt. But now Nims spelled it out, implying that it was a conspiracy to do PTL in. "Somebody was thinking that out quite well, and the end result would have been the total destruction of this organization," he said.

That was a message to a judge named Rufus Reynolds in South Carolina's federal bankruptcy court, the next battleground in the struggle for PTL. And the partners' claim was the key to the battle.

Lucille Bogan, seventy-six, a retired school administrator from Fenwick Island, Delaware, watched the Bakkers on "Nightline." "I couldn't see any repentance," she said. "I think of all the little people that send their very hard-earned money in, thinking they will help spread religion and do good things for people. It's disillusioning.

"I'm not a follower of Jerry Falwell either; but he comes across as a sincere, religious person, and he seems to have a sense of mission here."

Chapter 11

Farewell, Falwell

Norman Roy Grutman swaggered into the South Carolina bankruptcy court like Ivan Boesky making his move on a ladies' investment club. He left without his pants.

Even by New York measure, Grutman is abrasive. He uses his booming baritone and florid vocabulary as major weapons, never missing a chance to drip a little venom on the foe of the moment, and his insults range from juvenile to Shakespearean. In the days when he was opposing Jerry Falwell, he invariably referred to the preacher as "Foulwell," and among his many other targets in the PTL case, Grutman casually sideswiped Tammy Faye: "The woman is an incessant cataract." Portly and round-faced, he affects granny glasses, a red bandanna handkerchief, and a floppy hat reminiscent of the Scarecrow's in *The Wizard of Oz.* One of the Carolina lawyers recalled with glee that at first meeting, Grutman was wearing suspenders with naked women on them—a New York in-joke that doesn't translate well more than three blocks west of Madison Avenue. And his legal tactics are confrontational: He concedes no points, lets pass no tiny errors, mercilessly attacks any flaw in law or logic, and fights to the death for each ounce of flesh. "I asked myself, What is a Baptist fundamentalist preacher doing with this mad dog for a lawyer?" said one attorney involved in the case. The answer was that they suited each other.

There is an air of genteel regret about the bankruptcy court in Columbia, South Carolina; it is a place where dead dreams can be

decently buried, with as little acrimony as possible. A failed enterprise is a sad thing, the ethos goes, but it needn't be tragic. The aim
of the court is to spread the pain as fairly as possible, saving whatever can be salvaged and making sure nobody profits indecently
from the wreckage. In the big cities things may be considerably more
adversarial, but that isn't the way it works in courtly Columbia. "It's
a good old boys' club down there," Jerry Falwell was to conclude,
with a touch of bitterness.

The clubbiness comes naturally. South Carolina is a small state,
and it doesn't generate much bankruptcy work. There is one permanent judge in the federal bankruptcy court, a regular visitor handles
any case that might pose a conflict for the presiding judge, and a
tight fraternity of perhaps two dozen lawyers specialize in bankruptcy. They work together all the time, representing one side or the
other in a case or serving as examiner or referee, as chance and the
whims of the court decide. They have learned to speak quietly, deal
openly, and trust one another. These lawyers aren't the tobacco-
chewing hicks of southern courthouse legend; they include scholars, art lovers, and opera buffs, and they value the down-home
virtues of craftsmanship, moderation, and integrity. They do business on a handshake and a telephone call, and they don't cut one
anothers' throats. And as the *National Law Journal* remarked, they
study the moods and inclinations of the judge "as farmers study the
weather."

The complex PTL case, with more than fourteen hundred creditors and nearly two hundred million dollars in assets, involved
practically every lawyer in the South Carolina bankruptcy bar. As
PTL's local counsel, Falwell had hired Walter Theus, Jr. But Theus
was the son-in-law of the permanent bankruptcy judge, and that fact
made it necessary to assign the case to the visiting judge, Rufus W.
Reynolds, of Greensboro, North Carolina. At eighty, Reynolds was
the oldest active judge in the nation's federal bankruptcy court, a
shrewd, unpretentious storekeeper's son with Carolina roots going
back two centuries. He got into bankruptcy practice more or less by
chance, because not much else was going on when he hung out his
shingle in the depression year of 1933, and the lessons of those hard
times stayed with him. In Judge Reynolds's court, a debtor in bankruptcy was held to the judge's own frugal standard of living, which
meant until very recently that the debtor couldn't keep a color TV.

The judge officially retired in 1986 but immediately volunteered for extra service. Characteristically, he gave up his luxurious chambers and moved uncomplainingly into a windowless cubbyhole to signal the change.

It was probably inevitable that Judge Reynolds would collide with Grutman. And when it came, the collision was over an ethical question: Did Grutman have a conflict of interest in the case?

That was an arguable point. Whether or not Grutman had actually been Falwell's agent in persuading Bakker to turn over the ministry, he had acted previously as Falwell's attorney. He was recommended to Dortch by Falwell's men. He had told several people that he represented Bakker and Dortch as well as PTL, and Jim and Tammy both filed affidavits saying Grutman had assured them that he was their lawyer. Jim said Grutman had actually drafted his resignation statement and advised him to urge the other members of PTL's old board to resign. Tammy said she had argued against the resignations, but Grutman had repeatedly reassured her "that my husband and I would get PTL back in a few weeks. On one occasion, he told me to quit thinking and sent me a book to read instead." Now Grutman was opposing Bakker on behalf of PTL and Falwell.

Bakker's lawyers, headed by San Francisco's flamboyant Melvin Belli, maintained that Grutman should be thrown off the case and forced to return nearly five hundred thousand dollars in legal fees to PTL. Grutman argued that he had represented only PTL, never the Bakkers as individuals. He said he was looking forward to cross-examining Jim, who "may wind up in jail for perjury." The whole issue of conflict was a red herring, Grutman said, "simply made up out of the emptiness of what is in Mr. Belli's aging mind." That could have been more tactfully put, since Judge Reynolds was the same age as Belli: eighty. In any case, the judge told Grutman tartly, "This is a very serious matter. . . . If I were in your shoes, I'd take the money you've earned so far and go home." Grutman chose to tough it out, boasting about his nerve in risking the fee. It was just the old game of "get rid of the New York lawyer," he told the *National Law Journal*; when they got down to depositions and arguments on the conflict issue, "I don't anticipate an adverse outcome. I think Judge Reynolds will enjoy having me in his courtroom. I'm an excellent lawyer." That set the tone of the case: It was

to be high-stakes poker, with bluff and counterbluff all the way to
the final showdown.

At Tega Cay, the Goodman clan was on the rise all summer,
leading a squad of hotheaded Bakkerites who were pining for a
restoration. Jim and Tammy might be having another bout of depression, but the Goodmans were mad as hell on their behalf; they
wanted to make a fight for the house and for PTL, and on occasion
they meant that literally. When Tammy visited the evening prayer
session at Heritage USA, the gospel singer Howard Goodman saw a
local TV cameraman, Keith Rumph, trying to get the scene on
videotape. For all his sixty-five years, Goodman came on like a
sheriff's deputy in mirror sunglasses. Rumph, a small man at 130
pounds, said the 320-pound Goodman bore down on him, saying,
"Hey, boy, you better get that camera out of here before I punch
you down." Then, said Rumph, Goodman "hauled back and el-
bowed me hard in the chest and I buckled over." Rumph filed
assault charges and later sued for damages.

Howard's wife, Vestal, was equally ready to do battle. Once, after
a taping of the Falwell-style PTL show, she charged to the front of
the auditorium and loudly advised: "If you give to this man, you're
giving to a thief." And she was ready to take on Don Hardister's
security functions along with his adviser's role. Vestal was driving
Tammy Sue and Jamie to the Gatlinburg house one day when a
network news van gave chase, a scary, high-speed pursuit along the
twisting mountain roads. She solved the problem by stopping at a
truckers' restaurant and asking the drivers for help. Two big rigs
fenced in the TV van in the parking lot, and she drove on
unimpeded.

Eventually the loyalist crowd persuaded Jim and Tammy to fight
for Tega Cay. Tammy proclaimed defiance. They had been "hunted
like a scared animal" ever since the Falwell takeover, she told the
reporters, and loss of the $1.3 million house would be too much to
take. "I hope that Jerry Falwell never has to suffer the way he's made
us suffer," she said. She and Jim were down to their last $37,000;
Falwell's people had taken two of their dogs to the pound and
auctioned off the go-cart that Jim had given Jamie Charles for Christmas. As Jim told it, "The children keep crying, saying, 'Daddy,
please don't let them take our house away.' " Falwell's man DeMoss

called the charges "ludicrous," saying that the Bakkers had refused to answer repeated letters and phone calls and that "Our concern is not so much that they move out, but just that they communicate with us." Jim said the communications would come through a lawyer.

That was the last straw for Don Hardister, who was feeling increasingly shut out of the Bakker household and at ease in the Falwell camp. He quit the Bakkers with a succession of parting shots. Months later, he repented that; what he had said wasn't Christian, he regretted then, and he should have given Jim the benefit of the doubt, "but I said it." Hardister questioned the whole premise of prosperity theology and the Bakkers' life-style. He stopped short of saying he believed Jim was homosexual, but he denounced Jim for the money he had taken. "That's the part I can't deal with," Hardister said. "We've got staff on food stamps." And Nims quoted Hardister as saying that Jim and Tammy were holding cultish prayer meetings. They "were called sort of blood covenants," Nims said. "I don't think there was any blood shed, but observing to-the-death loyalty to the Bakkers to start a new ministry." Hardister did deny that story; Nims had misunderstood him, he explained.

Jim and Tammy didn't know what to do. Every time they made a move or a statement, Falwell trumped them. Jim lamented, "We know if we say something, there'll be a bigger mudball thrown back at us." So he returned to his pacifist line: They wouldn't fight; Falwell could keep the ministry; there should be peace in the body of Christ. "If Jim and Tammy have to go somewhere and fade away, if that will bring peace to the church world, all right. Let that be," Jim said late in June.

But other times it seemed they would have to fight. The Falwell people were practically inviting federal criminal charges against Jim and Tammy. "We've got documents and a lack of documents that we think somebody should come in and take a look at," Nims told the press, and the agencies willing to oblige included the FBI, the IRS, the Postal Inspection Service, the U.S. attorneys for North and South Carolina, and the South Carolina Tax Commission. The Justice Department said there would be no hiding behind the First Amendment if criminal violations were found. A federal grand jury was to begin hearings in August, and already there was talk of Jim's being indicted on charges of tax fraud, mail fraud, and wire fraud. Piously Falwell hoped the worst could be avoided. "I believe that it would be damaging to the cause of Christ in this country for a minister to go to jail," he said.

The danger was pointed up for Jim by a businessman friend from Charlotte who came to visit at Tega Cay, sneaking in by boat to avoid the reporters. He told Jim a story about a man trapped in his house by a flood. When rescuers arrived in a boat, the man refused to leave. "I'm believing in God to save me," he said. The water rose, and a helicopter came by. Again the man declined rescue, saying God would perform a miracle. But the water rose again, and he drowned. He arrived in heaven righteously indignant: "Hey, God, I was waiting on you." But God told him, "Well, I sent you a boat and a helicopter. What more did you want?" Perhaps, Jim concluded, it was time to accept some of the offers of help he was getting.

One of them came from a hotel executive in San Francisco, who sounded out Melvin Belli about Jim and his problems. Belli was a celebrity lawyer whose show business clients had ranged from Mae West to Lenny Bruce; he had defended Jack Ruby in the nationally televised murder of John Kennedy's assassin, Lee Harvey Oswald, but he hadn't had much national exposure in recent years. His prominent cases lately had been high-stakes ambulance chasing— damage suits after the 1984 Bhopal disaster in India and the Soviet downing of a Korean jetliner in 1983. Belli said he would be interested in the Bakkers, and soon they were having lunch at a restaurant called Filibusters in Rock Hill, South Carolina. Belli already knew a local lawyer, James Toms, a former employee; Toms would do most of the work on the case. It was the restaurant owner, a friend of Vestal Goodman's, who suggested one of the Columbia bankruptcy lawyers, W. Ryan Hovis, to help out. As things worked out, the aging Belli served mainly to help set strategy, fulminate to the media about Falwell, and host the Bakkers on his yacht, the 101-foot *Adequate Award,* when they visited San Francisco. Toms and Hovis were to be the boat and the helicopter to save Jim from drowning.

Meanwhile, Jim and Tammy's lives were on hold. They spent their time mainly plotting, brooding, and denying reality. They spun fantasies for the press, for their friends, and for the talk shows. The Assemblies of God had cleared Jim of homosexuality charges, he said on "Good Morning America." He had never given his ministry to Jerry Falwell; he had meant Richard Dortch to have it, and Falwell had betrayed him. They had seldom used credit cards, Tammy said righteously, never asked for an offering, never put money first. By midsummer, they probably believed all that.

Plans for their new ministry kept getting stalled in a maze of postponed promises and evasive excuses. Now they were talking about deciding whether to start over in California, Florida, or Tennessee. At one point, Jim announced grandly, "I've been invited to the great pulpits of America, but I'm not ready to speak." It was just one more symbol of frustration when the name Jim and Tammy had chosen for their ministry, New Covenant Partners, turned out to infringe the trademark of a charismatic magazine in Michigan, which threatened to take steps if the Bakkers used the name.

They left Tega Cay, saying they were going on vacation in Gatlinburg and would soon be back. But their claim to the lakeside house was shaky at best. The PTL board had indeed voted to give it to them, but that was to take place over several years; by the time they resigned, they had arguably earned only 5 percent of the place. So it wasn't long before the Falwell team packed up their goods, seven truckloads full, and sent them off to Gatlinburg, too. The Bakkers' equity in the house there had been deeded to Roe Messner, in part payment for the alterations he was making; but he said Jim and Tammy could stay there indefinitely, and the place silted up with furniture and movers' cartons. It was a jumble of piled-up belongings: lamps too big for their tables; too many chairs and sofas; fluffy pillows and stuffed animals everywhere; a kitchen so full of gadgets that there was hardly space to cook. The guest bathroom was the least crowded room in the house, but even it had a couple of stuffed dogs in residence.

Their finances were a mystery. Falwell's people hinted that there might be secret bank accounts in Switzerland and Greece, but the Bakkers kept talking about how broke they were. They were living on their retirement funds, Jim said once, and on the charity of friends. The Palm Springs house reportedly sold for six hundred thousand dollars, but it wasn't clear how much equity they had in it or what they did with the proceeds. Their salaries from PTL had been cut off. Still, they traveled compulsively all through the summer and early fall, visiting San Francisco, stopping in Palm Springs to empty the house there, driving east with the entourage. Tammy turned up in Nashville, where she recorded a new album: *Singing in the Rain.* And they talked of a "farewell tour" of the country, still dreaming of a comeback. "If the partners really get behind him," said Jim's brother Norm, "he'll be back—with a new ministry or at PTL."

In San Francisco there were parties on Belli's yacht and a shopping expedition for Tammy with Belli's wife, Lia, who supervised a new closer-cropped hairdo and a toning down of Tammy's makeup. Belli and the other lawyers held strategy sessions, war-gaming their court tactics and media battles. Jessica Hahn had tarnished herself badly with the *Playboy* photos, but should Jim accept *Playboy*'s offer to respond to her long story? Mike Clifford, an Arizona charismatic who was advising on public relations, counseled against it. Jim's loyal fans would be outraged if he had any dealings at all with *Playboy,* Clifford said; a reply could be good, but do it in another magazine, maybe *Esquire.*

The lawyers decided that when the time came for depositions, Jim should be allowed to tell his story, and they wouldn't object to wide-ranging questions even if the other side seemed to be fishing. "It may not be good from a legal standpoint, but it's better from a media standpoint," said Belli. They set up a nationwide 900 number, with a daily message so the faithful could call in and hear Jim and Tammy tell their side of the story in installments. The recorded chats were mainly diatribes against Falwell, mixed with pieties, prayers, and Tammy's gospel songs. One song, "The Ballad of Jim and Tammy Bakker," united all the themes in one bathetic burst of doggerel:

> Now Jerry Foulwell came with Grutman to Jim's home in
>   California one fine day
> They said, "Beware, Jim and Tammy, of a plan Jimmy
>   Swaggart is to play.
> "We want to let you know the plot and tell you we are
>   here to help in any way,
> "We want to help you Jim and Tammy, help you save
>   your Heritage USA." . . .
>
> They told lies about Jim Bakker, tried to ruin him and
>   his life in every way
> Let's send Foulwell back to Lynchburg and rebuild
>   our Heritage USA.

Callers would pay $2.20 to listen for three minutes, and 25 cents of that would go to the Bakkers, to help pay Belli's fee. Back at Heritage USA, Don Hardister called it the "whine line."

It wasn't the best of times for Jerry Falwell either.

PTL's fiscal seesaw was still bobbing: The "May miracle" in donations was followed by an "awful June," and some of the ebullient figures of early summer were being revised. It turned out that attendance at Heritage USA wasn't up 21 percent after all, but down by 10 percent in June, 15 percent in July, 24 percent in August. There had to be a hundred more layoffs from the staff, and a round of paychecks was deferred for a five-hundred-thousand-dollar saving. Another crisis was announced in late July, and Falwell promised a stunt of his own: If the faithful would send in enough to meet PTL's summer target of twenty-two million dollars, he would plunge down the 163-foot water slide at Heritage USA. In due course the triumph was announced. PTL was "over the top," Falwell said. He took the promised slide in his preacher's dark suit, with hands crossed prayerfully on his chest and much comic opera trepidation: "Now I lay me down to sleep. . . . Oh, oh, oh, my goodness. . . . Twenty-two million dollars—was it worth it? . . . I pray the Lord my soul to keep. . . ." It turned out on closer examination that the money actually came up four million dollars short, but the TV footage was memorable.

Falwell was also having problems winning hearts and minds. Most of the staffers at PTL had been with him from the time they learned of the Bakkers' fiscal marauding; but lines were hardening between the Falwell troops and the remaining Bakkerites, and it made for a poisonous atmosphere. Falwell himself told *Newsweek* that he taped all his phone calls, and the habit was catching. Jim's friend Kevin Whittum, the handicapped eighteen-year-old, was called in by Harry Hargrave to be told, he said, that his continued use of such perks as a specially fitted van would be contingent on his loyalty to the new regime. Kevin wired his wheelchair for the interview; unfortunately the tape proved inaudible.

Among the ministry's contributors, sentiment was harder to measure. The Association of PTL Partners said its telephone poll found 52 percent favoring the return of the Bakkers. The methodology was flawed, but the headline was damaging to Falwell. And there was a major embarrassment at the first meeting of PTL's creditors, when the Bakkers' attorneys dramatically forced Hargrave to admit that several of PTL's mailings had been produced in Lynchburg, at a cost of hundreds of thousands of dollars to PTL.

That transaction seemed to confirm some of the worst anti-Falwell suspicions. PTL had its own highly sophisticated mailing room, which had been functioning efficiently for years, but Falwell had bypassed the operation. At least one batch of mailings had been handled by the Lynchburg advertising agency owned by Falwell's brother-in-law, Sam K. Pate, and PTL's crown jewel mailing list had been sent to Lynchburg for the addressing. Some dissident partners complained that they were now getting Falwell's mailings, proof that the list had been compromised, but Falwell denied that, arguing that it would be foolish to send his literature to the PTL crowd. Hargrave confirmed that PTL had paid the "Old Time Gospel Hour" $240,000 for one mailing in May but balked when he was asked to account for a total of $731,000 in payments from PTL to the "Gospel Hour."

Falwell's man Mark DeMoss argued later that the whole operation had been a blessing for PTL. For one thing, he said, the new regime wasn't satisfied with the loyalty, security, and quality of PTL's mailing operation. For another, PTL didn't have the cash on hand to pay for the work. The "Gospel Hour" did it on credit, laying out its own funds for materials and postage and getting repaid when donations came in. In essence, DeMoss maintained, that amounted to an interest-free loan to PTL. Furthermore, the work had been done at cost; neither Falwell's ministry nor its contractors had made a penny on the deal, just as Falwell himself took no salary from PTL and didn't even bill the ministry for the use of his airplane.

As usual, there were no figures to back up the reassurances. For all his calls for financial candor, Falwell didn't release the accounting of his own ministry, promised in April, until August 20. It turned out then that in spite of his repeated vows to keep his ministry separate from his political activities, Moral Majority and the Liberty Federation had given the "Old Time Gospel Hour" $6.7 million in the past three years. And Falwell concealed until October the fact that the ministry, in turn, had been fined $6,000 several months earlier for buying Bibles at an inflated price from the I Love America political action committee, thus providing an improper political contribution of $28,000.

Among the partners, anti-Falwell sentiment was escalating in both venom and effectiveness. Falwell scoffed that the dissidents were only a few "horned toads" and shrugged off a demonstration of five hundred marchers on the grounds of Heritage USA. But late in July he was forced to cancel a "New Beginning" telethon after nine days, explaining that PTL's toll-free lines were being jammed by a wave of death threats and prank callers, "saying very bad things to our operators." There was also hate mail, full of the peculiar crabbed fury that religious disputes produce. "In the name of Jesus, may you rot in hell," one writer told Falwell.

Falwell named two charismatic directors to the PTL board and a charismatic entertainer, Gary McSpadden, to be host of the show, but that didn't quiet his clerical critics. The harshest and perhaps most damaging words came from James Robison, a Baptist of the charismatic branch and a nationally televised preacher, who wrote a savage open letter to Falwell with copies to thirty-four other religious leaders and several magazines. In ten single-spaced pages, Robison challenged Falwell either to confess faith in charismatic gifts or to step down from PTL. "How under heaven can you justify saving a ministry if you believe its doctrines are of the devil?" he demanded. And he urged Falwell to stop the flood of leaks about Jim's fiscal and sexual excesses. "When will you let the man up?" he wrote. "If you are trying to help him, for Christ's sake, why don't you get off his back?"

In a testy telegram, Falwell told Robison that he wouldn't be welcome at PTL until "God changes your heart and you no longer covet the pulpit here . . . which is, of course, your point of contention." Robison denied any interest in PTL and brought out the heavy guns of gospel: He advised Falwell to consult Obadiah 10–15. That passage reads, "For the violence done to your brother . . . shame shall cover you, and you shall be cut off forever. . . . You should not have gloated over his disaster. . . . You should not have looted his goods. . . . As you have done it will be done to you; your deeds shall return on your own head."

That prophecy was about to come true in the bankruptcy court.

With deceptive simplicity, the case was called *In Re: Heritage Village Church*, 87-01956. It was a colossal battle by South Carolina standards, and a big one anywhere. The stakes were a fifth of a billion dollars in assets, and as the *National Law Journal* quoted one of the lawyers, turning the other cheek had nothing to do with it. "There are no angels in this. . . . We are talking about big, big dollars," he said.

On the Bakker side, the aim was to protect Jim and Tammy from liability, to prove that Falwell had taken over illegally, and perhaps even to persuade the court to undo the transfer and reinstate the Bakker board of directors. If possible, Grutman should be thrown out of the case, not only to get rid of him but to establish that Jim had been tricked by a man who had conflicting interests. Melvin Belli was to be the figurehead in the fight; he was vague about the hard details of the case but trigger-quick with a sneer or a wisecrack on his client's behalf.

Jim Bakker, said Belli, was "a pussycat—he's not an old warthog like Falwell." Bakker had never been a moneyman, Belli said; he was a preacher with big visions who entrusted the details to others, and he shouldn't be held accountable for them. His flock wasn't bothered by what he had done. Said Belli: "They like their ministers to be well taken care of." And whatever Jim's faults, "I like a minister who's been tempted and sinned. He can counsel his flock better. He understands the meaning of redemption. Give me a sinning minister every time." As for Grutman, said Belli, "The bar association should be very concerned about a lawyer who says he is your lawyer when he represents the other side."

That was strong stuff, but Belli had met his rhetorical match. Neither Bakker nor Belli, Grutman fumed, "can be trusted for a single word of truth." He had never represented Bakker or advised him to resign, and "Nobody came to steal his ministry from him. . . . Mr. Bakker lied, lied. . . . I'm getting a little fed up with Mr. Bakker's revisionisms and his fantasies and his Johnny-come-lately irresponsible counsel." Warming to the subject, Grutman continued: "Really, Melvin Belli has been found . . . not to be a shining human being. I am trying not to become personal. I'm not talking about Melvin Belli and his multiple stewardess wives, or about the arrogance of naming one's son Caesar. Every step that Belli makes is one step lower down."

Thus it may have been simple prudence that led Belli to duck when the two finally came mouth to mouth. The occasion was a local New York talk show hosted by the Fox network's Maury

Povich, with Grutman on the set and Belli on-screen from San Francisco. Belli hadn't been told that Grutman was appearing, and he balked: "What he did to my client was perfectly dishonorable, and I'm not going to lend him credence by going on the air with him."

"Mr. Belli, you are as uninformed as you're arrogant," Grutman retorted.

"I want no part of him," Belli said. "I'll talk to Falwell. I'll talk to anybody else, not you." With that, Belli yanked off his microphone and stalked away. But if that was a rhetorical victory, it was also pyrrhic: Grutman was left to dominate the show, as he did for ten minutes.

Ryan Hovis was considerably more effective than Belli on Bakker's behalf, if less colorful. Hovis is a slight, soft-spoken lawyer, a longtime student of the bankruptcy court and Judge Reynolds. He is also Carolina-born and -bred, with an almost intuitive understanding of the local ethos, the Pentecostal scene, and the way the two fit together. And early in the case, Hovis proposed what turned out to be the masterstroke in the whole proceeding: He suggested that the judge name Billy Robinson as examiner, with broad powers to investigate the case and recommend solutions.

An unflappable, professorial lawyer with a penchant for restoring houses and a reputation for bone-crushing hard work, William E. S. ("Billy") Robinson is a longtime member of the Columbia bankruptcy fraternity who has often been Judge Reynolds's examiner in hard cases. The two have a special relationship of trust, and Robinson said later he had turned down offers to represent several creditors, hoping that he would get the central role. "I hold out on the better cases, don't take a client, because I like the whole case rather than just to have one part of it," he said. "That's where the creativity is. That's where the fun is."

In the PTL case, Robinson may have found just a bit more fun than he bargained for; even his old friend Judge Reynolds wound up barking at him. But as examiner, he played the crucial part in shaping the outcome.

Under bankruptcy law, a nonprofit organization like PTL can't be forced into court involuntarily, as a commercial venture may be. But if it appeals to the court for protection from creditors' lawsuits while forming a plan to settle its debts and reorganize, the nonprofit enterprise is treated in most respects like a company in bankruptcy under Chapter 11 of the federal law. The goal is to keep the enterprise running, protecting jobs and the continuity of operations, while working out a plan to sell off assets as needed, pay the creditors as much as possible of what they are owed, declare the debts settled, and put the organization back on a healthy, self-sustaining footing. Judges in bankruptcy cases have very nearly dictatorial powers while a case is before them; they can appoint examiners to look into any aspect of the businesses or even referees to manage them if none of the interested parties can be trusted.

As the incumbent management, Falwell's board asked Judge Reynolds to be allowed to run PTL during the proceedings. Hovis didn't object, but he did propose that Robinson be named examiner, with broad powers to poke around. Grutman opposed that, arguing that it was a thinly disguised ploy to make Robinson the effective manager, but Judge Reynolds gave Robinson most of the power Hovis had asked.

Robinson was told to investigate PTL's financial condition, to look into any incompetence or misconduct, to seek out fraudulent transactions by present or former PTL officials, and to consider filing lawsuits against the Bakkers and others. He was to report to the judge on what he found. But he wasn't supposed to plan the reorganization; under the law, the PTL management had three months to work out its own plan. If the creditors disagreed with those proposals, they could produce a plan of their own, and the judge would decide which alternative—or what combination—would be imposed. In the end, each class of creditors had to consent to the plan. If no realistic plan emerged or PTL couldn't be kept afloat in the interim, the case would turn into a Chapter 7 bankruptcy: PTL's assets would be liquidated, the creditors would be paid whatever the sale brought, and the ministry would come to an end.

But as Robinson explored PTL, he was impressed by what he found. He calculated the assets at $200 million to $230 million, enough to pay all the creditors nearly in full even if the partners were taken into account. Contributions had dropped by 40 percent since Bakker's resignation, and as summer wore on, Heritage USA looked more and more like a ghost town. Still, Robinson thought there was a good chance that the ministry could continue to operate. It wasn't clear that the remaining donors were endorsing Falwell, but the fact that they were still giving money proved that PTL could exist without Jim Bakker. "This is not a cult based around one person," Robinson concluded. "There is a deep institutional loyalty."

From the beginning, it was Robinson's goal to settle the case in the comfortable Carolina tradition: Get all the parties to agree on a single plan, execute it speedily, and get PTL out of bankruptcy as fast as possible, to sink or swim on the partners' donations. But it turned into a confrontation at the outset. Robinson said he told Hargrave the first day he met him, "The only way to make it work is to involve all the creditors." But the creditors were telling him that "there was this gap, this stone wall the Falwell people had thrown up. . . . [The creditors] tried to say, 'Here we are. We've got a right to do a plan, but we're willing to come up and talk to you for a day.' They got no response."

Robinson himself was having trouble getting information from PTL's new auditors, he said, because they had been told not to release it. He could have taken Falwell to court and forced him to give up the data, but he decided that would just mean long, combative hearings on every point, slowing up the case and raising costs even higher. By Robinson's standards, the legal fees were already horrendous.

Part of the problem was Grutman, whose preferred style was intimidation. The preacher Mike Evans had a taste of that when he first appeared on a talk show with the lawyer. Grutman turned up at the last minute before the camera went on, looked at Evans, and dismissed him contemptuously: "You're nothing." Robinson learned from his friends in New York that Grutman had a well-earned reputation for similar tactics in court. When it came to bankruptcies, he was told, Grutman's attitude was "My plan or no plan."

That posture suited Grutman's big client down to the ground. Evangelicals say it isn't Christian to take your brother to court, but Jerry Falwell has done well there, and not by sweet Christian charity. In the PTL case, he said later, he made the mistake of discussing legal strategy in the presence of his local counsel, Walter Theus, "only to find that it was put immediately into the hands of the other side." Falwell said he didn't fault Theus for leaking; Theus had to live in Columbia for the rest of his life and had to keep his peace with Robinson, the judge, and the rest of the good old boys. But "We don't play that way," Falwell said. "We play to win. The element of surprise is so necessary when you're playing against thugs like Bakker, Messner, and company. And you don't pass anything to anybody until you're in the ring." After the first leak, Falwell said, Theus was cut out of the strategy loop.

When Theus heard about Falwell's accusation—in effect, saying that he had betrayed a client's confidence—he was outraged. It was "utterly ridiculous" to say he had leaked anything to anyone, he said; he had tried to maintain good relations with Robinson but frequently disagreed with his positions in the case. And, said Theus, "If I was ever cut out of the loop, I wasn't aware of it. I liked Falwell." Somewhat lamely, Falwell responded that he was only repeating what somebody had told him. It seemed likely that Theus betrayed no confidences and leaked nothing of consequence, and that Falwell, with his adversarial approach, simply read any friendly contact with the other side as fraternizing with the enemy.

Given that mind-set on the Falwell side, Robinson soon gave up hope of coming up with a unified plan to reorganize PTL. He had met most of the major creditors individually in the early going, and at their first joint meeting, he told them that in his opinion they were going to have to work out their own plan. "If that's exceeding my authority, then I did," he said unrepentantly.

Robinson also decided that the key factor in any plan was going to be the role of the partners. In a sense, he thought, they were like shareholders who had put money into a company; in another sense, the lifetime partners could be thought of as creditors. Falwell and Grutman acknowledged that the lifetime partners had a claim to three nights' lodging every year, but they weren't about to add that up as a debt of $160 million—$1,000 for each of the 160,000-odd partnerships sold. After the other creditors had been paid, there would be no assets for PTL to work with. Beyond that, there would be a technical problem if the partners were admitted as a class of creditors: They would have veto power over Falwell's plan. Under the law, if any class of creditors rejects the final plan, the plan can be approved only if those creditors are paid at least as much as they would get in a total liquidation. If the partners insisted on getting that much, the other creditors would have to accept fewer cents on the dollar for themselves.

Falwell had often argued that charismatics weren't all that important in supporting PTL since they accounted for only 21 percent of the donations. But that figure came from a survey Dortch had quoted to Falwell back in March, and most people thought it was dubious at best. Robinson wanted to know more about the partners and their role in supporting the ministry. He asked Judge Reynolds for permission to run a comprehensive telephone survey. Grutman opposed both the poll and its fifty-thousand-dollar cost, but the judge approved a less expensive survey by mail. The results were startling: Not only were the lifetime members overwhelmingly charismatic, but they were the backbone of the ministry.

PTL had a total of 1,030,867 names in its files, and about half of them were frequent correspondents, or partners. About 250,000 were committed to make regular monthly contributions of fifteen dollars or more. There were 114,224 people who had bought lifetime partnerships, many of them taking more than one; one woman had bought a record seventy-four lifetime partnerships, and 23 others bought more than twenty-five each. The surprising thing to Robinson was that 80 percent of the lifetime partners continued to make donations to PTL even after sending in their thousand-dollar payments. Since the sale of life memberships began in 1984, he found, the lifetime partners had put up 69 percent of all PTL's contributions, including the sale of partnerships.

Thus, when Robinson turned in his report to Judge Reynolds on September 14, his key conclusion was that the partners were going to have to be treated well. Whether they were called owners, creditors, or just donors, Robinson said, they were the ones who kept the ministry going. "If there is to be survival of the PTL ministry in the present form, the key to this survival is the support of the lifetime partners," he reported to the judge.

Apart from that crucial point, Robinson's report was a surprisingly bland review of the PTL books. He accused the Bakker administration of having an "unsettled management style" that created "very serious irregularities and problems," but he actually had harsher words for the Falwell regime, accusing it of an "adversarial approach . . . which has contributed materially to the lack of progress toward compromise." In particular, he said, the new management had alienated the partners, and that "could create grave difficulties in confirming a plan."

The report led to some hard words between Robinson and his old friend the judge, who observed accurately that Robinson hadn't turned in three-quarters of his assignment. Where was the investigation of misconduct or incompetence? What fraudulent or illegal transfers had been made? What suits might be brought against the Bakker regime? "When he got my final report, he was livid. 'There's not one thing in here about Bakker!' " Robinson said months later. "I'm still getting chewed out about it every time he doesn't have something else to talk about."

In fact, Robinson said he had concluded that Bakker's management of PTL was "a disaster"—that Jim himself was an irrational recluse with serious emotional problems and that despite the earnest efforts of good people at lower levels, the management structure wasn't designed to show what was going on. He said he had decided that Dortch was "pure Satan. He was a leader, vain. He was exposed late to fine things, money. Over a period of time, he was consumed by it. . . . Dortch's management was to keep people at each other's throats. Scary. A scary man." Robinson found no evidence that Jim was trying to defraud anybody, but he had heard about two secret PTL bank accounts, one in Switzerland and one in Dallas, and he said he was trying to get the U.S. attorney's office to turn over information about that.

But in his "central role," Robinson was more concerned with keeping PTL going and contributing to a final compromise than he was with carrying out his precise assignment. And he argued that publishing his harsh conclusions would be counterproductive. It would risk losing support from the pro-Bakker faction, thus forcing the collapse and liquidation of PTL. "I had looked at the contributions. We'd lose half the dollars," he said.

After the report was filed, Falwell was harshly critical of Robinson as "a very unethical person" who had told the judge that "we wanted the ministry, that we were there to steal it. Just a case of bad translation, bad interpretation, bad perspective." But when Falwell's team produced its own plan two weeks later, it did nothing to dispel that impression. In fact, Robinson saw the Falwell plan as the final evidence that he and his men wanted to keep control of PTL and freeze the partners out.

The plan was designed to appear careful, consistent, and reasoned, and it promised to bring a healthy PTL out of bankruptcy in five years. All the small creditors would be paid in full within ninety days; large creditors would get their money in the longer term, with one exception: Roe Messner's $14 million claim was not only disputed, but Grutman was suing him and Bakker for allegedly skimming $20 million from PTL's construction bills. The ministry would pledge itself to follow the National Religious Broadcasters' financial guidelines, to negotiate and litigate state and federal tax claims, and to sell off 868 acres of undeveloped land to raise money for settling debts. A detailed five-year budget projected total revenues of $473 million and a profit of $36 million in the fifth year.

The key question was who would control PTL and its assets, and here the plan spoke mainly by implication. Falwell had already flagged his intention to leave PTL's management. But he was leaving it to a handpicked board made up mostly of fundamentalist Baptists, and he might well keep his own board seat. The board would supervise a management team that Falwell had brought in, headed by Nims, Hargrave, and Marcus. They in turn might not be able to use the board quite as the rubber stamp Bakker had enjoyed, but since there were no shareholders to account to, the board would almost surely defer to the officers in most cases. It might not be fair to call PTL a puppet of Falwell's, but it would be surprising if the new setup didn't reflect his views.

The partners were given short shrift. In essence, they had three choices. They could declare their thousand-dollar payments a gift to the ministry, as many no doubt had done already on their tax returns. Falwell's people said they expected half the partnerships would be written off this way. Alternatively, each partnership could be worth a two-thousand-dollar credit toward the purchase of a condominium or other property at Heritage USA. As a final choice, a partner could accept a thousand dollars' worth of PTL stock or join a new club for an additional payment of two hundred dollars a year and enjoy a discount of 50 percent on PTL admission fees, hotel bills, and rentals.

With the partners mostly out of the ownership picture, the profit lane was open for Falwell's team. "They were all going to get immensely wealthy," said Robinson. "All the equity—a lot of it, anyway—would eventually have ended up in the hands of Nims, Hargrave, Marcus, and others they selected. Enough of it could have gone into Falwell's entities so that he could have had some indirect financial gain. . . . They'd be fat and happy."

Robinson explained that the heart of the scheme was its proposal to split PTL into two halves, the profit-making side (including the park and the network) and the nonprofit ministry. On the surface, this sounded both fair and overdue. From the time they moved in, Falwell's people had been saying there were a good many activities at PTL that ought to be paying taxes. "Christians should render unto Caesar those things that are Caesar's," Jerry Nims quoted Christ, and it seemed to him Caesar had a claim on a lot of PTL. Why should the water park go tax-free when the competing amusement park called Carowinds just down the road had to pay?

But that righteous argument masked the real objective, Robinson said. If Falwell had ever hoped to liquidate the PTL empire and buy the network for a few cents on the dollar, his men now saw a larger opportunity. The new for-profit segment of PTL could legitimately issue stock, and the majority was to be owned by the nonprofit segment. The lifetime partners would also get some shares, but PTL could issue more to raise capital or for any other purpose the directors approved. According to Robinson, after some of the stock got traded on the open market, establishing a market value, other shares could be issued to PTL executives, in the form of restricted stock that couldn't be sold until the restrictions were lifted. If the enterprise prospered and grew, executives who were in on the ground floor could profit enormously when the restrictions were lifted and the time came to sell. As Robinson told it, that was the lure for the Falwell team. "Warren Marcus told my accountant that he wasn't getting a salary because his deal was for stock—a lot of stock," Robinson said.

"This was Jerry Nims's idea, not Falwell's," Robinson explained. And the scheme did bear a marked resemblance to one of Nims's earlier operations. His Nimslo camera venture had begun with the backing of several minority investors. When Nims later sold the company to a firm registered in Bermuda, some of the minority backers had objected, even though all of them got a profit on their stock. Soon after that, however, Nims had emerged as chairman of the Bermuda company. After further maneuvers the stock had traded publicly for considerably more than the minority investors had been paid, and some of them had sued Nims, arguing that they had been squeezed out of their legitimate profits. The suit had been settled for $1.2 million.

Nims contended that the original investors got a profit of ten dollars for every one they had put up. And when they were bought out, it was not a sure thing that the public stock would later go up. But the net effect, as in the PTL scheme, was to dispose of a large claim on potential profits from the people who had put up the money in the first place.

Similarly, there would be nothing illegal about the deal Robinson said he had uncovered. In fact, free enterprisers argue that such stock incentives reward creative talent, and they don't pay off unless the beneficiaries can make their companies a success. But as Robinson saw it, this deal would enrich the Falwell troops with the fruit of a bankruptcy that left the partners holding the bag. And even though the partners had no legally recognized stake in PTL, Robinson had come to think of them as the ministry's true owners. "One day I was talking to Harry [Hargrave] about turning it over to the partners," said Robinson. "He said, 'What about our stock?' "

Did such a plan ever exist? Both Marcus and Hargrave denied making the remarks Robinson had quoted, and Nims said, "No. There was nothing like that. That goes back to one of Billy's old canards." The whole scheme was a figment of Robinson's imagination, according to Marcus: "There was never any hidden agenda. There was never any discussion, public or private, of stock options or restricted stock for executives." But Robinson was convinced that the deal had been cooked, and when he wrote his report, it came down to this: It just wasn't the way Billy Robinson played the game.

Falwell's men had known for weeks that they had a problem with Robinson, and they were fighting an escalating campaign to undermine him. Nims took the lead in the early going, complaining to Judge Reynolds that Robinson was exceeding his instructions by drafting his own reorganization plan. Robinson replied that he had talked only about theories, not about plans. But later Grutman turned up with more suggestive evidence that Robinson was playing a devious game: the tape recording of a phone call between Roe Messner and Deborah Watkins, president of a sometime dissident group called PTL Partner Majority. In a long conversation, Messner told her repeatedly that Robinson was "not for Falwell. . . . Just believe me that he is working behind the scenes for us." A bit lamely, Messner's own attorney explained that the tape didn't mean anything, that Messner was in no position to know what Robinson believed.

And after Robinson had filed his report, Falwell himself took a hand, planting a story with the *Observer*'s editor, Rich Oppel, while both were attending an editors' convention in Seattle in mid-September. Falwell told Oppel he would ask for a meeting with the judge to complain that Robinson was too chummy with Bakker's lawyer Ryan Hovis and was "spending too much time with a few lunatic fringe dissidents." Oppel wrote in a front-page story that Robinson was telling the judge that PTL's board should be made up of two groups, half of it representing Falwell and half the creditors, and that Falwell himself should "resign graciously" by the turn of the year. That would pave the way for bringing Bakker back, Falwell predicted, which would mean the destruction of the ministry. And he warned through Oppel that he would quit PTL and take his board with him if Judge Reynolds endorsed any such plan.

That was Falwell's last bet in the poker game: all or nothing, table stakes. Robinson retorted that he had made no such recommendations and denied being overly friendly with Hovis, though he said he had never had any trouble believing Hovis, who was "a far cry different from Nims." For the rest, Robinson said he was spending 99 percent of his time talking to Falwell's people. "If I'm concentrating my time with lunatics, then maybe I was talking with the wrong people," he said acidly.

Falwell didn't press the judge for a meeting; his man DeMoss said Falwell figured Reynolds had got the message. The judge kept his counsel, waiting for Falwell to file his plan. It arrived on the last day of September, along with a request that Robinson be told not to make any more remarks to the media. The judge pondered that for a week. Then he called Falwell's bluff and backed Robinson's play. Falwell's plan wouldn't fly, Reynolds ruled officially, because it didn't have a firm base of support from the partners and wasn't a cooperative effort with the creditors. He invited the creditors to submit their own plan. Since Robinson had already advised them to be ready, they had one drawn up, and its key provision was the naming of a new board of nine directors: five from the Falwell camp, four representing the creditors. The judge endorsed that approach, sending a message of his own to Falwell: "You might as well bite the bullet now."

Instead, Falwell chose to quit. Grutman said he ought to appeal, arguing that the ruling was improper and could be overturned, but

Falwell said he wasn't ready to take on the federal judiciary. So he persuaded his fellow directors to resign, and along with them Hargrave, Grutman, and Marcus. As a parting land mine against Bakker's return, the board voted to restore the celebrated reversionary clause, this time stipulating that ownership of PTL would revert to the Assemblies of God in the event of "moral default." And in an emotional two-hour news conference, Falwell unleashed his bitterness and dropped any remaining pretense of brotherly love for Jim Bakker.

"Our first goal was to deliver this ministry to financial and spiritual health," Falwell said. "We believe we are right near the goal on that. Our second goal was to guarantee that never, never again that Mr. Bakker or someone like him could sit down at this chairmanship of PTL and rape the American people as has been the case in the past." Judge Reynolds's ruling made both objectives impossible, he said. The big lenders he had lined up wouldn't put up money if a second plan was pending, and the divided board would pose a real threat that Bakker might return.

Jim's ministry, said Falwell, was "probably the greatest scab and cancer on the face of Christianity in the two thousand years of church history. . . . I could not sit at the table with him, or look into this lens and ask you to pay our bills, knowing that one year from now, or less, Mr. Bakker could be sitting here." Then Jerry Falwell went home to Lynchburg, with a parting prophecy that sounded more like a curse: "Probably in the next six months, barring a miracle of God, Mr. Bakker will be sitting here running this ministry. And I cannot think of a more tragic thing."

In the Tennessee mountains, Jim was more than willing to head back. He and Tammy were the only hope for PTL now, he said; without them it couldn't survive, but after the crisis, they could get the largest audience ever. "We literally could end up with a megaministry," he said. And he gloated to a caller, "If we headed toward Charlotte now, they'd panic."

Tammy wasn't sure. She said she was afraid to believe good news. Once again she was right. They weren't going back.

As long as Jim and Tammy might be indicted, the judge wouldn't even consider giving them back their throne. Even the creditors who liked them, including Messner, weren't talking about anything grander than an occasional fund-raising appearance on the show. And there was considerable fear that even that might do more harm than good. Early returns from Robinson's poll had shown that the partners were willing to support PTL but hopelessly divided over the Bakkers: Some wouldn't contribute unless they were part of it, but at least as many would quit PTL forever if Jim and Tammy were there.

Their time was over. They weren't wanted anymore.

Ruby Jones, fifty-four, a barber in Tulsa, had realized sometime ago that there was phoniness and greed in TV evangelism. "But I still watched Jim and Tammy because they put on a tremendous show," she said. "I'm not going to say they're not sincere because that's between them and God. But that was my belief, that a lot of it was put on just for the show. I feel that anybody who makes a sham of God's work will be punished more greatly than any sinner. That if people preach his word and take money under false pretenses, he will take care of them in his own way. No, I didn't lose faith in God.

"I never did care for Falwell. I felt like he got in there and realized there were millions to be made, and he wanted it. They're all basically about the same. Money and power make them do a lot of things an ordinary person wouldn't do."

Chapter **12**

Tribulation in the End Time

The holy war was over, and everyone had lost.

It wouldn't be the end of the story. PTL would flounder on through the shoals of bankruptcy, shedding pieces of itself and pleading constantly for more money from the partners. The legal actions could go on for years: There would almost surely be criminal indictments, trials, and appeals, and the lawsuits could last as long as any possible defendant seemed worth taking to court. Jim and Tammy were talking about launching a new TV ministry; Jerry Falwell was denned up in Lynchburg like a bear with a wounded paw. All of them would be heard from again. But at least for a while there was peace in the body of Christ.

Lives had been changed forever. Jessica Hahn was in the Playboy mansion, recovering from extensive plastic surgery to her face, nose, and breasts; like Elizabeth Ray, Rita Jenrette, and Fanne Foxe before her, she was preparing to parlay her short-lived notoriety into a Hollywood career. Also like them, Jessica was almost surely on her way to becoming a question in next year's trivia quiz. Meanwhile, *Playboy* and *Penthouse* were still waging their war over her tattered virtue. The third installment of her own story was yet to come in *Playboy,* and *Penthouse* was rooting around for more lurid tales of her past. Jimmy Swaggart was enmeshed in his own sex scandal; the avenging Marvin Gorman had trapped him with a prostitute in a seedy New Orleans motel, and Swaggart had quit the Assemblies of God rather than do penance for a year. With that, Mike Evans had yet another abrupt change of heart: If his old friend Swaggart could behave like that, he must have been on a raid for PTL all along. Evans apologized publicly to Falwell. Richard Dortch had gone public to denounce Falwell and plead his own good intentions, but John Wesley Fletcher was starting a new ministry and staying away from reporters. Jerry Nims was putting his inimitable stamp on Moral Majority. Doug and Laura Lee Oldham had moved to Lynchburg, where Doug was working with Jerry Falwell's TV operation. Don Hardister had found a new job, handling security for a department store in Charlotte.

A new trustee was named to run PTL during the bankruptcy: David Clark, an Assemblies of God minister who had been an executive with Pat Robertson's Christian Broadcasting Network for more than a decade. He had helped draw up the National Religious Broadcasters' guidelines on financial accountability, and he got high marks from practically everybody for competence, fairness, and ethical sensitivity. Judge Reynolds approved the creditors' plan for reorganization, with a few modifications; that meant PTL would be split into two pieces, the nonprofit ministry and the profit-seeking network and theme park, much as Falwell had proposed. But there would be a troika in control. Clark was to be chairman of the board, naming two more members of his own, while the creditors and the lifetime partners each would name three board members to terms of varying lengths. By the time PTL emerged from bankruptcy in five years, the partners would be in full control, naming all the directors.

Like everyone else who put his hand to PTL, Clark found it a well of optimism. His trusteeship was yet another new beginning, he said, the "beginning of a whole new resurrection." But everything depended on the partners, and they would have to clear some major hurdles if PTL were to stay out of liquidation.

The first problem was simply to keep operating. In the last eighteen weeks under Falwell, PTL had run $3.3 million in the red; contributions had fallen to an average $495,000 a week, while at least $700,000 a week was needed to break even. In the confusion after Falwell quit, donations dropped to $403,000 a week. But Robinson and Clark cut back operations, paring payroll and expenses so sharply that in spite of the reduced revenues, PTL piled up $900,000 in operating profit in the two months after Clark took over. Furthermore, the partners hadn't given up. Donations rebounded a bit under Clark, averaging $480,500 a week, and Heritage USA had a good Christmas season in 1987, with record numbers of visitors on the peak weekend to view the display of 1.5 million lights. In the spring, however, costs would head back up. The payroll would have to rise again to get the water park running and prepare Heritage USA for the new season.

The next crisis point would be May 2, 1988, when the reorganization plan was to take formal effect. By then, PTL had to come up with $6 million, over and above the cost of operation, to pay the overdue interest on its mountain of debt. Unused land and other assets had been sold off to cut the debt; but the easy steps had been taken, and the debt was threatening to grow again: The IRS filed a claim to $55.7 million in back taxes. Clark was hoping to bargain that down considerably, and the agency had already shown its willingness to help keep PTL alive; but at least some taxes would surely have to be paid. And after May 2, the debt was to be retired at the rate of $1 million a month. That meant PTL would have to pull in an absolute minimum of $1.5 million every month, more than triple what contributors had been sending recently.

In Jim Bakker's heyday, he had been attracting more than $8 million a month, and his loyal fans saw an obvious answer to PTL's problems. "The solution is Jim Bakker," said Ryan Hovis. "Put Bakker back on the air to raise money."

Billy Robinson had had the same thought and even tried to persuade Jim to make an appeal for funds. He called Hovis, he said later, hoping Bakker would agree to urge his followers to keep giving, but also that he would say he was not trying to come back—something like "If you love me and Tammy, don't withhold your support, don't hold it back. And if it works, we'll let the future be the future, let God decide." Bakker's people wanted a personal meeting to talk that over, but Robinson said no. *God, that's all I need,* he thought. *As sure as I do that, there'll be four thousand photographers. I'll be finished.*

So Jim called Robinson at home in Columbia one night. The talk was inconclusive. Jim didn't agree to make the tape, but he never flatly ruled it out either. He kept saying, "Well, there are things you have to consider." But he passed on some interesting observations about the art of fund-raising. Years ago, when he was naive, he told Robinson, he thought that if the show was good, people would send money as a matter of course. But he learned that you have to ask for it, and also that it's necessary to have a central figure on-screen: "Ministries follow a person. It may not be me, but that's how it works." For that reason, he was skeptical about the latter-day PTL show, with no clear central character and several singers taking turns as host. He was also dubious about the new management's decision not to hawk any more books, trinkets, and souvenirs. "You have to give people something tangible in addition to spiritual fulfillment," Jim told Robinson.

But they couldn't agree on the appeal, and when David Clark got the results of the poll of partners Robinson had ordered, he lost all further interest in Jim. The flock didn't want Jim back at all. Fully 60 percent of the lifetime partners said they would stop giving to PTL if he returned; only 14 percent said they would give more if Jim were on-screen. Clark didn't say what percentage of the partners had returned their questionnaires, but it seemed likely that if the survey overstated anything, it was the support for Jim. His backers were passionate, whereas a partner who was disgusted and disillusioned was more likely to throw the questionnaire away.

To Clark, it was not just decisive but conclusive: "I don't think Jim Bakker has any role at PTL." Jim was certainly not above reproach, as a Christian leader should be, Clark added; he should be worrying about the grand jury. "We must drive a wedge, slowly but inexorably, between Jim and this place," said Clark.

The thin end of that wedge was already in place. The IRS had concluded that Jim and Tammy had been treating PTL like their own wholly owned corporation, stripping off its net earnings as their salaries and bonuses. The agency said PTL had paid $14.9 million in excess wages and bonuses to the Bakkers and their friends, and $9.4 million of that had gone to Jim and Tammy. Clark filed a lawsuit to get it back, along with millions more that Clark said had been squandered or misspent; in all, the suit claimed an astonishing $53 million. Jim and Tammy responded by saying they were nearly bankrupt anyway. They had already filed a claim with Judge Reynolds for $3 million more from PTL, including $1.3 million for the Tega Cay house. "I am amazed at their gall," said Clark.

By this time, even the Bakkers were running a little short of gall. They had rented a house on the beach at Malibu for a while, at seven thousand dollars a month, and then moved to yet another home on the grounds of a country club in Palm Springs. But things were not going smoothly.

In October, Jim had tried to repeat his triumph on Ted Koppel's "Nightline." This time Koppel mugged him. Koppel had taken a good deal of criticism for his limpness back in May, and now he came on like a district attorney, beginning with a few choice comments about the 900 phone number and the plans for a twenty-five-city tour. Jim wasn't showing contrition at all, Koppel charged, but just "doing what Jim Bakker has always done, and that is hustling a buck." "Well, I'm sorry you feel that way," Jim said lamely.

Koppel drove on, with question after question: "You can't seriously be thinking about going back, are you?" Why did Jim refuse to meet his accusers on the homosexuality issue? If several churches had offered to ordain him, "Why not name the denominations?" Why should Jim be restored to the ministry at all? "Why does Jim Bakker inflict himself on the American public?"

Jim looked stricken, stumbled several times, apologized for his sins. "I know God has forgiven me, and I hope the American people will forgive me for what I did wrong," he said; he could only hope people would see him as "a sinner saved by grace, and there's hope for me and there's hope for everyone else." But when it came to actual sins, he ducked again, denying most of the charges against him. Jessica was not telling the truth, he said; he wasn't homosexual; Falwell had perpetrated a hoax. The interview was a disaster, and worse was to come.

If people still wanted to hear Jim and Tammy, they were no longer willing to pay for the privilege. At prices up to twenty dollars, tickets for the "Farewell for Now" tour were going begging. It was to be a two-hour variety show, with a trick waterfall onstage, an orchestra and a chorus backing up songs by the two Tammys, and Jim telling his story. They promised not to take a collection. But in Nashville, where the tour was to open, just thirty-two tickets had been sold two weeks before the date, in an arena that would hold ninety-nine hundred people. The early sales figures were similar all through what used to be the solid Bakker belt: twenty-four tickets in Norfolk, thirty-three in Birmingham, forty-four in Kansas City, eighty in Dallas. Early in November the tour was "postponed." And the 900 number was quietly cut off. No figure of receipts was ever announced.

Jim had told Koppel that he wanted to clear up the homosexuality charges and was willing to confront his accusers before the Assemblies of God, and he actually asked his old friend Charles Cookman, the North Carolina district superintendent, to arrange a meeting to begin the process of reconciliation. But when the appointed day in January arrived, Jim failed to show up. Cookman said Jim's people had explained that Tammy was afraid to fly. That hadn't prevented her many flights in the past; in fact, she had published a book on how God had helped her overcome her fears, that one among them. But "I know for a fact that Tammy had a terrible fear of flying and always takes medication before a flight," Cookman told reporters. She was trying to be drug-free now, and "Bakker said he did not want to attend without his wife."

Without benefit of the Assemblies of God, Jim was a minister again. Early in November, he was quietly ordained by the Faith Christian Fellowship International Church, Inc.—a denomination not listed among the 302 in the *Yearbook of American and Canadian Churches*. The church said it had accepted a fee and was satisfied that Jim met its standards of wisdom and morality. He was being "restored" to the ministry, said Dr. Robert Lemon, national director of the ten-year-old church, and would not practice until that process was finished. "He is not actually in the pulpit right now and won't be until God says it is time," Lemon said when the news got out in December.

A month later, Jim's people said he and Tammy would be back on the air in February. They planned a late-night religious talk show originating in Palm Springs, to preempt the David Letterman show in the local market. It would also go by satellite to other markets where Jim and Tammy had done well, including Detroit, Atlanta, and the Carolinas. They wanted to minister to the downtrodden, a spokesman said, but they hadn't decided whether they would raise money on the air or accept corporate sponsorship. No names of would-be sponsors were discussed. In any event, that date also fell through.

Jim was facing major legal problems. He claimed to be unworried about the possibility of criminal indictments, but he was angry at the IRS for its tax claims and the whole idea that the government could decide what was "reasonable" to pay him and Tammy. The PTL board had set their salaries and bonuses, he insisted, and the board had every right to do that. "We made one percent, basically, of the money we raised for the ministry," Jim said. "Johnny Carson makes probably twenty million dollars a year. I'm not comparing myself with him. I work harder than Johnny Carson."

Jim also argued, with some justification, that the figures on his "excess income," issued by the IRS and gleefully quoted by Falwell's people, were highball estimates that were meant to be bargained down. "The IRS throws everything but the kitchen sink at you; then you have to prove yourself innocent," he said. Among other things, he said, the money listed as his income and cash advances included air travel and hotel bills for guests on the PTL show, and he was being billed for use of the parsonage and for production costs for a record by Tammy Sue that actually belonged to PTL.

Jim was still talking about going back to PTL. "I believe," he said, "if Tammy and I are allowed to return and speak to the people, that with God's help, the bills can be paid and Heritage USA and PTL and the satellite network can be saved." He had met with bankers, he said, and he had promises of enough money to buy and run the place if the court would let him back in. Or his old friend Roe Messner might help; early in 1988, there was talk that the builder was lining up financing to buy what was left of PTL if the reorganization plan failed. But Messner wasn't about to give Jim the key to the cash register, and given the outright hostility of the PTL staff and the partners in Robinson's survey, Messner would have to be cautious even about letting Jim and Tammy back on the air. If the new show from Palm Springs actually came to anything, one possibility might be to buy it some time on the PTL network and see whether the old spark could be rekindled. There might be only 14 percent of the faithful left, but the faithful used to send in ninety-six million dollars a year, and 14 percent of that was worth a shot.

Some people thought PTL might have had a better chance if Jerry Falwell hadn't given up on it so abruptly. Jeffrey Hadden, the University of Virginia sociologist who has followed Falwell's career for years, said Falwell got frustrated and nervous and walked out too soon; he could have dealt from a stronger position than Clark's, particularly with the IRS, whose claim would probably determine PTL's fate. "He should have held on just a little longer," Hadden said. "The creditors' plan would have happened anyway, but he could have cut a better deal. He could have claimed victory and walked away as a hero instead of ducking out."

As it was, Falwell had done pretty well. At a time when his political role was winding down and his revenues were already falling, said communications director William Fore of the National Council of Churches, Falwell "got the main thing he desperately needs over everything else, which is public attention. These electronic evangelists are no different from Zsa Zsa Gabor. They don't exist except as they exist in the media." And the attention was mainly respectful. In a surprisingly laudatory editorial, the evangelical magazine *Christianity Today* praised Falwell's willingness to take risks to build consensus among Christians. The fact that he had left PTL without any overt attempt to capture the network seemed to defuse criticism of his motives. In fact, Calvin College's Quentin Schultze said he thought Falwell had actually gained in public stature because of his involvement in PTL, and "The thing that helped him most is that he eventually resigned."

Falwell himself said he had no regrets. "I think I did the right thing when we went in," he told *Newsweek*, and he had no second thoughts about leaving either. "We gave it our best shot, built some bridges between Baptists and Pentecostals. We've got a lot of friends there. But I didn't like the idea that the court would not let us stay in and win, then pass it on to whomever." Judge Reynolds, he said, had been "in over his head. I don't think he ever understood it." But Falwell agreed that PTL after he left was "a disaster. . . . No way can they raise six million dollars, carry the staff. They've just shot themselves in the foot so many times. I don't know of anything they've done since we left there that I consider a right move." Falwell predicted that it would come to "at least a modified" liquidation for PTL, that "They'll have to sell off and sell off and sell off to keep the thing afloat, until it gets down to a small thing that they can handle. That small thing will probably be the network, maybe the church. That's about it."

So it seemed. By early 1988 it was clear that the partners weren't giving enough to pay the back interest and the monthly debt installments. But it looked for a while as if the network might go first: PTL started discussing a merger with Pat Robertson's CBN, itself floundering after Robertson left his ministry and "The 700 Club" show to be a full-time presidential candidate. CBN estimated that its contributions fell to about $90 million in 1987, down from $130 million the previous year, and after Clark went to PTL, he raided

CBN for a half dozen of its best people. CBN reportedly had a reserve of as much as $30 million, and a merger might make sense. As industry sources pictured it, the two networks could become one meganetwork; they could keep their most popular programming, including some of CBN's commercial reruns, and all their cable outlets, dropping the overlaps and cutting costs by a considerable margin. "The 700 Club" could be killed or reconfigured, and Ben Kinchlow, its popular cohost, could take over as host of the PTL show.

But that plan, too, fell through. After the collapse of his presidential campaign, Pat Robertson announced that he would return to CBN and try to heal it. His friends said he would have preferred to stay in politics, but he felt obligated to come to the rescue.

And PTL suffered what turned out to be its death blow. As the May 2 deadline for paying the arrears of interest loomed closer, it was increasingly clear that the money would not be found. By some accounts, donations were picking up in April, but PTL had run an operating deficit of $1.5 million in the first three months of 1988. It was the IRS that finally signaled the end, announcing that it was revoking PTL's tax exemption. Clark filed an appeal. While that was pending, donations would still be deductible from a donor's taxable income. But the impact was immediate: Receipts sagged from $700,000 a week to less than $150,000. Reluctantly, Clark bowed to the inevitable and filed a new plan with Judge Reynolds. This one followed Falwell's scenario. All of PTL's property would be sold; the religious functions, including the network, would be spun off as a new organization called Heritage Ministries. At least two potential buyers surfaced; one of them, a Charlotte businessman named George Shinn, thought he could make a go of the hotels and the water park if he could also build a stadium on the grounds for his minor-league ball team. But he made it clear that he planned to sell liquor in the hotels and beer in the ballpark—a plan that would surely end any further pilgrimages to Heritage USA by the faithful. Clark resigned his trusteeship, hoping to be named to head the shrunken ministry, and Reynolds appointed a new trustee, former Winston-Salem mayor M. C. "Red" Benton, to preside over the liquidation.

Even then, it wasn't clear that the network could survive. The flow of donations, at $22,000 a day, wasn't even enough to buy broadcast time for the PTL show, Benton warned; if more money didn't start coming in, the show would have to go off the air. "When we can't meet the payroll, we'll close the doors," Benton said. In theory, it might be possible to keep the network running with other preachers' shows, but Benton insisted that this time, the familiar threat was real: "If we don't have the funds to operate, I'm prepared to close it all down."

If that happened, hours of religious programming would vanish from the nation's cable systems, and in the new era of cable TV, there would be no equivalent replacement. As Falwell had predicted, "We think it's whistling 'Dixie' to think that there are thirteen million homes that XYZ Christian cable could come in and pick up when PTL goes out." The competition for cable time had become too fierce, and the time correspondingly expensive. In fact, the electronic church seemed headed for a major restructuring. Some preachers were cutting back on commercial stations and buying less expensive cable time; Oral Roberts, for one, was in a new fiscal mess, trying to persuade local officials to take over his hospital, and was preaching only to the cable audience. But with cable operators actively trying to shed their religious shows and replace them with home shopping networks and other more lucrative programs, cable time seemed sure to get more costly, too.

So Falwell was charting a bold new course for his LBN network. The network as such would go out of business, to be replaced by a new operation run by Jerry Nims and known as Family Television Network—Family Net for short. Owned 79 percent by "Old Time Gospel Hour" and 21 percent by LBN, Family Net would switch its signal from the little-used Satcom 4 to a transponder on Galaxy III, a satellite that carries the MTV signal and several other widely viewed channels. Family Net was to carry Falwell's "Gospel Hour" and "Pastor's Study" shows, along with sports programming from the Southern Conference and several new shows to be produced by LBN. In the development stage, they included "On the Edge," a religious music program; the "Over the Hill Gang" with Doug Oldham as host; "Acted Out," a talk show aimed at high school and college students; and "Backstage," a variety show hosted by Gary McSpadden, another PTL alumnus. Family Net would sell some time to other preachers, but religious programming would be held to a maximum of six hours a day. Nims planned to sell advertising around the sports events and the new shows. And Falwell was intrigued by the idea of a Christian home shopping program, with viewers using their credit cards to buy books, cassettes, albums, and the like from his warehouses. "In fifteen seconds, money is in our account," he said. "We'll be using a lot of junk time doing that."

Falwell also had to repair his own ministry and the lingering disaffection of his fundamentalist constituency. The depth of the damage was far from certain. His ministry's financial statements showed that contributions had been on a steady slide for years, from a high of $52.6 million in fiscal 1983 to $44.2 million in 1986. No one knew for sure, but it seemed likely that at least part of that decline was traceable to unhappiness among the fundamentalists over his high political profile and his dealing with non-Baptists as head of Moral Majority. And the PTL imbroglio seemed to accelerate the damage, though Falwell provided no actual figures, just the usual welter of conflicting statements. He said that fiscal 1987 was the best year his ministry ever had, except for direct donations, but he also said that donations were down by as much as 60 percent, a calamitous loss if it reflected the whole year. He pledged to remedy that, launching among other efforts a $10 million campaign to build a new sanctuary for his Thomas Road Baptist Church.

And Falwell knew it would be a full-time job, at least for a while. Announcing his departure from Moral Majority and the Liberty Federation, he said, "My first love is back to the pulpit, back to preaching, back to winning souls, back to meeting spiritual needs." As for any more rescue work, he was done with all that. "I'm home for good," he announced. "And if Billy Graham, Pat Robertson, and Pope John Paul the Second all get into trouble on the same day, they need not call Lynchburg."

It would be a long time, however, before the evangelical flock, or the nation at large, could safely file away what Falwell called the "Watergate of the religious world." The damage done to other ministries was as hard to gauge as Falwell's own injuries; individual preachers blamed the PTL scandal for drops in income ranging up to 30 percent. Such figures weren't to be trusted: Some of the ministers tried to minimize the damage; others exaggerated it to promote a new crisis; some did both by turns. But even if they weren't evangelizing, who could pinpoint the cause of a decline? The only thing sure was that the ministries mired deepest in scandal were hurting most. In February 1988, the Arbitron ratings showed PTL with only 141,000 households tuned in for at least five minutes a week, which dropped it out of the top eighteen shows. Oral Roberts could claim only 677,000, but that was good enough for fourth place. Swaggart was still in the lead, but even he had lost 200,000 households at 1,961,000—and his own scandal erupted just as the survey was being taken.

But the damage went far beyond money.

"The quote that comes to mind," said conservative columnist Cal Thomas, "is from Jesus when he entered the temple: 'My father said this shall be a house of prayer, but you have made it a den of thieves.' That's the perception non-Christians are getting out of this, and it's very sad."

That was surely the perception. Shortly before the scandal, a national Gallup poll had found 46.6 percent agreement that Christian fund-raising is generally "ethical or honest," with 39.9 percent disagreeing. A month after the news broke, only 23 percent said TV evangelists in general were "trustworthy with money." The new poll also found heavy damage to individual preachers. Since 1980, Bakker's approval rating had plummeted from 58 percent to 23 percent. Oral Roberts dropped from 66 percent to 28 percent. Swaggart fell from 76 percent to 44 percent; Robertson, from 65 percent to 50 percent. Even Schuller, least damaged among the TV regulars, dropped by seventeen points to 61 percent favorable.

People who said they were regular viewers of televangelists were showing disillusion as well. A *New York Times* / CBS News poll just after the scandal broke found that three-fourths of the viewers thought the preachers were overly concerned with money. Even among those who sent funds—26 percent of the watchers—more than a third said their general opinion of televangelists was unfavorable. And well before Jim Bakker's sins were uncovered, there was beginning to be organized resistance to the televangelists. A group called Fundamentalists Anonymous, founded in 1985 in New York, said it would be a watchdog on the accountability of TV preachers and claimed forty thousand members who had quit evangelical churches. The group intervened in the PTL bankruptcy case on behalf of three hundred of Bakker's contributors.

There was also vigilante action. In 1985, Edward Johnson, a computer systems analyst in Atlanta, was exasperated because his sixty-seven-year-old mother was a regular in the electronic church and seemed on the verge of signing over the family peanut farm to Falwell. So Johnson programmed his home computer to call Falwell's toll-free number at thirty-second intervals night and day. Allowing for the time it took Falwell's operators to answer and for Johnson's computer to disconnect and redial, that could come to five hundred thousand calls a year. Falwell's office said the calls cost a dollar each. Falwell threatened to sue, and the telephone company told Johnson to cut it out or be disconnected. Johnson stopped the calls, but by then he had been chipping away at Falwell for nine months.

As usual after any scandal, some said there ought to be a law to crack down on the TV preachers. It was outrageous, said Richard Yao, one of the founders of Fundamentalists Anonymous, that "people go on television, raise hundreds of millions of dollars, and are not required to issue financial statements to anyone."

However, the First Amendment prohibits the government from interfering with religious organizations, and over the years the courts have read that as a very broad ban indeed. Ministers can certainly be prosecuted for fraud or other criminal activity, but although there is fairly wide agreement that a church's tax exemption probably shouldn't extend to purely commercial activities, there have been remarkably few cases testing that theory. In general, lawmakers and prosecutors at all levels of government hesitate to poke the hornets' nest that would erupt if they seemed to move too vigorously against any church. And although the IRS receives voluntary reports from some religious groups on their activities, there is no general rule requiring them to file and probably won't be anytime soon.

Even so, it was probably inevitable that the PTL headlines would trigger a congressional investigation. Texas Congressman J. J. Pickle, chairman of the oversight subcommittee of the House Ways and Means Committee, leaped into the breach while the holy war was still raging, announcing an in-depth investigation of the TV preachers and their doings. Pickle said "many members of Congress and individuals" had asked him what was going on, and "frankly, I have not been able to answer their questions."

The prospect of such an inquest made sizable waves. Pickle's staffers conceded that they were venturing onto sensitive ground, and some of the preachers bristled protectively. Cal Thomas said his friend Billy Graham was "always a little nervous about government interference in religious matters," and Jerry Falwell warned that the hearings shouldn't become a media circus. Graham and Pat Robertson said they had other engagements and couldn't appear—and that was before Pickle set a date.

They needn't have worried. In the end, the Pickle hearings shrank to a one-day event, with the ministers righteously attacking the very idea of regulation and the congressmen on the defensive. "For the first time in the history of this nation, we're finding the Congress of the United States investigating churches," fumed D. James Kennedy, head of Florida's Coral Ridge Ministries and one of the top ten TV preachers. Jim Bakker had been defrocked by his church, Kennedy noted pointedly, but Representative Gerry Studds of Massachusetts was still sitting in the House, several years after being censured for having had sex with a teenage male page. "Amen!" cried Falwell. "Good preaching!"

With more than a dash of chutzpah, the National Religious Broadcasters used the occasion for a little fund-raising. Executive Director Ben Armstrong sent out a letter calling for contributions to a million-dollar "warchest" to defend ministers' rights to the airwaves, and he enclosed a copy of Pickle's invitation to the hearing as evidence that the money was needed. "I resent that," said Pickle. Perhaps the headlines were balm enough.

But there was no prospect for any legislation; even Pickle said he had none to offer. As a solution to the problem of televangelical abuses, that left self-regulation—something Falwell and Armstrong both professed to embrace.

Self-regulation is not a new idea. In 1979, under Billy Graham's prodding, the Evangelical Council for Financial Accountability was set up to enforce a code of ethics. The rules are far from draconian, but they do stipulate, among other things, that TV preachers should not have a majority of family members on their boards and that they should release audited financial statements every year. As of early 1988, however, none of the televangelists who are household words were among ECFA's 376 members. Jim Bakker had belonged but had quit in 1986 rather than disclose his figures. Falwell used to be a member, too, but he dropped out in 1983 on the ground that opponents of Moral Majority were harassing him by demanding huge numbers of audited financial statements.

These days, said the NRB's Armstrong, "The broadcasters themselves want to be more open." Several preachers said the scandal made them realize they would have to open their books; early in his PTL adventure, Falwell accused himself and most of his brethren of having "been very independent and arrogant as far as accountability to the public is concerned. . . . We deserve to get our hands slapped." (Nonetheless, it took him almost four months after that to release a new set of figures.) Armstrong warned that the alternative to self-policing would be government intervention, and observers seemed to agree. "If they try to stonewall, it's going to be trouble," said Jeffrey Hadden. "Direct mail fund-raising is not going to be a private matter anymore."

So the NRB set up EFICOM, a new Ethics and Financial Integrity Commission. It was in the works before Jim Bakker's problems were public, but Armstrong maintained that the code approved in early 1988 was considerably tougher than it would have been if the scandal hadn't happened. Even so, it was notably lacking in teeth. The code requires member ministries with more than five hundred thousand dollars in annual income to provide "full disclosure of financial information and an annual report, to be made available to anyone who asks for it," Armstrong said, and family-dominated boards of directors would be banned. But there would be no public disclosure of the preachers' compensation. Members would be given two full years to come into compliance. After that, the penalty for members who flunked the tests would be that they couldn't use the EFICOM logo, a seal of approval to be displayed on letterheads and TV.

It remained to be seen whether the auditing would actually be tough enough to catch abuses. PTL, for example, managed to pass the ECFA's tests during several years of Bakker's most flagrant behavior. Some prominent evangelists, including Oral Roberts, haven't even felt it necessary to belong to the NRB and have made no pretense of financial openness; there was no reason to expect them to change that stance. Finally, there was the open question whether any of the Grandma Grunts would notice or care if EFICOM denied its seal of approval to their favorite preacher. In the past, many ministers have brushed off harsher criticism than that as no more than the devil's work and have gone right on collecting. In the end, the only way to make the code stick would be to persuade the preachers that it would pay to police themselves.

*   *   *

What did it all mean? Did the great PTL scandal have any lasting effect on the nation, and was there a lesson to be learned from Jim and Tammy?

The story was endlessly fascinating, a study in hypocrisy. Gospel-gate wasn't just Jim and Tammy playing out their depraved soap opera. It was the self-destructive hubris of Jimmy Swaggart, right-eously denouncing his fellow ministers for the sexual obsessions that were actually hounding him. It was the parade of backstabbing preachers across the TV screens of the nation, Jerry Falwell playing power games for PTL, Pat Robertson denying his own words and rewriting his biography to play up Jim Bakker's old sins. It was the cynical fund-raising game and the duping of the faithful. It was a morality play about the seductions of money and power, the corrup-tion waiting to ensnare people who set themselves up as moral leaders.

It was also a study in the national character. Here we are, said Ted Koppel at one low point in the scandal, "claiming to be incensed, even outraged by what we hear, all the while clamoring for more." That was an accusation of prurience, and the charge was just. But perhaps the hypocrisy went deeper. As ministers know, they are set up to fail; their people first demand that the pastor be better than his flock but then probe relentlessly for signs of failure. There is a kind of wicked glee when a priest is taken in sin; if he is no better than we are, we are somehow licensed to go on sinning, too. The contract between priest and people is full of hidden clauses and anything but simple. In ancient times, some tribes are said to have sacrificed the priest-king every year and chosen a new one. It might be a more straightforward transaction.

Perhaps the scandal was inevitable, one of those periodic correc-tions of the excesses that seem endemic in American life. The televangelists were riding for a fall, said William Fore of the Na-tional Council of Churches: "If the Bakkers hadn't come along, it would have been something else—like Oral Roberts and his nine-hundred-foot Jesus." Across the country, evangelicals and main-stream leaders alike were hoping that the lesson had been learned: That preachers would walk more carefully and that they and their flocks alike would know better how to tell glitz from God.

There was some worry that the scandal had subtly damaged the nation's moral fiber. Religious historian Martin Marty of the University of Chicago warned: "Events like this contribute to a climate of cynicism, to a feeling that there seem to be no refuges, no islands, no pure places to turn to." Such cynicism is bad for any nation. It undermines the social contract, and there is too much of it going around anyway.

Gospelgate certainly gave the American mainstream an eye-opening look into the evangelical world. "Suddenly the whole culture knew these people," Marty said of Jim and Tammy, "and the first vivid sense they got of it was not that the Bakkers were part of a subculture that was different but that they did some truly egregious stuff—climbing into bed with a church secretary, earning millions a year, and having air-conditioned doghouses."

As the mainstream learned more about evangelical values and beliefs, the new knowledge reinforced the old liberal fear of the moral absolutism of the religious right. It is hard for evangelicals to compromise on questions of right and wrong, and that stance is at odds with the pragmatic spirit that makes democracy work. Liberals fear that the evangelicals aim only to impose their rules on everybody else. John Buchanan, chairman of the liberal lobby People for the American Way, calls it the "mind-set of inerrancy—'I speak for God and this is scripturally sanctioned and nonnegotiable.'" That attitude certainly contributed to the corruption of the preachers. "You report to nobody but God. You lose your perspective completely," said Billy Robinson. It happened to Jim Bakker, he said, and "That's Falwell's mentality, too. You could never tell him he's wrong. He'll never admit it. You just give up."

Thus the scandal helped underline the wisdom of separating church from state, a doctrine that is not just a part of our political heritage but a real issue in contemporary politics. As a Southern Baptist official warned years ago about members of Moral Majority, "They not only want a theocracy, but every one of them wants to be Theo." Moral Majority itself had already been largely discredited before the scandal; in Falwell's own state of Virginia, few candidates wanted his support unless it could be given secretly. Pat Robertson's campaign ran into the same problem of polarization: Those who weren't for him tended to be vehemently against him. Even in Iowa, where he threw the primary race into turmoil by running a strong

second in the Republican caucuses, Robertson got unfavorable ratings from 54 percent of his own party's likely voters.

But Robertson's campaign also proved the power of evangelical
zeal in American politics and social issues. True believers may not
amount to more than 6 percent of the population, but they are the
shock troops of the religious right: They give money, they turn out
to canvass and vote, and they lobby elected officials more efficiently
than any other group, with the possible exceptions of the National
Rifle Association and the Israeli lobby. The difference they make is
at the margins. The movement doesn't expect or need a majority,
according to Robert Grant, founder of the conservative Christian
Voice. "All you need is perhaps three percent in order to influence
any election, from dogcatcher to president," he said.

What sustains this zealous minority is the tacit support of a far
more diffuse and divergent group. The third of the nation that
identifies itself as evangelical will hum to the same music as the
hard core, but nowhere near as loudly. And the tune is one that the
preachers have been playing for years. The nation, they say, is
turning from God. It is moral decay that threatens America's greatness; our problems trace to our sins—divorce, loose sex, drink,
drugs, and crime.

The moderate evangelicals tend to agree. These voters are troubled by abortion, they want their children to be allowed to pray in
school, and they don't want homosexuals teaching there. But as a
practical matter, most of them are far more open to compromise
than the hard core. In a study of evangelical college students, sociologist James Davison Hunter of the University of Virginia found
significant concerns among them about the intolerance and closed
minds of Moral Majority. Even among seminarians, 57 percent
disapproved of Moral Majority's goals and methods, and fully 87
percent of the future preachers opposed the idea of a constitutional
amendment making Christianity the state religion.

Thus the liberal alarm over jackboots on the religious right is
considerably overblown. What gave edge to Moral Majority was the
pent-up resentment of the moderates it claimed to represent, people
who felt ignored and disenfranchised by the rest of the nation.
When they heard their values being voiced from the Oval Office by
Ronald Reagan, much of that resentment evaporated, even if he
didn't cement their agenda into law. The key to dealing with the

evangelicals among us is simply old-fashioned compromise and accommodation. If they feel their concerns are understood and being addressed by the majority, they will be much less easily mobilized in far-right political causes.

This kind of compromise will not come easily. Liberal activists tend to their own kind of absolutism, fearing, for instance, that any mention of God in the classroom could be a camel's nose under their tent. But it is clearly in the liberals' interest to accommodate their neighbors. The social and political power of the evangelicals isn't likely to diminish. In fact, it will probably grow in the years to come, and televangelism is likely to flourish, too.

Most experts dispute this view. They see the waning of Moral Majority and the declining audience of the TV preachers as proof that evangelical influence in America has already peaked, and they think it will continue to diminish for the foreseeable future. The older people who watch televangelism are simply dying off, said Quentin Schultze of Calvin College, and the shows have never appealed effectively to young people.

But the shrinking of the audience is only temporary, a demographic interlude. Because of the low birthrates during the 1930s, the number of people reaching prime age for the religious right has declined in recent years. In 1996, however, the first of the baby boomers—that huge postwar cohort working its way through the population like a pig being swallowed by a python—will turn fifty. And just as they have at every age since they started using diapers, the boomers will stamp the nation with their new demands. "The demographic truth is that we are aging, and aging affluently," said Jeffrey Hadden. All through the 1990s, the number of Americans over fifty will be rising fast; demographers estimate that by 2010, the fifty to sixty-four age-group will be 20 percent of the population.

Nobody can predict for sure that these Americans will follow their parents and grandparents in turning to religion as they grow older. Any number of events—war, hard times, yet more spectacular scandals—could change the trends. But "When people get old, my reading is that they are more likely to turn conservative and to turn or return to religious groups," said Hadden. If they do, the TV preachers will find a message to appeal to them. The religion that attracts the next generation might well contain more self-gratification or New Age mysticism than Old Testament fundamentalism, but Jim Bakker and Robert Schuller have already taken large steps along that path. In any case, religious broadcasting of some sort will not only survive but almost surely grow as a cultural force. Somehow, we will have to come to terms with it.

But not with Jim and Tammy. The future for them seems bleak, even if they avoid indictment for looting PTL and defrauding the faithful. If it's any consolation to them, they will probably not be forgotten. "The Bakkers have entered the folk consciousness," said Martin Marty. "Americans have a great capacity for fascination with the wounded, the gross, the besotted and the burned out. The indomitability of the Bakkers is part of their fascination."

Jim and Tammy can find some hope in the record of disgraced preachers in America. They tend to survive; after the great scandal of 1926, when Aimee Semple McPherson was charged with adultery, her national image faded, but her following kept growing. When she died in 1944, she was still preaching the Foursquare Gospel—and talking about trying the new medium, television.

But the most recent case was Billy James Hargis, a nationally famous crusader for Christ and against communism in the mid-1970s. He was seen every week on 140 TV channels and heard on 500 radio stations; there were several hundred students at his American Christian College in Tulsa, and his newspaper had a circulation of two hundred thousand. Then *Time* reported that two of his students had married each other and confessed on their wedding night that each had had sex with Hargis. A college official said he got similar confessions from three more male students.

Late in 1987, Hargis was still vehemently denying the charges. "I was guilty of sin, but not the sin I was accused of," he said. "I got hung for the wrong offense." He wouldn't say what he had done, except that his ego had done him in: "I was so sincere when I started. But I got to believing what people were saying about me. I got to believing I was one of the messiahs."

Whatever the sin, Billy James's ministry was derailed by the scandal. Thirteen years later he was still running the Christian Crusade, but his old campus had become part of the University of Oklahoma. By his own account, readership of his newspaper had fallen to fifty thousand, and he had to drop his daily radio show when costs got too high. At sixty-two, Hargis was spending most of his time on a farm in the Ozark hills of Missouri, in a log cabin office and chapel he had built himself. The office was filled with memorabilia from the glory days: a sword once owned by the late Spanish dictator Francisco Franco; plaques thanking Billy James for starting leprosy colonies in Korea; a certificate from Alabama Governor George Wallace making him an honorary officer in the state militia in 1971. "I don't keep up with national leaders anymore," he said.

Hargis was planning to publish a book, and if he could get just five hundred thousand dollars for a satellite uplink and other equipment, he said, he could get back on TV. He planned to bypass both commercial stations and cable networks, beaming his program directly to about two million houses with backyard antennas. "All I want is an opportunity for God to use me," he said. "I will frankly die if I don't see some of my visions become a reality."

Billy James had a word of advice for Jim and Tammy: Avoid self-pity. But already they sounded a lot like him, waiting in their gilded Palm Desert exile, lamenting their lost empire, spinning visions of another ministry, another flock, another two-billion-dollar theme park in the California desert. "I know there's people who want to kill my dreams," Jim told a reporter from the *Observer* who had tracked them down for an anniversary piece, and Tammy said, "You just wonder how people could hate us so badly that they just keep crucifying us over and over." For Hargis and the Bakkers alike, the cinders of their downfall are like debris from a nuclear accident: The radioactive glow fades slowly, but it never quite dies away.

Gail Jauregui, the laundry worker in Tulsa who found her new life in Jesus, is a member of the Faith Christian Fellowship International Church, the sect that recently ordained Jim Bakker. She is happy to have him. "It's incredible! I heard it on the radio. The first thing I thought was: Praise God! Great!"

The scandal doesn't bother her. "That's between them and God, really," she said. "Whatever he's done, he's going to answer to God, not to man. It hurts the body of Christ. But what can you do? Just have to go through it all. Go through the fire and come out. We all need to just pray for them and move on.

"He made a mistake. They just missed God. I've missed God myself. And you can't dwell on it. God doesn't want you to dwell in the past."

Index